AVENUES OF TRANSLATION

AVENUES OF TRANSLATION

The City in Iberian and Latin American Writing

EDITED BY
REGINA GALASSO AND
EVELYN SCARAMELLA

Lewisburg, Pennsylvania

Library of Congress Cataloging in Publication Control Number: 2018049876

A British Cataloging-in-Publication record for this book is available from the British Library.

This collection copyright © 2019 by Bucknell University Press.
Individual chapters copyright © 2019 in the names of their authors.

All rights reserved

No part of this book may be reproduced or utilized in any form or by any means, electronic or mechanical, or by any information storage and retrieval system, without written permission from the publisher. Please contact Bucknell University Press, Hildreth-Mirza Hall, Bucknell University, Lewisburg, PA 17837-2005. The only exception to this prohibition is "fair use" as defined by U.S. copyright law.

∞ The paper used in this publication meets the requirements of the American National Standard for Information Sciences—Permanence of Paper for Printed Library Materials, ANSI Z39.48-1992.

www.bucknell.edu/UniversityPress

Distributed worldwide by Rutgers University Press

Manufactured in the United States of America

CONTENTS

Prologue: The City and the Translator   vii
SUZANNE JILL LEVINE

Introduction: Translation and the City   1
REGINA GALASSO AND EVELYN SCARAMELLA

1. Un Walker en Nuyol: Coming to Terms with a Babel of Words   15
ILAN STAVANS

2. Translation as a Native Language:
The Layered Languages of Tango   23
ALICIA BORINSKY

3. Lorca, From Country to City:
Three Versions of *Poet in New York*   32
CHRISTOPHER MAURER

4. "Here Is My Monument": Martín Luis Guzmán and
Pancho Villa in the Mexico City Landscape   52
NICHOLAS CIFUENTES-GOODBODY

5. On Languages and Cities: Rethinking the Politics of
Calvert Casey's "El regreso"   69
CHARLES HATFIELD

6. A Palimpsestuous Adaptation: Translating Barcelona in
Benet i Jornet's *La Plaça del Diamant*   81
JENNIFER DUPREY

7. Montreal's New *Latinité*: Spanish-French
Connections in a Trilingual City   97
HUGH HAZELTON

8. Translating the Local: New York's Micro-Cosmopolitan
Media, from José Martí to the Hyperlocal Hub   112
ESTHER ALLEN

9. litoral translation   **traducción litoral**   133
URAYOÁN NOEL

| 10 | Coda: The City of a Translator's Mind
PETER BUSH | 142 |

Acknowledgments 145
Bibliography 147
Notes on Contributors 157
Index 161

PROLOGUE
The City and the Translator
SUZANNE JILL LEVINE

> This scholarly outlook might be sustainable in certain great cities, in which curiosity could lead one to exercise any geographical, cultural, linguistic, or historical vocation. In my world, cultural space was too small and fragile, and the idea of pursuing poetry, dance, art, or anything not connected to business and dreams of financial fortune, seemed laughable.
> —Eduardo Lalo, *Uselessness*[1]

Would I have become a translator if I hadn't been a native New Yorker, if I hadn't spent my first thirty-five years in this city, this "melting pot" of people from all nations, religions, and ethnicities? Having lived in California for more than thirty years now—decades that seem to have gone by at breakneck speed—I would answer the question posed with the same answer I have often given to students when they ask, "How did you become a translator?"

That is: I cannot imagine having translated, as I did in my early twenties, a writer like Guillermo Cabrera Infante, from Havana, or Manuel Puig, from Buenos Aires, had I not grown up in Saul Steinberg's center of the universe—New York, city of salvation and rebirth for exiles. Here I was immersed in cultural and literary discoveries high and low as a student attending the High School of Music and Art from ages 13–16 and, starting at age twelve, as a young pianist on scholarship at the Prep Division on Saturdays at the famous Juilliard School of Music. Where but in the city could one be so intensely exposed to books and libraries, theaters, museums, pulsing street life, and the amazing people I was to meet in those post–Cuban Revolution 1960s?

While I went to college up the Hudson at Vassar, I spent my junior year in 1966 in Madrid—when Spain was (to my good fortune) not yet a destination for global tourism—and there is no doubt that learning to speak Castilian like

vii

a native was essential to my adventure into translating Spanish writing into English. Madrid, the traditional center of the Hispanic world then, was a city I explored as a girl, discovering not only romance with boys but a romance language, all part and parcel of immersion in its street life, its bookstores, and its rich history.

After college I returned to the city Manuel Puig called Gotham. At age twenty, I was a graduate student in 1967 at Columbia University and attended a course on the Latin American novel taught by Gregory Rabassa. In those agitated late 1960s in New York, before the funky 1970s and in an atmosphere that was both stimulating and competitive, I picked up a research job at the newly founded Center of Inter-American Relations on Sixty-Eighth and Park Avenue, where I began to meet major figures of Latin American culture. Learning, living, and working in a major city were indispensable to the birth of my life as a translator, scholar, and writer.

* * *

Maurice Blanchot once wrote about the translator as a nostalgic person, experiencing her language as missing something that can exist only in the original work. This is an interesting way to look at the translator, both as a general statement relevant to translators everywhere (especially in the Americas, lands of immigrants) as well as to myself as a native-born New Yorker and grandchild of Eastern European immigrants. Like many from a similar background, I knew relatively little about my "roots." (Cabrera Infante would quip that only teeth and trees had roots.) Those persecuted people fleeing pogroms didn't have the luxury of sentimentalism, I'm guessing, and they knew that upon settling in America, they had to "assimilate"—therefore, they did not pass down that invaluable data, those traditions now lost to my generation.

Translation is historically colored with loss (of the original), a tired cliché but nonetheless always waiting in the wings to pounce. More interestingly it also connects with nostalgia: for those in the literal state of exile and for others who are not totally at home in the city of their own language yet somehow missing their original place of origin—in my case, probably a mixture of Central and Eastern European languages or maybe just Yiddish. With the ghosts of these languages in the background, the impulse in the midsixties to absorb or immerse myself in another European language and culture made sense even though English is where I live and write. Having a deep sense of the foreignness of language can turn words into an escape from pain and loss, a place to play, as they were for a James Joyce or a Guillermo Cabrera Infante. Some translators are as subversive as the authors they interpret.

My affinity for Latin American writers had been, it now seems, an affinity for a certain rootless urban spirit. Writers like Guillermo Cabrera Infante, Manuel

Puig, and Severo Severo were displaced or exiled; all three of these writers were from the provinces (two of them from Cuba, one from Argentina), yet with cosmopolitan spirits, they ended up as citizens of big cities: Buenos Aires and Havana and, later on, Paris, London, New York, and Mexico City. Their books and novels that I translated are imbued with the street wisdom of the city dweller, and after having visited Buenos Aires and Havana, I realized, particularly in the case of Buenos Aires, how much these places and their people were reminiscent of New York.

Manuel Puig and Guillermo Cabrera Infante, like many writers of the twentieth century, shared a grand passion for the movies, especially Hollywood movies. Those movies were capable of giving the multitudes from different corners a kind of home away from home that all people could share. Cinephiles such as Henri Langlois, founder of the Paris Cinematèque, have often observed that their love for film is motivated by nostalgia. Like Infante and Puig, I was a movie fan at an early age. These writers associated the movies with their respective childhoods, seeing the movie house almost as a safe haven, a place to recapture, momentarily, the dreamworlds of childhood and early adolescence. Puig spoke of his early failed career as a filmmaker in Rome as the place he discovered writing and as a way to return to the "paradise" of his childhood adventures at the movies; Cabrera Infante's principal books feed off the nostalgia for the city of his past as well as those afternoon childhood idylls in the darkened theater where life danced on the screen. The cinema for many spectators, myself included, translates us momentarily into a desired past or a longed-for present or even future, and let us not forget that the cinema, at least back then, was mainly an urban site of adventure.

A city-born translator, I celebrate this volume that takes us on a journey to explore the rich dialogue between translation and the city.

Santa Barbara, California, June 2018

NOTE

1. Eduardo Lalo, *Uselessness: A Novel*, trans. Suzanne Jill Levine (Chicago: University of Chicago Press, 2017), 88.

AVENUES OF TRANSLATION

INTRODUCTION
Translation and the City

REGINA GALASSO AND EVELYN SCARAMELLA

This volume of scholarly essays and creative writing is a significant and pioneering contribution to Iberian and Latin American studies. It is not only the collection's content that makes it unique but also its range of participating authors, scholars, and translators. *Avenues of Translation: The City in Iberian and Latin American Writing* is not just about the representation of the city in literary texts. Rather, this volume proposes that thinking about translation and the city is by and large a way of telling the backstories of the cities, texts, and authors that are united by acts of translation. This particular approach slows down experiences that are often taken for granted in the cultural and literary spheres of the city. At the same time, *Avenues of Translation* does not attempt to offer a definitive map of the translation paths of Iberian and Latin American cities. The essays gathered here are by literary scholars for whom translation as a critical lens and creative activity is an integral part of their work.

Overall, the goal of this volume is to highlight avenues of research that, on the one hand, prioritize the space of the city—as seen in the recent works of James Scorer, Edgar Illas, Enric Bou, and Susan Larsen, to name but a few.[1] At the same time, we look to translation as a theoretical frame to further explore transnational, multilingual, and interlingual networks of literary circulation—building upon the works of Jonathan Mayhew, Vera Kutzinski, and Gayle Rogers, among others.[2] James Clifford, in his book *Routes: Travel and Translation in the Late Twentieth Century* (1997), speaks of location as "an itinerary rather than a bounded site—a series of encounters and translations."[3] Borrowing from Clifford, the conceptual location that shapes this book is the avenue. Sharing the kind of restless movement within a given site, avenues can, at times, seem

1

endless to the sight of pedestrians and other travelers within the city, contributing to the imaginative possibilities that cities present to individuals. Yet their limited width also creates boundaries in which creativity must develop. It is on these avenues of literary and artistic activity that translation inspires movement, interaction, and creative confluence.

Avenues of Translation highlights several possibilities for literary studies in both Iberian and Latin American spheres. First, together the essays showcase the contemporary period, spanning the turn of the twentieth century to contemporary media trends. This inclusive chronological approach highlights an understudied area—that of translation studies—and how translators fit in to the literary history and culture in the Iberian and Latin American world. Translation is the ideal idiom for studying the city because of the rich interpretive space of cultural and historical diversity that it generates. Next, because this volume spans more than one region and multiple historical circumstances, it illuminates how translation expands and diversifies the literary production of cities. This volume examines how translation shapes an understanding of a city's recent past and present literary and cultural practices via acts of travel. All the contributions discuss travel to and within various cities during the contemporary period and highlight the importance of travel to translation practices. Finally, beyond the emerging theme of travel as a unifying factor, instead of adhering to a specific type of theoretical analysis or framework, the individual authors of the following essays analyze the specific historical circumstances that surround their authors and texts, thus allowing this volume to offer a range of theoretical and analytical possibilities that will hopefully inspire more to come.

TRANSLATORS OF THE CITY

The Galician-born writer Julio Camba (1884–1962) authored over fourteen books, which contain many of the pieces he wrote during his years as a foreign correspondent for Iberian Spanish newspapers. His writing was published almost regularly over the course of forty years in at least ten different newspapers. Camba left the small town of his birth at the young age of sixteen, traveled to Buenos Aires, got himself deported, returned to Spain, and then went on to travel to numerous cities, from Istanbul and Paris to Berlin and New York. He initially wrote about all these cities and more for a Spanish-language, newspaper-reading audience back in Spain. Travelers are seldom recognized for the amount of translating that they must do—be it interlingual or intralingual translation—when they write about their experiences in literature.[4] Camba never referred to himself as a translator, although translation is a major aspect of his writing. But as a traveler, Camba participates in the translation process, undertaking a "translation act" each time the city's sights and sounds are interwoven into his literary landscape. These "translation acts" of a traveler in his work have not received the attention they deserve from critics of Hispanic literature. What has widely been omitted from criticism of his work or from most discussions of travel writing is the way travelers to cities often act as translators. Camba does not yearn for the tranquility of the countryside in order to write—"en plena Naturaleza soy hombre muerto" (in the middle of Nature, I am a still man).[5] Instead, Camba noted that he was at complete ease while writing in the company of the noise produced by all that the city is made of.[6]

In addition to Camba, a host of examples arise when we think about travel and translation within cities in Spain, Latin America, and the Caribbean and from those sites to other major cities across the world. Several writers from Spain, such as Federico García Lorca, Juan Ramón Jiménez, and José Moreno Villa, visited New York City during the twentieth century and, as a result, wrote their most notable works, which ultimately altered the literature of their homeland and created a distinctive cultural sisterhood between the two places. These dialogues have also led to rivalries between cities. For example, in the first half of the twentieth century, Lorca opted for New York at a time when Paris was in vogue, and Manuel Puig's writings from the 1970s find London's theater scene second-rate as compared to what was happening on New York stages. These connections and disconnections between cities have often been established as the result of acts of translation.

For African American modernist writer Langston Hughes, travel from New York to Havana, Mexico City, and Madrid in the 1930s not only caused important political and artistic collaborations among the Hispanic writers he met along the way but also inspired his own translations of writers such as Gabriela Mistral, Nicolás Guillén, Nellie Campobello, and Lorca. Hughes's interaction with Hispanic writers within the space of the cities in the Hispanic world even brought the Spanish language into his own poetry and prose via bilingual wordplays and multiple narrative voices. When Hughes arrived in Spain in July of 1937, one year after the start of the Spanish Civil War, he joined writers and intellectuals from across the Hispanic world and internationally who had come to the aid of the struggling Spanish Republic. Soon after arriving in Spain, Hughes set up camp with some of the world's foremost modernist writers at the Alianza de Intelectuales Antifascistas (Alliance of Antifascist Intellectuals), where he was given a gift from Rafael Alberti—a copy of Lorca's *Romancero gitano*. Just one year had passed since Lorca was assassinated at the hands of nationalist troops. The gift from Alberti, which the poet had recently reissued with a new prologue that served as an homage to his slain friend Lorca, allowed for Hughes to undertake a translation of Lorca's text. During his time in Madrid, Hughes completed his translation of *Romancero gitano* as *Gypsy Ballads*, with Alberti and Manuel Altolaguirre assisting him with the project along the way.

Hughes also translated Lorca's *Bodas de sangre* and several of the Generation of 1927's Spanish Civil War ballads in 1937 while traveling among Madrid, Valencia, and Paris.

The bustling translation activity that Hughes accomplished in Madrid at the Alliance was a strategy to align American and Spanish literary traditions across linguistic and cultural boundaries for the purpose of Republican political propaganda. During the war, many Republican writers viewed translation as a key method of international political mobilization and organization. Not surprisingly, Hughes's life-writing in English became increasingly interlingual as a result of his translation work within the city of Madrid. In his second autobiography, *I Wonder as I Wander* (1956), as Hughes described his time in Spain during the civil war, he frequently interwove new Spanish expressions he learned in Madrid into his English prose. These heteroglossic moments offer glimpses of his efforts to translate aspects of the culture he experienced during his travels to Madrid. As songs about the defense of Madrid resounded in the streets, the Spanish words and phrases of these lyrics filled his head and heart and soon became incorporated into his writing: "'Madrid, you wondrous city!' were words the Brigade boys had put to an old Spanish folk song, 'Mamita Mia.' The Madrileños had previously put wartime Spanish words to it, too, about the way their city was holding out under siege: '*Madrid, que bien resistes! / Madrid, que bien resistes, / Mamita, mia, los bombardeos!*' The will to live and laugh in this city of over a million people under fire, each person in constant danger, was to me a source of amazement. [...] City without heroics, Madrid, *que bien resistes!*" Hughes was just one of many bilingual Spanish, American, and British writers who worked in Madrid and passed through the Alliance of Antifascist Intellectuals during the Spanish Civil War who used the translation of literary texts in Spanish and English to foster international awareness of the Republican cause.

Translators, in this way, can become special mediators in the material circulation of cultural ideas in urban communities. Langston Hughes's translations of *Romancero gitano* put Lorca's work on the literary map in the United States, allowing for the wide circulation of Lorca's work to an Anglophone audience at an important political moment when Republican Spain desperately needed support. As in Madrid during the Spanish Civil War, the city can mark "encounters with modernity" through translation during times of intense political and cultural change.[8] In other words, translators can place the authors and their texts that they translate into the circulation of political and cultural ideas, acting as liaisons facilitating interaction, circulation, assimilation, and exchange. Sherry Simon has discussed that some cities are connected by a "common structure and spirit" and that as travelers, we are always translating the values of our home city and mapping them onto another city when we visit (*Cities* xix). Likewise, when a writer travels to a new city and embraces its cultural and political history, the author and traveler begins to translate aspects of that city into his own life and work. Expanding upon Doris Sommer's notion that bilingualism benefits and enriches the civic life of a city, Simon explores how the "accents, code-switching, and translation" of multiple languages within cities become a crucial element of that city's identity (*Cities* xix). Simon urges us to understand a city's history beyond the visual and spatial markers of its monuments and urban design. Just as it did for Hughes and Camba, for Simon, translation encourages the traveler to listen to the distinct soundscapes of cities and their diverse languages.

Edith Grossman, the celebrated translator of Hispanic letters (1936–), shared a similar sentiment about the relationship a writer has with the city. In a 2010 lecture at Manhattan's Yale Club, Grossman, one of today's foremost translators of some of the monumental works of Spanish-language literatures, shared with the audience that the city was central to her role as translator. She explained that the close contact of individuals in New York City was preferable to their isolation in the countryside. She remarked how city sounds, songs, and voices heard on the streets, subways, buses, cafés, and restaurants are resources for her work. When she is searching for a word or a phrase for a literary translation, she at times finds it rolls off the tongue of an individual moving through the city alongside her. The city gives words, and gives life, to her translations, helping her to locate the colloquial expressions of the city space that her characters need to say.[9]

Her story is intriguing because it speaks to how well successful translators *listen* to what is being said around them. This careful listening to the soundscape of the city undercuts and challenges the notion that translation can simply be done with access to dictionaries and a basic knowledge of two languages. By revealing that the sources that a translator relies on to do his work are to be found outside heavy hardcover books and beyond computer screens, Grossman takes the translator out of the solitary environment where he or she is often thought to be and into a dynamic urban space.

What is more, the scene Edith Grossman described to a New York audience in her lecture places the translator in the city, waiting for an individual to utter the words of an existing character who speaks another language, thus adding a playful level of fictionality to the city's occupants. The translator considers the city just as we might imagine any other writer would: as a well of inspiration from which the language of stories emerges. Surveying the city and its audible surface thus becomes one possible strategy available to translators, and the city is revealed as an infinite and unpredictable creative resource. Sherry Simon elaborates, "Translation is the key to citizenship, to the incorporation of languages into the public sphere. This means seeing multilingual, multi-ethnic urban space as a translation space, where the focus is not on multiplicity but on interaction. Understanding urban space as a translation zone restores language to the picture and offers a corrective to the deafness of much current urban theory (*Cities* 6–7)." Expanding upon Simon's and Grossman's theoretical frames, this volume discusses the intersection between literary translation and travel within the space of the city and between cities. The examples of Camba, Hughes, Grossman, and the works gathered in this volume illustrate that translation in the context of a familiar or foreign city can be understood as an act of creative expression. Translation, especially during an era in which it is all around us, has many ways of shaping and affecting cities. As cultural and capital centers, cities have a high concentration of individuals and languages moving in and out of them as well as within them.

Therefore, the primary aim of this volume of essays is to explore how translation perpetuates, diversifies, deepens, and expands the literary production of cities in their greater cultural contexts, as well as how translation shapes an understanding of and access to a city's past and present literary and cultural practices. *Avenues of Translation: The City in Iberian and Latin American Writing* defines translation not only as an art carried out by translators and writers but also as an analytical tool that opens new ways of understanding the literary experiences and representations of Iberian and Latin American cities. This volume celebrates a wide range of translational phenomena that mark writing and literary texts, exploring how those translation acts help us to better understand the cultural and historical contexts of the urban spaces that are described within those texts. The focus on Iberian and Latin American cities aims to show the intellectual and artistic discoveries that result from interactions and connections between writers and their cities. We have also included cities that have been places of historical and imaginary importance for Iberian and Latin American literatures in general, such as New York and Montreal. We hope that by exploring the theoretical framework of translation and its relationship to the city, we can clear new pathways that challenge one-dimensional representations of the role of languages in urban spaces.

THEORETICAL AND CONCEPTUAL FRAMEWORK

Avenues of Translation celebrates a variety of approaches to reading the city through translation, recognizing scholars who are established and emerging experts on their respective cities and the literary and cultural histories of them. Besides the work of the literary scholars and translators previously mentioned, this volume has been inspired by discussions that go beyond the visual aspects, the iconic representations of the city, to focus on the languages, or texts, that emerge from it. Going back to the biblical story of the Tower of Babel, the city has long been associated with language. Prominent philosophers such as Walter Benjamin, Ludwig Wittgenstein, and Roland Barthes, who are also often cited for their translation theories, all regard the city as an expressive form bearing strong connections to human language (Darroch 26).[10] Much of the abundant literature on cities, however, neglects to tune into "the audible surface of cities," favoring the visual aspects of urban life (Simon, *Cities* 1), and, if only with a few exceptions, has not widely discussed them as a privileged space of translation.

As evidenced by the previous discussion of her work, Sherry Simon has had the most immediate impact on the theoretical and conceptual framework of this volume. Her book *Translating Montreal: Episodes in the Life of a Divided City* (2006) brought translation to the analysis of urban-centric literature and made way for novel possibilities of critical inquiry.[11] Five years later, with the publication of *Cities in Translation: Intersections of Language and Memory* (2011), Simon broadened her interest in cities and translation and furthered critical views of language relations in urban life. During those same years, Simon spoke in public fora in which she defined translation in the context of the city as "writing at the intersection of languages, writing under the influence of, in the company of, with or often against other languages."[12] *Avenues of Translation* indulges in the breadth of this definition as one that gives opportunities to thinking about translation as an integral and forceful shaper of city writing and literary interactions.

Simon has noted elsewhere that "like the train voyage that brings travelers to their destination, translation is part of the evolving history of the cultures it links" (*Montreal* 6). Being a central part of translation on etymological, practical, and metaphorical levels, travel's association with translation has also influenced the making of this volume. Travel, as what happens to texts when they move from the mind to the page, from one language to another, from one medium to another, and from one city to another, spotlights translational acts, as does the writer who (re)presents urban life. In this regard, to further call attention to the role of language in travel, scholars of translation studies such as Michael Cronin, Loredana Polezzi, and Susan Bassnett[13] have specifically framed the study of translators as travelers. Cronin, for example, addresses travel accounts in his book *Across the Lines: Travel, Language, Translation* (2000) to underscore the amount of translation that travelers must do.[14] Drawing from Roman Jakobson, Cronin identifies instances in which travel writers use intralingual, interlingual, or intersemiotic translation to produce their works. The centrality of translation in travel and in travel writing, coupled with Simon's urge to shift analyses of the city and literature from their visual offerings to the linguistic actions and interactions that also define the city, have informed the types of essays included in this collection.

Moreover, Iain Chambers has called the modern city a "perpetual translating machine" (27–29),[15] arguing that "the city continually proposes the urgency of considering life, both ours, and that of others, in the transit proposed by translation" (27–28). In the city, Chambers sees the "forces of translation" apparent in "multiple forms and formations" (28). His views—which derive from the premise that cities, both ancient and modern, have primarily been sites of cultural encounter—have been helpful in making sense of the larger ramifications of this volume. Thinking of the city in terms of translation illuminates confluences that deepen the ways in which the city participates in surprising facets of literary culture. In many cases, this perspective reveals compelling moments in literary history and points to an intriguing present and future. If translation is recognized to have always been a part of the city, it also intensifies how the city is experienced and portrayed. In his book *Translation and Identity in the Americas: New Directions in Translation Theory* (2008), Edwin Gentzler proposes that "translation is not a trope but a permanent condition in the Americas" (5) due in part to the many mistranslations that are part of the language used to name and talk about the Americas as well as the "movement and maneuver" (7) that characterizes the way in which individuals experience them. In the context of the city, translation can also be thought of as a permanent condition, since the fragmentary nature that defines cities continuously offers possibilities to create new versions of them.

CONTRIBUTIONS

This volume's essays include studies of the multiple voices of the city—translators, writers, poets, publishers, and other artists—and their contributions to cultural production. It also incorporates a range of voices of scholars, writers, and translators who contribute to a critical dialogue on how we think about the ways translation helps us understand the dynamics of interactions within a city's literary milieu. The essays in *Avenues of Translation* loosely follow a chronological organization based on the publication date of the principal text or period studied in each of the chapters. We frame the essays with a prologue and coda by Suzanne Jill Levine and Peter Bush, two celebrated literary translators and scholars of Iberian and Latin American literatures as well as of translation studies. Their reflections as both translators and scholars highlight how the city has deeply affected their personal and professional development.

The volume opens with a brief autobiographical essay by Ilan Stavans titled "Un Walker en Nuyol" that sets the scene for this collection's exploration of examples of language changes and exchanges in urban centers throughout the Iberian Peninsula and the Americas. Stavans's essay follows a walk he took with his roommate Franco, from Italy, while moving through the city's avenues from one Manhattan neighborhood to another and off the island, on one of his first winter days in the city. During the trek, Stavans and his companion are exposed to the rhythms of the city and the sounds of the various languages encountered along the way, from Italian, Russian, and Chinese to variations of the Spanish language. Moreover, Stavans's text pays homage to Alfred Kazin's *A Walker in the City* (1951), a book that both physically and intellectually accompanies Stavans on his walk through an urban environment to which he does not yet belong. Born in Mexico City, Stavans, also the son of Yiddish-speaking immigrants like Kazin, shares with him the desire to bring the city closer to himself. Inspired by Kazin, Stavans's essay uses the textual surface as a space in which to represent his linguistic journey with the use of quotations, italics, "Espanglish"—a term introduced to him by Franco—and other visual markers to identify the multiple languages of the walk. Stavans's piece ends with a pertinent question that all individuals with a keen sensitivity to the soundscape of cities might ask themselves once they return from a walk: "Am I back where I began?" This question is a relevant one for opening the exploration of translation and the city because it calls attention to movement throughout or travel in the city as being synonymous with change. Federico García Lorca's New York poetry was keenly aware of this in what have come to be the opening verses of his celebrated *Poeta en Nueva York*. The poet of "Vuelta de paseo" ("After a Walk") announces voluntary transformations, such as "dejaré crecer mis cabellos" (I'll let my hair grow long), as well as continuous transformations that the city returns to the poet— "Tropezando con mi rostro distinto de cada día" (Bumping into my own face, different each day; 6–7).[16] The city invites translation by allowing the traveler opportunities to explore different versions of the self.

Next, in a brief although vigorous piece that calls attention to the interactions of individuals in the city, Alicia Borinsky further develops her scholarship and writing on tango and its place in Buenos Aires. In "Translation as a Native Language: The Layered Languages of Tango," she dismantles Buenos Aires's signature artistic expression, which she claims makes no room for translation in the Argentinian city's context. In her essay, however, Borinsky pauses the music and movement of tango—developed in city spaces such as jails, dance halls, and brothels—and discovers opportunities in the multiple components of tango to translate its creators, performers, voices, and languages. In her essay, she decodes not only the very vocabulary associated with tango but also some of its intriguing lyrics. While she respects the originality and original form of the lyrics, she tells what selected lyrics mean and their significance in the larger picture of tango. Tango tells the stories of the city, and as a result, tango embodies translation. A tango artist, like a literary translator, knows the most intimate secrets of a text.

A volume on translation and the city in the context of Iberian and Latin American urban spaces would not be complete without a discussion of one of the most frequently cited texts when thinking about Spanish-language literature and New York City—or any city for that matter: García Lorca's *Poeta en Nueva York*. The poems of this collection were written during his less-than-one-year visit to the United States and Cuba in 1929–1930, but they were not published until 1940. When it was first released to a widespread audience in the United States, it was done so in a bilingual edition bearing the title *The Poet in New York and Other Poems*, with English translations by Rolfe Humphries. The publication of the English translation before Bergamín's edition in Spanish indicates that translation has always been a key factor in the image and reception of Lorca's source text, as well as the instability surrounding the history of the manuscript. Christopher Maurer studies these aspects in his essay "Lorca, From Country to City: Three Versions of *Poet in New York*," based on newfound correspondence from editors, translators, scholars, and advisors. What is more, Maurer presents a fascinating backstory that tells how translation into English, along with all the personal and political interpretations it entails, aided in promoting a cosmopolitan, urban García Lorca, who went on to initiate an entire cohort of urban-inspired verses echoing Ben Belitt's version of *Poet in New York*. This essay is exemplary not only because of Maurer's intensely deep understanding of Lorca and his worlds but also because of what it reveals about the history of the decisions made in a city about the image of a poet in the city.

Nicholas Cifuentes-Goodbody focuses on one of the world's largest cities as well as one of the most important in all the Americas, Mexico City, while exploring translation as a way of making sense of the relationship between text and physical space. In "'Here Is My Monument': Translation, Urban Space, and Martín Luis Guzmán's *Memorias de Pancho Villa*," Cifuentes-Goodbody studies Guzmán's biography of Villa, calling attention to its extratextual circumstances as well as to the curious relationship that Guzmán and Villa have with Mexico City. Guzmán's reference to himself as the translator of Villa's biography is a fertile point of departure in addressing translation as the shaping of familiar names of a city. Cifuentes-Goodbody offers a richly multifaceted discussion on topics including translation in the New World, autobiography in Latin America, urban architecture, and monuments and argues that space, like translation, is neither neutral nor empty.

In his essay "On Languages and Cities: Rethinking the Politics of Calvert Casey's 'El regreso,'" Charles Hatfield revisits Casey's most famous short story and considers it in relation to a broader set of discourses about language, politics, and identity between Havana and New York. Casey's story deals with a bilingual Cuban-born cosmopolitan who lives in New York and decides to return to a prerevolutionary Havana in order to recover his *Cubanidad*. The story ends badly for the protagonist, and thus it has often been read as a rumination on the complexities of identity and the various forms of belonging. Moreover, because the protagonist in Casey's story so closely seems to resemble the author, critics have tended to see the story as a vehicle through which Casey attempts to resolve his own conflicted multilingualism and multiculturalism. Hatfield, by contrast, argues that the story points toward a vision of difference anchored in the structural and the political rather than the cultural and the linguistic—and ultimately, the personal and the individual.

Jennifer Duprey studies another literary classic, this time by Mercé Rodoreda (1908–1983), in "A Palimpsestuous Adaptation: Translating Barcelona in Benet i Jornet's *La Plaça del Diamant*." As a classic also among the ever-increasing number of literary texts of Barcelona, Rodoreda's 1962 novel has been adapted for the big screen and the stage numerous times and translated close to twenty times from the Catalan into over a dozen languages, most recently by Peter Bush in English (*In Diamond Square*, 2013). In her chapter, Duprey moves away from literary translation to focus on the 2007 theatrical translation, or adaptation, of *La Plaça del Diamant* by the award-winning playwright and screenwriter Josep M. Benet i Jornet. Duprey's analysis of this "intersemiotic transposition," to use Linda Hutcheon's term, develops from the premises that for Barcelona, theater has been a place to dissect urban life and for oppositions to play out, and that Barcelona holds onto the sociopolitical events that have shaped the city, thus creating a palimpsest. Benet i Jornet's theatrical adaptation celebrates these characteristics of the city while carefully intertwining the story of the main character with that of Barcelona and Catalonia. In her richly insightful review of the play, accompanied by striking images, Duprey argues that this "theatrical adaptation materializes history, and spatializes time in the very process of translation from the novel to the dramatic form and the stage." Benet i Jornet's *La Plaça del Diamant* provides an opportunity for a collective audience to not only experience a new reading of a literary classic but also revisit historical events that have deeply transformed the city and to consider how they resonate with individuals and groups today.

In "Montreal's New Latinité: Spanish-French Connections in a Trilingual City," Hugh Hazelton—a scholar, translator, and poet who has dedicated a large part of his career to unifying and facilitating the Latin American literary presence in Montreal—offers a succinct bibliographical and biographical overview of the historical and current conditions that shape the making of a contemporary trilingual Montreal in terms of literary production and circulation among French-, Spanish-, and English-speaking spheres. Hazelton poignantly outlines the chronology of contact among Quebec and Iberian, Latin American, and French explorers as well as the connections and conflicts with Anglophone Canadians and the British. Above all, Hazelton emphasizes how Quebec's link with Latin America has allowed Montreal to become a city in which the movement among the three languages continues to influence creative choices, translation, and affiliations among writers and within the publishing industry. As Hazelton argues for the unique place of Montreal within Latin American letters because of its milieu of creative and translation opportunities, his contribution to this volume will be an article of reference for years to come.

The city, with its wide offering of imaginative possibilities for writers, has always been an inspiration for some of the best fiction writing. Nonfiction, however, and more specifically journalism, a key type of writing of the urban environment, has received less scholarly attention. Similar to travel writing, the amount of translation that happens in journalism has been obscured. Esther Allen highlights the place of nonfiction in the context of the city in "Translating the Local: New York's Micro-Cosmopolitan Media, from José Martí to the Hyperlocal Hub." Her essay carries this volume to the present with a discussion of the place of nonfiction in translation while at the same time exposing some of the historical currents of New York's marginal journalism with the case of one of the city's most outstanding residents of all time: José Martí. Allen deepens our knowledge of Martí's roots in New York by highlighting the ties between his journalism and translation work in a broader discussion about the role of translation in local media spheres, acknowledging the city's non-English media outlets. Besides calling for greater consideration of nonfiction and translation, she triggers new directions for translation studies that prompt reaching beyond the domestication-foreignization binary. At the same time, she promotes the idea of the media as a space where multidirectional translation conversations can take place and bring together local and international communities. Allen's examples of current initiatives and glimpses of the past New York display translation as an ever-evolving way of experiencing, writing, and reading cities.

Just as this volume opened with a creative essay, we close it with a provocative creative piece by Urayoán Noel, one of today's leading urban poets and performers. Noel's "litoral translation   **traducción litoral**" is the transcription of a long smartphone improvisation that is envisaged as both poetic prose and a quirky quasi manifesto on translation and the embodied city. Noel does not walk the city streets with an interlocutor, as Stavans did, nor does he rely on notes from the journey to later write the city. Instead, he carefully records the poetry he creates as he walks the city, a poetry that itself moves from English to Spanish and Spanish to English. Noel's piece is in a sense a self-translation, but it is also a text that translates itself. Motion is detected as the text shares the changing urban locations of Noel as a walker-poet-translator, thereby making every move between languages become a representation of progression or travel in the city. Noel's contribution pushes the question of how to represent today's city in writing as well as explores the possibilities that the city gives to the actual look of a text. For Noel, it is not only rock formations that make a city but also voice formations. Additionally, "litoral translation   **traducción litoral**" is not only an example of one of the ways in which the city is translated but also leaves us wondering what it would mean to translate this "translated city."

NOTES

1. For example, see James Scorer, *City in Common: Culture and Community in Buenos Aires* (Albany: SUNY Press, 2016); Edgar Illas, *Thinking Barcelona: Ideologies of a Global City* (Liverpool, UK: Liverpool University Press, 2012); Enric Bou, *Invention of Space: City, Travel and Literature* (Madrid: Iberoamericana Vervuert, 2013); and Susan Larson, *Constructing and Resisting Modernity: Madrid 1900–1936* (Madrid: Iberoamericana Vervuert, 2011).
2. See Jonathan Mayhew, *Apocryphal Lorca: Translation, Parody, Kitsch* (Chicago: Chicago University Press, 2009); Vera Kutzinski, *The Worlds of Langston Hughes: Modernism and Translation in the Americas* (Ithaca, N.Y.: Cornell University Press, 2012); and Gayle Rogers, *Incomparable Empires: Modernism and the Translation of American and Spanish Literatures* (New York: Columbia University Press, 2016).
3. James Clifford, *Routes: Travel and Translation in the Late Twentieth Century* (Cambridge, Mass.: Harvard University Press, 1997), 11.
4. See Michael Cronin's *Across the Lines: Travel, Language, Translation* (Cork, Ireland: Cork University Press, 2000), in which he uses Roman Jakobson's three definitions of translation—intralingual, interlingual, and intersemiotic—developed in his essay "On Linguistic Aspects of Translation," in *On Translation*, ed. R. A. Brower (Cambridge, Mass.: Harvard University Press, 1959), 232–239. Loredana Polezzi furthers the link between travelers and translators in her book *Translating Travel: Contemporary Italian Travel Writing in English Translation* (Aldershot, UK: Ashgate, 2001).
5. All translations are ours unless otherwise noted.
6. Julio Camba, *Maneras de ser periodista*, ed. Francisco Fuster (Madrid: Libros del K. O., 2013), 61.
7. Langston Hughes, *I Wonder as I Wander* (New York: Hill and Wang, 1993), 345.
8. Sherry Simon, *Cities in Translation: Intersections of Language and Memory* (New York: Routledge, 2012), 5.
9. Edith Grossman, untitled lecture, Yale Club, New York, NY, Fall 2010.
10. Michael Darroch, "Language in the City, Language of the City," in *Circulation and the City: Essays on Urban Culture*, ed. Alexandra Boutros and William Straw (Montreal: McGill-Queen's University Press, 2010), 23–47. Darroch's essay provides an insightful discussion of how "the city itself is a cultural expressive form in which language and linguistic exchange play a defining role" (43). See also Ludwig Wittgenstein, *Philosophical Investigations*, 1953 (Malden, Mass.: Wiley-Blackwell, 2009); Roland Barthes, "Semiology and the Urban," in *The City and the Sign: An Introduction to Urban Semiotics*, ed. M. Gottdiener and Alexandros Ph. Lagopoulos (New York: Columbia University Press, 1986), 87–98; Walter Benjamin, "The Task of the Translator," in *Selected Writings, 1913–1926*, vol. 1, trans. Harry Zohn, ed. Marcus Bullock and Michael W. Jennings (Cambridge, Mass.: Belknap Press of Harvard University Press, 1996), 253–263; and Walter Benjamin, *The Arcades Project* (Cambridge, Mass.: Belknap Press of Harvard University Press, 2002).
11. Sherry Simon, *Translating Montreal: Episodes in the Life of a Divided City* (Montreal: McGill-Queen's University Press, 2006).

12. Sherry Simon, "Across Troubled Divides: Translation, Gender, and Memory" (presentation, Nida School of Translation Studies, Session Twenty-Two, San Pellegrino University Foundation, Misano Adriatico, Italy, May 27, 2013).
13. See Susan Bassnett, "Travelling and Translating," *World Literature Written in English* 40, no. 2 (2008): 66–76.
14. Cronin, *Across the Lines*.
15. Iain Chambers, "The Translated City," *Translation* 1, no. 1 (2011): 101–106.
16. Translation of Federico García Lorca by Simon and White in Christopher Maurer's edition of *Poet in New York: Bilingual Edition*, trans. Greg Simon and Steven F. White, ed. Christopher Maurer (New York: Farrar, Straus and Giroux, 2013), 6–7.

1 · UN WALKER EN NUYOL
Coming to Terms with a Babel of Words

ILAN STAVANS

> Exaggerate to exist.
> —W. H. Auden, *The Age of Anxiety* (1948)

FROM EL GUETO

Friday, January 4, 1985. It's 7:50 a.m. The temperature outside is below freezing.

"The city" isn't altogether alien to me. I've seen it featured in a thousand movies. As a boy, I came with my father, a theater actor, to buy Broadway plays. I'm familiar with its grammar. Indeed, I make my way through conversations, although, in all honesty, my English is still precarious.

This time around, though, I'm alone, and I'm learning to cope with it. I barely have any money. The $67 a week I make shelving books at a local library is barely enough. Collect calls are expensive. I used to write long letters while I lived in the Middle East, but I've lost practice. Plus, for now I don't feel like sharing my thoughts with others.

I've landed in a small apartment on Broadway and 121st Street, next to the Jewish Theological Seminary. They have given me a scholarship to study philosophy. I share the apartment with three other young men: Francesco, from Italy with a heavy accent; Arno, from Canada; and Ritchie, from the United States. It has taken us time to get acquainted with one another. I understand what they all tell me, though I'm at a loss every third or fourth word, especially with Arno's lingo. He speaks fast and uses strange words. He says I talk in English like a "primitive." Franco's syntax isn't good either. His accent is heavy. Yet he helps me when I fumble.

Even though the closest subway station is on 125th Street, I'm told it's safer to walk a few extra blocks to 116th Street. Spanish Harlem is dangerous. But to me, it doesn't feel like it. I hear lots of Spanish on the streets—a different kind of Spanish from what I'm used to in Mexico. The last syllable in every sentence tends to vanish.

I'm fresh out of *El gueto*. In my native Mexico, I was raised far from the Jewish enclave, yet I'm a *judío* through and through. My parents are Yiddish-speaking descendants of Ashkenazi immigrants and refugees. The majority of Jews in Mexico lived first in middle-class *colonias* like Roma, Del Valle, and Condesa; later, their offspring moved to higher-end neighborhoods: Polanco, Tecamachalco, and Herradura. My house was across town, though, as far away as possible from *El gueto*, in Colonia Copilco, because my parents, artists and hell-rousers, didn't want anything to do with *El gueto*, as they often described the Jewish areas.

I always dreamt of making it out. And *out* meant New York.

In my room, I've found a bunch of books. A previous renter left them behind on a shelf. I disposed of most of them but kept a copy of Alfred Kazin's *A Walker in the City*. It was published in 1951. I've never heard of Kazin before. As I browse through it, I think to myself, This isn't a travel guide; nor is it a full-fledged memoir. *Vos is dos?* I can't figure it out.

Even so, I'm enjoying it. One night, I open it up in the middle. I have a dictionary next to me, just like when I tried reading *Moby-Dick* in English. The back-and-forth between book and dictionary means that I spend a long time plowing through each page.

Kazin reflects about leaving his neighborhood in Brownsville, Brooklyn, in order to discover "the city" block by block. It is before the Depression, and he, also a Yiddish-speaking Jew, is eager to seize the day. Carpe diem.

TO THE SUBWAY

I haven't peeked outside. It must be around twenty-eight degrees Fahrenheit, I hear Franco say. I'm still used to counting in Celsius, and I don't know how to get the conversion right.

Francesco is up early too. He is in the kitchen, frying eggs, reading *L'Unità*. I open the refrigerator and sit next to him while spooning a yogurt.

"Eh, Stavans, da ya want to taik a wolk wit me?" he asks. I immediately say yes. "But d'ju kow, it is veeery cold. Don't maind, eh?" I tell him I'm game. I show him the Kazin book. He smiles, saying he knows about it. "I write a tesis in Naples about Bernard Malamud," he tells me. I ask him who Malamud is. Francesco talks about a group of New York intellectuals: "Malamud is no part of it, but Kazin yes. Do yu want mee to call yu Ilancho? I don't like Francesco. Ma, it's the name of a gigolo."

Franco asks me to bring along my copy of *A Walker in the City*: "Maibee if we rest yu reed a paragraf, yes?"

Each of us returns to his room to get ready. I'm wearing the heavy winter jacket my father bought for me at a discount store before he said good-bye on Lexington Avenue. In the jacket's left pocket, I have my wallet and a pair of leather gloves, and in the left, I put the book. I also have a wool scarf and, though I dislike hats, I take a beret that, with my longish hair, makes me look bohemian. Plus, I'm using my construction-worker's boots. Not comfortable but warm.

Soon, Franco and I are out the door, talking our heads off. Our journey starts as we walk up Broadway to 125th at a good speed. There is an employee-owned bakery not too far away. We stop by to get a loaf of sourdough. A pair of Dominicans attends us. I marvel at their speech. They are from *El Barrio, en* Washington Heights. "La perla de Nuyol," one says. I smile. Franco wants to know if *perla* means she-dog: "No, they talk of El Barrio. They say it's a jewel."

I look around. Big paper bags of bread are ready to be picked up. A truck is double parked outside. I look at the door Franco and I came through a few minutes ago. On top of it, someone has written: *Por cada hombre en prisión, el resto de nosotros pierde la libertad.*

I marvel at how one of the Dominicans inflates his mouth when he talks, as if he was about to play the saxophone.

We leave the bakery for the train. At the station newsstand, I look at the headlines: Tip O'Neill is elected House Speaker. A big snowstorm in Memphis. Then I look at the Spanish newspaper: a police officer was gunned down in the Bronx. I notice a typo in *El Diario / La Prensa*.

Endlessly moving his arms, Franco tells me about being a Communist in his youth. I respond that I participated also in protests in Mexico, though I was never a rank-and-file member of the party. He talks of Diego Rivera, Frida Kahlo, and Italian photographer Tina Modotti. Then he switches to another topic: his awkwardness with women. "I never know wat tey want from mee!" he says, looking at me. I exhale vapor. "Come stai, Ilancho? Bene?"

We have almost reached the Seventy-Second Street station. He is now talking about being a non-Jew in the Upper West Side. In fact, as a boy affiliated with the Jewish Theological Seminary, he says it's just like being a fish out of water.

We exit on Canal Street and walk to the Lower East Side. Franco tells me of a synagogue he entered in this neighborhood the last time he visited. Around us I see Orthodox Jewish women pushing baby strollers. I notice two of them talking in English with the occasional Yiddish word thrown into the mix. "Tey in the Warsaw ghetto, no?" Franco asks.

We pass by a pickle store with huge barrels displaying pickles of all kinds. A merchant is discussing the price with a customer. A homeless black man is pushing a nearby cart full of stuff: bottles, plastic bags, a broom, a rearview mirror stolen from some car, and a kid's lunch bag with Sesame Street characters. There is a sign next door that reads *Kosher*. Not too far away, there is a staircase going down into a basement where a scribe is carefully writing Hebrew letters on a parchment.

We walk through Delancey Street, looking at garment stores. It is around 11:15 a.m. I'm hungry. This isn't a day to be outside, not for a Mexican boychik. I tell Franco that my nose is an ice cube. He describes a scene in an Italian World War II movie in which the protagonist loses three fingers to frostbite.

In Little Italy, the festive decorations are still up for Christmas and New Year's. It doesn't feel outmoded, as if one had arrived at a party after everyone was gone already. But in stores, prices are being cut to make way for new merchandise.

We enter an espresso bar. He talks in Italian with a waitress, then in Russian with the owner. "You think he is also Communist like me?" he asks.

Two cappuccinos arrive at our table. The busboy *es un mexicano*. He is short, with dark, greasy hair. I speak to him in Spanish. He's from Puebla. He left his wife and children behind. Every month, he sends them remittances. He says he feels lonely, but there is not much time for regret. He lives with seven other poblanos, all men, in a small apartment in the Bronx. Most of them came seventeen months ago. He asks me which Mexican soccer team I root for. "America," I tell him.

"¡Uff, que mala onda!" he replies.

THE BIG WONG

Past one o'clock. Blocks are short, but they multiply. We have made it to Chinatown. Everything looks strange. Fruit and vegetable vendors are selling their produce to customers. Their bargaining is done in Chinese.

I find it strange, I tell Franco. Why do these neighborhoods exist? Why haven't all Chinese assimilated? Have some rejected the American Dream?

That becomes our next topic. Is there such a thing as *el sueño americano*? Franco believes it is sheer propaganda. But it works, I reply, because people are still ready to sacrifice everything to make it here.

We enter a restaurant called The Big Wong. Neither I nor Franco knows what the name means. (I will learn it later, from my future wife.) It's a popular down-and-out joint with glazed ducks hanging in the window and a cook boiling noodles at high temperatures. Locals love it.

It is sweaty inside. We are seated at a large table with other clients. Taking my beret and jacket off, I look meticulously at what they're eating: dumplings, steamed broccoli, sliced duck, congee soup, and fried bread. The menu is in Chinese with undecipherable English translations. Prices are lower than anywhere I've been in the last few months. I try ordering. The waiter is impatient with me. I point at what the folks near me are eating and then ask where the item is on the menu. The waiter leaves without writing anything down.

Finally, Franco explains what he wants. A few minutes later, the plates arrive. We eat slowly. The food is delicious.

Everyone around me is Asian. I like being a stranger in this place.

I take *A Walker in the City* out. Franco smiles. "Wai ar we alwais becomin stories?" he asks. At first, I don't understand what he implies. But then I realize it: Kazin's journey from and to Brownsville wasn't only about wonderment. It was about enlightenment. In traveling the distance from the place he was raised in to "the city" itself, he went from being a Jew to becoming an American.

I try explaining this to Franco, but words fail me.

Soon I ask myself, In what language should I describe *este* walk in Nuyol? There is a *mare magnum* of slangs coexisting all around. Everything is lost and won in translation. But New Yorkers don't translate. They just erupt into the world in whatever tongue they feel most comfortable in. And I? Is my stream of consciousness still in Spanish? I imagine myself talking to a mirror. Should it be in my newly acquired English, even if it isn't mine yet?

The bill comes. Franco and I each put half the amount, counting each dollar we have as if it were our last. Then we dress up again and leave the restaurant.

It's crowded outside. An African man is selling fake watches on the corner. In a nearby stand, another one is displaying scarfs, gloves, and sunglasses. Across the street, there is a telephone booth with Chinese characters on top. Nearby, I see a bank in the form of a pagoda. Further down, a somber-looking woman is preaching on a corner. "I am the resurrection and the life," she says as she browses through a Bible.

Two policemen patrolling the area, one probably Irish, another Puerto Rican, stand at her side. She falls silent. "Mira, mujel. Ya te dije que no puedes 'star aquí," the Puerto Rican officer advises her. "Understand?"

Now an Argentinian family is passing by. I immediately recognize the *porteño* accent. The young daughter is trying to formulate a sentence in English. "Where is movie teatro with Chinese?" she asks. Do I sound the same? I sympathize with her.

There are lots of tourists nearby. Several look German. One of them points to the west, explaining to the Argentinian family where a certain location is.

Chinatown looks like a relic of another era, like a living museum. Its nostalgia is clearly a source of revenue for the locals. Is that why they don't assimilate?

A piece of chewing gum sticks to my shoe. ¡Ay, qué joda!

IS THIS QUEENS?

The temperature is a bit warmer. We are walking across a large bridge. I tell Franco that the first visit I ever made to New York was when I was thirteen. I stayed for a month. I want to explain where, but my memory is fuzzy. I know it was Queens, but I say Brooklyn. The truth is, beyond Manhattan, the landscape looks exactly the same to me.

I'm eager to show Franco where the house I stayed in was, although I have no idea where. I pretend to walk with a clear goal ahead of me. I tell him there was an Alexander's just three or four blocks away. From afar, I see an Alexander's, which in turn allows me to concoct a whole story about going to a baseball game in the summer of 1974, with my cousins Brent, Allen, and Richie.

Why am I redrawing the parameters of this story? Why am I telling Franco about a past I know isn't quite as I'm pretending it was? I'm a story machine.

"Yo, you promis' me, didnja? Didnja promis', pa?" A little boy is crying. His father has told him to go back to his room. No more playing outside. He is grounded. They were supposed to go that night to the Mets game, the boy says. "Whay y'achangin' now?"

Richie was an all-American boy. His room was always a mess. He liked playing chess with his father. In the ballpark, he tried explaining to me how baseball works: a man stands at home plate, bat in hand. The pitcher is not too far away. He throws a ball. His task is for the batter to miss it. If the batter does connect, his objective is to hit the ball as far as possible, hoping no one catches it.

I pretend to be interested but, truth be told, I'm bored to death. Baseball is slow, individualistic. I prefer *fúbol*, a team sport if there ever was one.

An Ecuadorian young man is talking to what I believe is a Puerto Rican woman. They are outside a pizza parlor. They switch back and forth from Spanish to English. I can't sort out what the topic is. Are they romantically involved? Or are they siblings?

"It's Espanglish," Franco announces. "Tey spik Espanglish."

I might be wrong, but this might be the first time I heard the term. Espanglish: it sounds atrocious. Why can't they make up their minds? The constant back-and-forth contaminates everything. I like the cadence, but *en México rempería los tímpanos*.

> In every cry of every man,
> In every infant's cry of fear,
> In every voice, in every ban,
> The mind-forg'd manacles I hear.

Franco is reciting a William Blake poem. Out of the blue, he is pretending to have a British accent. It sounds strange in his mouth. Yet the words came out far clearer, less bumpy, than I've ever heard from him.

I think of all the stories coalescing around me. Do they exist in order to be told? Otherwise, they would vanish into thin air. Stories, stories, more stories.

Which among them ought to matter? And to compete with real life, should they be embellished?

Franco and I talk about our common passion: literature. It is in literature where the soul of the people might be found. I tell him I'm in graduate school because I wanted to leave the Mexican Jewish *gueto*. Now that I'm in "the city," I'm ready to write about it.

"About what?" Franco asks.

"About my people," I reply.

"Ar tey funy, like yu?"

"No. And I'm not funny."

"No one wil believe yu, Stavans," he affirms. Mexican Jews: the concoction is absurd. You can't be both: either you're this or you're that.

I want to write, I tell Franco. About them, yes, but also about all this—about the noises I hear.

GETTING BACK

"And you thout you will improv yur English en Nu York? Com'on, amigo. English is now extinct," says Franco.

"I've heard a lot of English," I reply.

"Yea, but it is no correct."

As we walk to a subway train on Flatbush Avenue, I tell Franco about Yiddish always being a *fardreyte* tongue, with a twisted history, full of malapropisms, absorbing whatever is available in the environment. It was created by ignorant people—the *ignoramus*—mixing German and Hebrew and some Slavic languages, making a mishmash.

We sit on a bench. The train is slow. People are congregating on the platform. Work is over. Everyone is getting ready for the weekend. I pretend to relax by closing my eyes a few minutes, then I take out Kazin's book and open it on its first page: "Every time I go back to Brownsville it is as if I had never been away."

I marvel at Kazin's capacity to deliver his message in what looks like flawless English. He learned it in "the city," didn't he?

I imagine the day when I myself will also communicate in a syntactically correct way. Right now, it looks like an impossible goal. Nevertheless, I don't have any option but to pursue it. I didn't become an immigrant, like my grandparents were before me, in order to be a pariah. They spoke Yiddish and Polish and Russian and Hungarian, but they also learned Spanish, the language of their host country, Mexico. Whenever they used *español* with me, it was always clear. If they were able to achieve such a feat, I will surely be able to do the same.

To be a pariah, in my eyes, is to live in a place without understanding its secrets.

We jump on the train. It's packed. No way to talk: commuters are next to each other but not with each other. I just look.

Franco and I change to the express: a sardine can. Ay, it's hot: a steam room. I make it through one door, he through another. The train suddenly comes to a full stop.

After much delay, we reach Ninety-Sixth Street. There's no service on the numbers two and three. We exit and walk up Broadway. At this point, I feel dizzy. I'm running low on temperature. "Maibe we taik un taxi, Ilancho?" asks Franco.

Our funds are limited, though. Franco has a five-dollar bill. I have two twenties, but these must last me until the end of next week, when I'll get my next check.

Somehow Franco and I are talking now about the difference between the words *home* and *house*. They denote radically different concepts: one is a state of mind; the other is a physical place. In Spanish there is a similar difference: *hogar* and *casa*. "Che figata," Franco says.

It's 4:21 p.m. The sun is setting. In my mind, I see my apartment on 121st Street. It feels cozy, inviting. It is my home, I tell myself.

It's almost half past five when we make it back. Franco goes to the kitchen and starts preparing pasta. I collapse in my bed, thinking of all we've gone through. As I retrace every step of the walk we took through various boroughs, it is difficult for me to think of each person and each scene as something apart.

I don't know why, but I'm overwhelmed with anxiety. Did I make the right choice in leaving Mexico, where I have my family, plenty of friends, and a future, and moving to New York? Everything in "the city" feels alien to me.

I ventured far away today. Am I back where I began?

2 · TRANSLATION AS A NATIVE LANGUAGE
The Layered Languages of Tango

ALICIA BORINSKY

THE DANCE: RIVALRY AND COLLABORATION

Common depictions of tango highlight the lyrics and dance as sharing an alluring physical proximity, a promise of an enticing eroticism beyond the common grasp. Nevertheless, they trigger a passion that is within our understanding. In mesmerizing dance steps, couples intertwine and separate, following the ironies of a choreography that sometimes demands would-be initiatives—*el arrepentido*, the regretful step, for example—only to take them back. It is a dance made up of guaranteed flow and failed attempts. It is a walk, or *una caminata*, that does not go anywhere. It is a deepening of an ephemeral conversation as the hand of a man on a woman's back does the *marca*, or the prompting steps, because of its pressure. A successful dialogue in tango implies that partners glide across the floor as though they had always known each other. When it works, it looks natural and seamless. In tango, *marcar* is the equivalent of being understood in a language that is in no need of translation. Thus the *marca* is so beyond misunderstanding that women often dance with their eyes closed to better feel the invitation of the *marca* and the music. "It takes two to tango," goes the trite saying; however, "You do not want three to tango" would be more to the point. The illusion is that there is a perfect interlocution, that a collaboration without mediation is at stake. There is no need for translators. Or so it seems.

The term *milonga*[1] refers to several different things: a fast-paced tango, a woman of the night who dances the *milonga*, the space of the dance hall, and a special occasion organized by somebody with a particular repertoire. These meanings belong to the language of *lunfardo*,[2] a coded language born in Argentine jails and initially spoken by delinquents whose stories were told in the first tango lyrics. *Milongas*, with their quick pace and concomitant light touch, turned sleazy events into humorous occasions portraying different types of individuals. Tangos and *milongas* are discursive snapshots. Their taxonomies incorporate vocabulary from different languages spoken by immigrant groups in Argentina, especially French and Italian.

The dance adds a level of interpretation to the lyrics. *Las letras*, the lyrics, or the poetry of both tangos and *milongas*, frequently boast about pranks against the police, accuse individuals of being *batidores* (informants), sentimentalize stories of *cafishios* (pimps), condemn *niños bien* (mama's boys), and praise *minas* (beautiful, generous women)—often prostitutes—whose stories highlight the economic difficulties faced in their places of origin.

Tango and *milonga* in their *canyengue*, or low-class, streetwise manifestations, use a code for communication: the sharing of a secret language, or *lunfardo*, that brings interlocutors together to form a fictional intimacy. In the execution of the *marca*'s message, they appear to understand one another, to have always known each other. But the stories told in tango are of outsiders, and as the dance partners of the *milonga* separate after five tangos to mix with the others, anonymity is restored.

Some couples behave differently. They stay together because they have arrived as dance partners. They *get* each other, and there is no anxiety about the *marca* there. Their perfect understanding of one another's movements makes them the equivalent of the native inhabitants of a place. They are *in*. They have a natural language of movement, but like all natives, they do not experience the thrill that comes from overcoming the anxiety of failure. Aside from the obvious fall, hesitating about the *marca*, not knowing how to get out of a certain position, or getting entangled in your partner's legs, there is one form of failure that surpasses all others: not being able to find a partner. In a traditional *milonga* hall, women wait for the glance of a man who, from the other side of the room, makes eye contact and, if eyes meet, comes over to invite her to dance. It is common practice not to refuse. Héctor Mayoral (1937–),[3] one of the icons of tango, referred to his own apprenticeship in a group of *milongueros* as having been made possible because he was useful to his group. He would occasionally go to *milongas* dressed as a woman so that his male friends could show off their steps dancing with *him* as a *her* and, therefore, not be rejected by women with whom they wanted to dance.

Milongas are a meritocracy. Your potential partners feel like saying yes if they have seen you dance (well) before. Dancing the tango is like holding a conversation in any language. You learn by doing it, and your partner is essential. Everyone is a foreigner when not in a couple. Dressed as a woman, Mayoral was not giving up his manhood. In the dense world of the *milonga*, role switching is an admired feat. If you pull it off, it means that you can articulate the language perfectly, that you are able to follow as though you lead. With regard to the *marca*, tango masters say, "*El hombre propone; la mujer ejecuta*," or "The men suggest; the women do." In role switching, power shifts in the dance to produce an unsettling flow of gender roles that dismantles the certainties of heterosexual oppositions. Heterosexuality becomes an evocation, a way of quoting rather than an acquiescence to established male/female differences.

Jorge Luis Borges's book *Para las seis cuerdas* (1965)[4] includes *milongas* about male rivalries. He evokes knife fights, *la danza del cuchillo*, captured by Astor Piazzolla (1921–1992), with metallic sounds that he composed for the book. Even if the Piazzolla-Borges collaboration is not quite as smooth as a well-executed dance, it is suggestive of gender tensions at the heart of the genre. Men dancing tango together while they wait for their turn in a brothel is, for some, one of the possible origins of the dance. The fancy footwork is a source of pride and defines a neighborhood, as tango is closely associated with the very nature of the city of Buenos Aires. Whether women are pulled into the dance by a glance or kept out by a history that objectifies them, tango is a language structured by oppositions. An understanding of its origin as a male-only affair or a heterosexual matter is decisive in determining tango's mother tongue and in cracking the power code of the *marca*. Code-switching couples mock univocal interpretations and add a layer that unfolds ironies in the dance. They redefine or translate the story in such a way that the earnestness of clear-cut interpretations is swept up by parody.

DANGERS OF LOVE

The tango "Malevaje"[5] is one of the most celebrated examples of how a man falls for a woman: "Te ví pasar tangueando altanera / con un compás tan hondo y sensual / que no fue más que verte y perder / la fe, el coraje y el ansia 'e luchar" (I saw you pass me by in a tango step, so haughty / so deep, so sensual / that as soon as I saw you / I lost my faith, courage, the urge to fight).[6] The male voice addresses a woman who has mesmerized him; her sensuality has transformed him. He went from being a swaggering rabble-rouser to attending mass, leaving his friends—losing, in fact, his way of life. The magnetism of the woman as she defeats his male posturing by turning him into a lovesick suitor is seen as a fall from grace. "Malevaje" understands manhood as distinct from love. Being a man is staying with the boys in the rough knife-wielding neighborhoods where violence gains respect. By sheer magnetism, she has been able to turn him inside out. Perfectly attuned to the cadences of tango, her body suggests a path to pleasure exclusively for two: no male friends, no visits to mother. Tango reveals that a seductress, sinuous and promising but never quite truthful, is capable of altering the paradoxical harmony of the violent male world. A man's success at conquering such a woman is equal to the deterioration of his life. In this sense, tango is deeply suspicious of love, which is frequently portrayed as a maddening infatuation.

Borges's short story "La intrusa," translated into English by Alistair Reid as "The Intruder," depicts two brothers in a rural setting.[7] Their lives are harmonious until a woman appears. Although she is not particularly attractive, each of them desires her. Their peace is disturbed. One of the brothers sells her to a brothel only to realize that that is not enough to erase her influence. *Resolución*, or resolution, is a position you always return to when you dance tango: feet parallel, facing your partner. It allows you to continue by starting again. In "La intrusa," the brothers find a literary resolution for their plight: one of them kills the woman. His act reaffirms that they are ready to restart their lives: "A trabajar, hermano" (Now, brother, to work).[8] They go back to the harmony of male friendship. The intruder is gone. Through this story, tango suggests one of the avenues by which to construct its own history. The men may start again and affirm life without interference. It only takes two to tango.

The majority of tango lyrics, though, refer to the ups and downs elicited by an urban environment. It is easy for one's financial fate to change because of the many temptations the city offers. Edgy male characters, or *malevos*, share the city space with dangerous women capable of heartless betrayal. Love for a woman dismantles the *malevo*'s bravado and threatens to domesticate the neighborhood.

La ingrata herself, or the ungrateful, undeserving woman, may turn out to be a prostitute or an adulteress. She may also disappear from her lover's life, leaving him in debt and subject to ridicule from male friends who warned him of the dangers that awaited him. The lyrics of "Aquel tapado de armiño," a tango that has been around for decades whose title in English literally means "That Ermine Coat," eloquently tell of how a jilted lover was left:

Aquel tapado de armiño
todo forrado en lamé
que tu cuerpito abrigaba
al salir del cabaret.

Cuando pasate a mi lado,
prendida a aquel gigoló
aquel tapado de armiño
¡Cuánta pena me causó!

As he sees the woman coming out of the nightclub on the arm of a gigolo and sporting an ermine coat that he is still paying for, its cost is the evidence of his mistake. As the woman's victim, he recalls the sacrifices he made to buy her that present even as she dons it in a life that humiliates his original hopes for their future. The woman in the ermine coat is no lady; she has left him to go out cavorting with sleazy nightclub characters. Here, as elsewhere in tango, the streets of the city provide a stage for glances, criticisms, betrayal, and disapproval—or the solidarity of friends and lovers. If the woman of "Malevaje," glanced at as she sashays by on the dance floor, promises an intensity of pleasure that she betrays by turning her man into a domesticated suitor, the sin of the one berated in "Aquel tapado de armiño" is the opposite: she goes from being a humble woman to a tango bar star after she gets the coveted coat. The dance floor and the city are a writing pad on which the failures of love are inscribed and the mirages of infatuation forged.

BUENOS AIRES AS A STAGE

Observing and being observed, the ones telling us their stories are, at the same time, bringing us into the city. Their love is intertwined with the streets as walking becomes a rehearsal of false starts (as in the *arrepentido*, or regretful step) and intermittent successes. The city streets are a dance floor for tango. When they leave or are left, these characters are thrown back into the streets, their paths now traced by the wisdom of their stories.

Humble women and humble neighborhoods carry the ethical conviction of tango, providing a momentary escape from the betrayals of glitter. They allow tango lyrics to lose their sharp-edged sarcasm and skepticism and wish for the return of the one who holds a key to the particular state in which love and the good and simple pleasures all coexist. Words also change. Language becomes more transparent, opting for metaphor rather than the multiple layering of *lunfardo*'s allusions. Tango provides examples of good women. Mothers and sick sisters tend to be beyond reproach, since they do not trigger the turmoil of passion for money and sex or the anxieties of betrayal. They constitute points of nostalgia. They are one with the cherished street scene and romantic serenity.

"Victoria," one of Carlos Gardel's most celebrated renditions, features a man who sings of his joy, voicing victory, upon being left by his wife because he will be able to see his old friends again and go back to living with his mother: "Volver a ver mis amigos / vivir con mamá otra vez." Loyalty is found in the mother's nurture after love is defeated by the absence of one of the members of the couple. Getting dumped is not embarrassing. Being victimized by a woman naturalizes the male presence by coloring the tone of city conversations.

A table in a bar or a café or in the lover's home is the preferred locale for telling such a story. Pascual Contursi (1888–1932) wrote the most representative of these compositions, "Mi noche triste":

> Percanta que me amuraste
> en lo mejor de mi vida,
> dejándome el alma herida
> y espinas en el corazón,
> sabiendo que te quería
> que vos eras mi alegría
> y mi sueño abrasador,
> para mí ya no hay consuelo
> y por eso me encurdelo
> pa' olvidarme de tu amor.

Jilted by the flower of his life, a drunk sitting alone in a bar tells his story. The explanation for his deterioration is invariably the wound inflicted by a woman. In "Mi noche triste," the evocation of what she has left behind is given in terms of the breakdown of the cozy domesticity of the room they once shared. Since he is unable to recover alone in their place, he is thrown into the streets. The departure of the "good" woman redefines the space in which the romance took place; longing for her is synonymous with bemoaning the gloom of his surroundings. The serene harmony of the everyday rather than the anxiety because of the provocative *milonguera*'s sort of sexual harassment is the mark of the worthwhile woman who is, nevertheless, bound to disappoint. While the departure of the unworthy objects of infatuation is a relief, although it is associated with moral and financial ruin, the loss of a good woman permeates every aspect of daily life. This is why the singer says that when he goes to sleep at night, he leaves the door open so that she may come back in. He still brings home the little pastries she used to enjoy and feels that the bed is angry because it does not have them both there:

> De noche cuando me acuesto,
> no puedo cerrar la puerta,
> porque dejándola abierta
> me hago ilusión que volvés.
> Siempre llevo bizcochitos
> pa' tomar con matecitos
> como si estuvieras vos,
> y si vieras la catrera
> cómo se pone cabrera
> cuando no nos ve a los dos.

The wealthy are regularly denounced by tango's populist lyrics. Men and women who dress up in fancy clothes and show off their money and jewels in nightclubs are shown to be fakes or mere parasites. These male characters of the sort who abound in the city are called *niños bien*, while the women are referred to as *pitucas*.

The woman worthy of tango is, then, humble in appearance. Her attributes offer an alternative to the nocturnal glitter and sexual density of the relationships between pimps and prostitutes. In this manner, to miss this woman of tango also brings on nostalgia for an original uncomplicated relationship in which money does not play the decisive role that it does elsewhere. Descriptions of appearances become keys in defining the moral profiles of characters evoked by tango, creating a complicity with a listener who shares the judgments made by the singer in his confession. Thus the shabby brown coat and hat of the departing María in the composition also called "María" are emblems of her kindness:

> Acaso te llamaras solamente María,
> no sé si eras el eco de una vieja canción,
> pero hace mucho, mucho fuiste hondamente mía
> sobre un paisaje triste, desmayado de amor.
>
> El otoño te trajo, mojando de agonía,
> tu sombrerito pobre y el tapado marrón.
> Eras como la calle de la melancolía
> que llovía... llovía sobre mi corazón.

Perhaps her name was just María, the singer tells us; she might have been the echo of an old song, but he knows that a long time ago, she was deeply his. Autumn brought in María in her humble clothes. The landscape was sad and rainy, just like the melancholy street raining on the singer's heart. María is, then, the medium through which an absent young woman is woven into the landscape with the certainty of goodness lost. Her aura of moral uplift is a result of her attire. She has left a wound that defines autumn as well as the streets in which she appeared.

Returning women, though, seen passing in the street years after the love affairs are over, show that time has erased the beauty of youth, with traces that bespeak the misleading nature of all love. A ubiquitous lament is one expressed in a tango by Carlos Gardel as "y pensar que hace diez años fue mi locura / que llegué hasta la traición por tu hermosura / que esto que hoy es un cascajo fue la triste metedura / donde yo perdí el honor" (and to think that ten years ago I was crazy about her / that I went as far as betrayal for her beauty / and what is today an empty shell / was once the sad infatuation / for which I threw away my pride). Better not to come back, tango teaches us, because the drunk wallowing in his pain in a bar will be further disappointed by the looks of his beloved. The young woman who left her poor origins for the allure of money and nightlife is portrayed as heartless and ugly after her youth and innocence are snatched away by *la farra*, or the pleasures of the cabaret. Such is the lesson of Contursi's other tango, "Flor de fango," which in English literally means "Gutter Flower." This tango tells the story, in *lunfardo*, Buenos Aires slang, of a beautiful girl who gives herself up at the age of fourteen to "las delicias de un gotán" (the indulgences of tango) and ends up losing herself night after night in the ongoing party, portrayed in contrast to the domesticity of her previous simple, worthy existence. Like other women in the tango tradition, she has been coaxed into believing in love only to be left alone, old and disillusioned. Tango punishes all its characters: men and women age and decay; men face the added burden of the loss of their lovers' beauty.

Tango wishes for returns that are to be regretted later because true distances are measured in terms of time and not space. Something decisive and morally abject resides in the pleasures of the night. In tango lyrics, dancing, drinking, dressing up, faking different origins, and enjoying fast money are each simultaneously the source and the obstacle to happiness.

The hesitation of tango is the source of the very flow of its lyrics and dance steps. It is a conversation constantly threatened with incomprehension. Who is good? How will the other answer? What would be the right word? How to find out where the joke resides? Frequently, the *marca* is successful in the dance, and *lunfardo*'s meanings are understood when sung. In every case, there is the suspicion that one more layer of interpretation will make the difference. *Dibujar* (to draw) and *barrer* (to sweep) are names of *figuras* with which dancers produce the silent and eloquent intimacy of implied conversations between strangers or foreigners establishing citizenship in a multilingual city.

NOTES

1. The history of the word *milonga* is remarkable in that it has tended to keep all its meanings and even added to them over time.
2. *Lunfardo* is a jargon born in jail during the early twentieth century. It incorporates words from many of the immigrant groups in Argentina and gives them a Spanish sound. The vocabulary abounds in terms used for the prostitution trade as well as with the many characters associated with breaking the law and assorted urban types. Today, there is a National Academy of Lunfardo in Argentina. Jorge Luis Borges mocked its institutional respectability.
3. Héctor Mayoral, together with his wife and dance partner, Elsa María, are icons of the tango stage and have extended their work to include therapeutic uses of the dance to treat heart disease, Parkinson's disease, and depression.
4. Tango scholars and enthusiasts continue to be intrigued by the musical collaboration among Borges, Piazzolla, and Rivero in the making of the album that attempts to flesh out the belonging of Borges's poetry in the tango tradition. Are they *milongas*? Are they quotations of the genre? The uneasy combination of three stars, each with his own definition of the music

and poetry of Buenos Aires, stands as an example of a language combination that does not work—a celebration of fissures and discontinuity, like the city itself.

5. In song, the tone redefines the lyrics of "Malevaje." Some singers add a note of irony, while others interpret the story as one of true loss.

6. In this chapter, I provide English translations for some of the quotes from tango lyrics. For others, I do not provide a translation of the tango quotes, but I explain their meanings in my own critique of them. For all other translations, they are mine unless otherwise indicated.

7. Jorge Luis Borges, "La intrusa," in *El Aleph*, trans. Alastair Reid (Buenos Aires: Emecé Editores, 1995).

8. Borges, "La intrusa"; Jorge Luis Borges, "The Intruder," trans. Alastair Reid, *Encounter*, April 1969, 15–17; 2.

3 · LORCA, FROM COUNTRY TO CITY

Three Versions of *Poet in New York*

CHRISTOPHER MAURER

I

A translation, like a traditional Spanish ballad, begins *in medias res*.[1] We don't apprehend a poem directly and transport it straight into the target language; the meaning is always mediated by an idea of the poet being translated. Questions of genre and precedent shape the translator's idea of the poet and, in the case of Federico García Lorca (1898–1936), render him rural or urban, Arab Andalusian, gypsy, or perhaps even Scottish.[2] "If there is an equivalent to the *romance* in English," argued the South African poet Roy Campbell, apropos of Lorca's *Gypsy Ballads*, it must be "our ancient popular ballad form."[3] "Canción de jinete" reminded him of "one of the Scotch-English border ballads" (82). A more recent translator, Carl Cobb, seems to have thought of the Lorca of *Primer romancero gitano* as an avatar of Wordsworth, Housman, or Auden: "Green grows my love, / my love grows green."[4] Some balladic Lorcas are laconic and halting, others Baroque. Almost all are at odds with the urban subject of *Poet in New York*.

It isn't only the image of the poet—rural or urban—that seems unstable. We often think of translations as variations on a theme or as though light from the original had been refracted through the prism of translation. In many a schema of literary translation, a single original gives rise to multiple versions. The source text—the supposed "best text" of a work in the source language—is often regarded as the more stable element in the operation (one original and a succession of possible translations). But obviously, the original, too, can exist in different versions, and even when there is only one known source text, our

32

readings are shaped by ever-changing images of poet, publisher, and translator. Questions worth asking: The "best" source text *when? For whom? For what purpose?* One measure of the quality of a translation is the translator's awareness of the history both of the source text and of its reception by previous translators and other readers. The late Edwin Honig, in a conversation with fellow poet and translator Ben Belitt about the latter's version of *Poet in New York*, had some interesting comments on textual instability: "I wonder what *is* the text actually translated? Put it another way: is the text always a stable quantity, or is it that, plus something else—a variable? And if one says that it's also a variable quantity, then does one have to adjust, as a translator, not only to a word-for-word persistence of the text, but also to its ups and downs, its hiatuses and gravitational shifts? . . . You can't expect faithfulness where there's not something to be faithful to; some redoubtable scenario. Not even the mind of God can be thought of as the single originating source."[5] Belitt agreed: "There is no single, originating, authentic locus of all the meanings. A poem is an *area*, a quantum, rather than a datum. . . . No one concludes a translation, any more than one does the original" (75–76).

Poet in New York reminds me, more than other texts, that we cannot step twice into the same original, that the textual river cannot be read or translated twice in the same way. In a curious book on Lorca's reception and re-creation by American poets, *Apocryphal Lorca: Translation, Parody, Kitsch* (2009), Jonathan Mayhew considers the Spanish text of Lorca's *Suites*, as reconstructed by Melissa Dinverno and as recreated in English by Jerome Rothenberg, and wonders in passing whether the textual theory of versioning might not be the "ideal approach" to Lorca's work and—one might suppose—to translation.[6] The history of some of Lorca's works makes it difficult to imagine a "definitive" text. The best we can do, in some cases, is to try to capture one particular version or moment. In each of those textual snapshots, sometimes just out of camera range, are a number of agents—copyists, typographers, cover designers, editors, and publicists—whose work sometimes seems at odds with what we imagine to be the author's intentions. As Borges writes, "There can only be drafts. The concept of the 'definitive' text corresponds only to religion or exhaustion."[7] The idea of versioning strikes me as particularly apt in the case of Lorca not only because he didn't like to be *bound* and sometimes thought of the printed page as the deathbed of the poem but also because his protean works "translate" more easily than those of other poets from the verbal to the visual or musical. When I think of García Lorca sitting in a New York theater in 1929, watching a play in English, understanding little but absorbed in the nonverbal world of lighting, movement, music, and audience reaction, I remember a comment made by his brother, Francisco, long before Carlos Saura's *Bodas de sangre* (1981): that scenes from his plays could be stripped of language and somehow survive, despite the "bárbara amputación de la palabra."[8] His plays and poems live not only in variants but, perhaps to a greater degree than those of other poets, in different media. The "original" is more stubbornly elusive in Lorca than in other poets, changing form like Proteus and challenging one's notions of authority and originality. In some cases, the Spanish original goes missing altogether: André Belamich performed his Pléiade edition entirely in French, giving both text and manuscript variants in that language, and Rafael Martínez Nadal published a book-length paraphrase and textual mosaic of *El público* before the original became available. In still other instances—for example, *Poet in New York*—one of the originals was lost for decades, leaving translators "without something to be faithful to" (as Honig might have put it), wavering, as we shall see, between earth and moon, city and country.

II

Poet in New York offers a particularly striking example both of an unstable original and of the different ways translators have imagined Lorca. As Andrew A. Anderson, Mario Hernández, Daniel Eisenberg, and others have shown, Lorca's ideas for structuring into a book, or books, the poems he had written in New York and Cuba in 1929–1930 were in flux until shortly before his violent death in August 1936. From the first translation of *Poet in New York* by Rolfe Humphries to subsequent ones by Ben Belitt (1955), Greg Simon and Steven F. White (1988, 2008), and Pablo Medina and Mark Statman (2008), the book's translators have puzzled over Lorca's originals and dealt, in different ways, with his sexual and political persona and with editorial circumstances I shall attempt to illuminate here by drawing on the letters and essays of translators, publishers, editors, and editorial advisors.

Humphries, the first to translate *Poet in New York* into English (*The Poet in New York and Other Poems*, W. W. Norton, 1940), had been drawn to Lorca during the Spanish Civil War as he gathered poems for his anthology "... *And Spain Sings": Fifty Loyalist Ballads Adapted by American Poets*.[9] In December 1936, Humphries writes Edmund Wilson that he is "doing a lot of Spanish guys in translation—mostly fellows who have either been shot by the fascists or are likely to be. I have done about 25 poems, all rather simple, ballad-y kind of things, not class conscious or revolutionary."[10] Humphries would retain his taste for those "ballad-y kind of things" in the months and years ahead, as he labored, in Mexico, Paris, and New York, to assemble, edit, and translate—with the help of Mildred Adams, Herschel Brickell, Ernesto Guerra Da Cal, Margarita Ucelay, and others[11]—what would become the first edition and English translation of *Poeta en Nueva York*, a book he disliked but whose publication by Norton had been meant as a gesture of sympathy for Republican Spain. Oddly, *Poeta*'s social dimension—the critique of American capitalism, racism, and anthropocentrism and the attack on the Church's alliance with the wealthy and with Mussolini—was barely commented on by Humphries and was sometimes dismissed by reviewers as "an extemporaneous flight into alien areas," one not to be "considered in the main stream of [Lorca's] poetic development."[12] The book's "forced" surrealism and "cosmopolitanism" seemed alien, too, allied, somehow, to Lorca's homosexuality, as though they were postures, "phases," or "modes" the poet would grow out of. "I don't like his later poetry much," Humphries confided to his friend, the poet Louise Bogan: "There will be a fine passage now and then, but in general I think the new world, and New York, were rather too much for him, and the surrealist stuff got up his nose too much; his rhythms [do] not shudder but shriek, when he had no form to impose some discipline on them, and some folk tradition. [. . .] It seems to me clear also that he was more and more having a hell of a time with his homo impulses and had a rather bad lot sucking up to him."[13]

The Lorca Humphries valued was not "the poet in New York," with his "show-off kind of bad Bohemianism"; it wasn't his "surrealist smarty side"; it was the "young Spaniard" who "managed to keep the simple folk-talk and the mystery" and "get at the inner stuff and sense of things, and to keep his cadences both strange and simple." Lorca, Humphries wrote Bogan, may have evolved later in life, improving on "the New York stuff" with the "later tragedies . . . in a strict and realistic vein." Or maybe not. In any case, *Poet in New York* was a "hysterical" book, the result of "homo tendencies" that had pulled the poet far from his rural origins.[14] It must have seemed to Humphries, who would later translate *The Gypsy Ballads*, that the poet needed reprogramming:[15] "The New York poems still sound pretty hysterical. I have not read his plays, so I do not know exactly what was happening to him in the work which he evidently had most respect for in his later days; but it is too bad he couldn't have been spared and put through a course in ballads and simple writing again. Maybe he couldn't have stood it; maybe his work was finished; maybe his homo tendencies had him stopped. I don't know—but I do know the best of the Gypsy ballads are very good (Gillman and Novak, *Poets* 156)."

I am not sure what Guerra Da Cal thought of the book, but another of Humphries's helpers, the journalist and translator Mildred Adams, would later confide to a friend that she felt guilty to have participated in the project: "I have a growing sense of guilt at having aided the translation of *Poet in New York*. I think those sur-realiste things [*Poet in New York* and *Así que pasen cinco años*] were only a phase, and a very passing phase, and that Federico's reputation will not depend on them in any way. I am sorry to have helped put them before the American public, and glad they didn't sell very well. It is a great tragedy that he had not emerged from that phase into another which would blot it out."[16]

III

The sexual, the textual, and the political—the "rural" poet's supposed inability to assimilate surrealism and translate the city—were still intertwined over a decade later, in the early 1950s, when Federico's brother, Francisco, living in exile in New York, teaching at Queens College, and fielding requests from all over the world for permission to translate Federico's poetry and plays, turned his attention to *Poet in New York*. On his desk at 448 Riverside Drive, among unopened letters, student papers, drafts of his own poems, and pages from the book of critical essays he was composing about his brother, were a proposal from New Directions to publish a *Selected Poems*; another from Donald M. Allen, then an editor at Grove Press, offering Ben Belitt's *Poet in New York*; and a third, from John Green, agent for South African poet Roy Campbell, who, scornful of previous translations,[17] claimed to have been authorized by Lorca's family to translate *Poet in New York* along with the rest of the poetry and was hoping—with the support of T. S. Eliot at Faber and Faber—to publish four volumes of his translations in England and the United States.[18] Two of those proposals did, in fact, materialize in 1955: the New Directions *Selected Poems*, edited by Francisco García Lorca and Allen, and Belitt's *Poet in New York*.[19] Not all of Campbell's translations were published during his lifetime, due in part to reservations, on the part of the poet's family and others, about his political beliefs.[20] To begin with, Campbell was the author of a number of fierce anti-Republican, pro-Franco satires in verse, filled with contempt for the Leftist sympathies and homosexuality of one of the poets—Stephen Spender, "leading poet of the Rear"—who would had written, and collaborated on, some of the earliest translations of Lorca into English. As Robert MacGregor of New Directions put it to Campbell's agent, Green, in May 1952, "Though Francisco recognizes that his brother's death was a long time ago he is still troubled by . . . rumors . . . to the effect that Mr. Campbell has not only been pro-Fascist and pro-Falangist in the past, but that he is at work on the official history of the Franco regime."[21] In their correspondence, New Directions and Francisco offer to put aside politics in the interest of poetry: if the Campbell translations are of high quality, MacGregor promises, Francisco will "do everything possible to persuade the rest of the family to allow them to be published." New Directions tended to "lean over backwards" when it came to political impartiality: "We republished Céline here at a time when he was under indictment in France for presumed collaboration with the German occupation authorities, and of course we publish Ezra Pound."[22] Campbell was quick to reply:

> If you print Pound or Céline you shouldn't find me a tough problem. I have no politics outside my religion, which is persecuted alike by Commies and Nazis. I

fought longer against, and killed far more Nazis, than I killed Commies, and was wounded far worse by them: having been crippled for life I was conscripted illegally by Spanish Reds when I wanted to escape from Toledo with my family. I was then put in the Tcheka of the Hombre de Palo and then in the Maristas at Toledo and sentenced to death—so I had some little cause for fighting in the Spanish war, having also been tortured in the Checka, only for being a Catholic. Also, as Don Francisco [García Lorca] himself can tell you—not a single bullfighter or *chalán* (as I am), or gipsy, ever joined the Republicans (that only happens in Hemingway's imagination); we all fought for the old order. When you think that Federico García Lorca made his best poetry out of this class of worker and the life we live, it should be easier to forgive, since it was not for politics that we fought but for a way of life, the life of the Christian peasant and cattleman, which is so ruthlessly being stamped out all over eastern Europe. I also partly undertook the translation as an expiation of the indelible stain on Nationalist arms resulting from the dastardy murder of Lorca. I would not dream, in my translations, of turning a single hair of Lorca's meanings politically, any more than I do in my translations of Eça de Queiroz's novels (which are furiously socialist) or of Baudelaire's blasphemies. The job of a translator is to *represent*, irrespective of his own feelings. I should always hold myself subject to correction by Lorca's trustees, if I did unwittingly transgress.[23]

As with Humphries, images of rural Lorca come to the fore, as though the slain poet, the son of a prosperous farmer and a retired school teacher, represented not, vaguely, the people, and certainly not the proletariat, but a rugged, loosely defined, rural class—that of the gypsy, the "Christian peasant and cattleman," and the *torero*—whose values Campbell admired and with which he identified himself.[24] *Poet in New York* was difficult to reconcile with that image. In New York, Campbell wrote, Lorca had attempted to follow Salvador Dalí "into the complex world of surrealism, and lost his depth." The "pulse" of his imagination falters, "metaphors and images fall out of focus; his verse becomes loose, plaintive, and slightly mephitic" (26, 95). It was the image—promulgated by John Crow, Humphries, Ramón Sender, Philip Cummings, and many others—of the balladeer in the big city, the earthy poet of the people, "a sort of Spanish Johnny Appleseed,"[25] an urban cowboy or "chalán," a "mere folklorist who should have remained singing gypsy ballads in Granada."[26] Campbell writes in 1952, "We are reminded, in Lorca's American venture, of Burns when he went into high society at Edinburgh and started to write like a courtier and gentleman of the world. It was a fiasco. Lorca's talent is not cosmopolitan, and it did not flourish far from the scent of the orange groves of the South."[27] Lorca could be universal "when he is writing at home about his native Andalusia," but paradoxically, his appeal "is never more parochial and provincial than when he is self-consciously trying to be 'cosmopolitan,' under the influence of Whitman, in the poems written in, and about, New York and the Caribbean" (*An Appreciation* 3). For Campbell, as for Humphries, the rural and "oral" Lorca mattered more than the urban, written one.[28] Campbell's Lorca—who had "grafted" (that country know-how!) Baroque Spanish poetry onto the popular oral tradition—the Lorca who meshed with Campbell's vision of a "timeless bucolic Spain,"[29] had gone astray, down the path of homosexuality, under "the influence of Whitman." Campbell's phrase "slightly mephitic"—"offensive to the smell, foul-smelling; noxious, poisonous, pestilential" (Oxford English Dictionary),[30] unlike the "orange groves of the South"—struck a nerve with Randall Jarrell, reviewing one of his books in the *New York Times* in 1955: "He [Campbell] loves to tell [his enemies] in the accents of 'English Bards and Scotch Reviewers' that they are stupid and homosexual and smell bad."[31] "Mephitic" is clearly an allusion to the poet's homosexuality, as in Campbell's satirical poem *The Flowering Rifle* (1939), where Lorca's death is seen as part of the nationalists' zealous cleansing of the left. Lorca was caught "bending over"[32]:

> And what if García Lorca died for this
> Caught bending over that forlorn Abyss
> For some mephitic whim his soul that spliced,
> As once he boasted, with the Antichrist?[33]

To the Campbell of *The Flowering Rifle*, Lorca was a hubristic flute-playing Marsyas, flayed by Apollo (Nationalism? Franco?) in an age of "fevered sin and languid eye" (homosexuality again) and supplanted by the memory of José Antonio Primo de Rivera, "new-fledged eagle," whose virtues more than compensated for "the genius lost" in Lorca:

> It was his fate with his own age to die—
> That of the fevered sin and languid eye.
> And let the new-fledged eagle take the sky. (*Flowering Rifle* 93)

Many years later, in 1957, after he had abandoned any hope of obtaining the family's authorization for his Lorca translations, Campbell attempted an explanation: "When the Nationalists entered Granada the unbelievable babooneries perpetrated by the Reds made them trigger-happy as they rounded up and shot all corrupters of children, known perverts, and sexual cranks."[34] An epigram in *Talking Bronco* (1946), "On the Martyrdom of F. García Lorca," had the poet simply "lose" his life, the victim of gunshots, removing all agency except that of translators:

Not only did he lose his life
By shots assassinated:
But with a hatchet and a knife
Was after that—translated![35]

IV

By the early 1950s, with Spain—and American poetry—emerging from isolation, García Lorca had become better known in the United States. Belitt was probably right to think that Lorca had contributed to "the internationalization of poetry" (Honig, *Poet's Other Voice* 66). The publication of Belitt's translation by Grove Press in 1955, and of the *Selected Poems* by New Directions that same year (both books initiated by Donald M. Allen), would give *Poet in New York* some remarkable traveling companions. In the 1950s, interest in Republican Spain would fade and, in new editorial company, *Poet in New York*'s supposed surrealism and defense of homosexuality became less objectionable. Grove Press was only a few years old and exploring new terrain. In the summer of 1955, Grove's director, Barney Rosset, brought out the first American edition of *Waiting for Godot* (1953). *Poet in New York* took its initial place, in a slender Grove catalog (1949–1955) among what its salesmen might have described as "distinguished foreign writing" of the nineteenth and twentieth centuries. In the early 1950s, Grove's list included David Magarshack's biographies of Chekhof and Turguenev and Spencer's life of Flaubert; nineteenth-century novels (the Goncourts' *Germinie Lacerteux*, Zola's *Earth*); the poetry of W. S. Graham; works by Nigerian Amos Tutuola; D. H. Lawrence's translations of Giovanni Verga; *The Poems of C. P. Cavafy*, whose "perversity" was mentioned by at least one reviewer[36] and who helped accustom U.S. readers to homoerotic poetry; and *Devil in the Skin* by another gay writer, Raymond Radiguet (Sommerville, "Commerce" 252). During its first few years, Grove's list tilted toward French literature; García Lorca was its first Spanish-language writer, one of relatively few individual poets, and one of the first published in Grove's new series of quality "Evergreen Paperbacks," a sign he was reaching wider audiences, particularly in colleges and universities.[37] That same year, 1955, Lorca's *Three Tragedies* inaugurated a new line of "Paperbooks" at New Directions and sold ten thousand copies (Sommerville, "Commerce" 427). The encounter between the Old World and the New—one of the underlying tensions in *Poet in New York*—must have seemed perfect for Grove, which, in the early 1950s, inserted American authors like Whitman into a *European* tradition and "quickly became a voice dissenting from American exceptionalism" (Sommerville, "Commerce" 251).[38] By the time another Spanish-language writer, Octavio Paz, joined the list (1961), Grove had assumed a very different image—that of a leading publisher of African and East Asian literature in translation and of transgressive fiction, poetry, and drama, including the novels of Henry Miller and William Burroughs; a line of "Victorian Erotica"; and eventually, the notorious film *I Am Curious Yellow*, which kept Rosset and Grove entangled in litigation about obscenity and gave the Andalusian "folk poet" more urbane editorial company than he had kept at Norton. While Belitt was working on his translation of *Poet in New York*, Rosset was beginning to plan the publication battle over *Lady Chatterley's Lover* and other novels that would challenge obscenity laws.[39] Moreover, Grove's "championing of authors such as Miller, Burroughs, Genet, Rechy and Selby '—some of whom, like Lorca, were introduced to Rosset by the gay Donald Allen—' indicates the homosocial contexts in which most of the postwar struggles against censorship were initially negotiated."[40]

For all of Rosset's and Grove Press's editorial openness, the correspondence of Belitt and Ángel del Río, who had agreed to write the introduction to *Poet in New York*, shows them stepping carefully around the issue of Lorca's homosexuality. "I am worried about the allusion to problems into which it might be advisable not to delve," Del Río writes Belitt in December 1954, sending him a copy of his introduction. "You know, of course, to what I am referring. I feel that a discreet allusion should be made, but by being *too* discreet I do not want to imply too much and, above all, I do not want to [stir up] a delicate matter which I know troubles Lorca's family and friends a great deal."[41] In his reply, Belitt says he has "given careful thought to your uncertainty regarding the single allusion to Federico's personal difficulties and I have suggested a revision which avoids the danger of defamatory innuendo which I think you are right to wonder about. Certainly, the little that is left needs to be said. And I hope that before long the much that has been omitted will be sympathetically and openly avowed by everyone concerned; of course it will have to be. The story is already written into the records in 'Tu Infancia' for anyone who can read English (or Spanish) and construe poetry."[42] Barely a sentence in the published version of Del Río's intelligent introduction mentions Lorca's sexuality: the sources of the poet's "emotional crisis are obscure, at least for those who knew him superficially. They touch delicate fibers of his personality, problems which cannot be hastily appraised or dismissed."[43] Both Del Río and Belitt were aware of Lorca's friendship with a young gay poet, a certain Mr. Cummings, with whom he had spent a week in the country—in Eden Mills, Vermont, in August 1929—and about whom Lorca seems to have told del Río very little. Reticent about Lorca's private life, del Río hardly mentioned him in the introduction for Grove's first edition—he was "a Mr. Cummings [whom] I have never been able to identify" (xiv–xv).

Cummings—who read those words and lost no time in writing to del Río[44]—insisted for years, to Lorca scholars and others, that Lorca's stay in Vermont had taken the poet back to his rural, Andalusian roots, had given him a glimpse of "the real America," and had left a deep mark on *Poeta en Nueva York*, inspiring the "Poemas de la soledad en Vermont." Belitt would have none of it:

> When I read the poems of Vermont, "Poems of Solitude in Vermont," the word that stands out to me is a very Spanish word, the word that is really one of the most untranslatable and indigenous words, the word soledad. I see almost nothing of Vermont in the poems, in contradistinction to what Mr. Cummings is saying, but I do see that these are poems about solitude in Vermont; in the same way that I see nothing of Columbia University in the poems written [there]. And solitude is a distinctly Spanish vocation. It is a word that has more context than it is possible to recover in a transla[tion]. But the one thing that is common to all the context is a special depth of introspection which I don't think is particularly Vermont, but I think is very Spanish.[45]

The idea of Lorca writing poems in "plena selva americana" (an expression used by the Spanish critic Guillermo Díaz-Plaja apropos of the trip to Vermont) was yet another variety of rustication; it seemed to Belitt "a neo-primitive regression to the world of Leatherstocking and Chateaubriand."[46]

Del Río's introduction and Belitt's adventurous and sometimes bombastic translation got mixed reviews,[47] but the book was vastly more influential than Humphries's, which had sold only a few hundred copies[48] and of which the translator himself was "never very fond."[49] Remembering the struggle to obtain permission to publish his own translation of *Poeta*—which Norton had allowed to go out of print—and wondering "what [was] the matter with my own version" and why it needed to be "done over," Humphries had advised Grove's Donald Allen to steer clear of publishing *any* Lorca in translation: "I think you will save yourself a lot of headaches if you decide to let Lorca alone."[50] Like Humphries, whose oral Spanish was barely up to hailing a cab or buying a newspaper,[51] Belitt was still learning the language when he "flung" himself at García Lorca (Honig, *Poet's Other Voice* 62–63). Help with the translation came—in person and in a list of tactful suggestions—from the critic José Fernández-Montesinos, who spent many summers at Bennington College and whose wife, Nora Hasenclever Montesinos, was a Bennington friend and colleague of Belitt. Both Fernández-Montesinos and the poet's brother, Francisco, who, later, hoped Belitt would translate some of his own essays, had kind words for the translation. Like Humphries, Belitt struggled heroically with the absences and uncertainties of the originals and for years gathered textual materials and followed the research of a cadre of *lorquistas* in the United States and abroad. By the early '80s, he was proposing a twenty-fifth-anniversary edition of his translation and asking Lorca scholars to help him assess the critical edition of Eutimio Martín, who had doubted the authority of Bergamín's edition and divided *Poeta* into two separate books, *Poeta en Nueva York* and *Tierra y luna*: a "city book" and a "country book,"[52] with poems inspired by New York and by Vermont, respectively.[53] Doing his best to make sense of the scholarly debate, the exasperated Belitt wavered, between 1980 and 1982, on whether to redo his translation entirely, following the Martín edition, or, as "an old-time religionist," adhere to the unified *Poeta en Nueva York* he had followed in his 1955 edition.[54] What he had settled on, by May 1981, was a bifurcated *Poeta*: "The book as I now envision it will contain the modified text of the *Poeta* (about half the length of the present one); the text of *Earth and Moon* (containing most of the other half of the *Poeta*, plus a number of 'miscellaneous' poems from the Lorca canon); a section of other poems considered 'supplementary'; the lengthy Introduction by [Piero] Menarini, both historical and interpretive in character; my own considered enlarged Chronology documenting Lorca scholarship since 1955; and maybe a brief prefatory note of my own. That is all."[55]

That was, in fact, the book submitted to Grove and to Lorca's nephew, Manuel Fernández-Montesinos, who, after the death of the poet's brother, Francisco, in 1976, had begun to act as the literary executor of the Lorca estate and who had asked Grove—as well as the family's agent in the United States, New Directions—to send the manuscript to him for approval. To Belitt's astonishment, after several months of silence, and with the book already scheduled for fall publication, in September 1982, Fernández-Montesinos wrote him a harsh letter, confessing that he had never been "satisfied" with Belitt's 1955 edition and refusing permission to publish the revised, bifurcated version: "Lorca's New York Poems: Poet in New York / Earth and Moon." A line-by-line, thirteen-page critique of Belitt's translation of the first two poems in the book brought an end to his long history of cooperation with the Lorca family—with Francisco, José Fernández-Montesinos, Nora, Tica, and her mother, Concha (Federico's sister), who, years earlier, had copied for Belitt the table of contents of *Poeta* from the still-unpublished Aguilar edition of the *Obras completas*.[56] A considerable amount of work was lost: not only Menarini's introduction but Belitt's well-researched "Chronology," his translation of the lecture Lorca had given about *Poet in New York* and of additional poems, and most important, an interesting revised translation based on galleys of the edition of Martín (Ariel, 1981). The need to accommodate the new edition by Martín had sparked Belitt to reexamine *all* his English translations and, in some cases, to revise them in order to bring them "closer to the literal."[57] Lines from the 1955 version that have been criticized by generations of critics—for example, "O heaven murdered one" as the translation for "Asesinado por el cielo"—are simpler in 1982: "Slain by the sky" (Vuelta de paseo).

In no case did Belitt's revisions satisfy Fernández-Montesinos, who refused to authorize the new edition and translation and began to distance the estate from New Directions and from Grove. In September 1983, when Grove defiantly brought out a new edition of the old translation—with an updated chronology and a postscript to the 1955 translator's foreword—Fernández-Montesinos angrily ordered them to pulp existing stocks of *Poet in New York* and stop reprinting the Belitt translation.[58] Although Belitt was unable to publish his revised versions, they were not entirely lost. Some time before his death in 2003, Belitt, who had the unwavering sense that he and Grove had made "Lorca history" and who wanted it preserved, handed or sent Honig a fat envelope of correspondence on the case of *Poet in New York*: "Some day scholars will be asking."[59] Accompanying the letters—to and from the family, Menarini, the publishers, and others—was a copyedited version of the aborted manuscript, with Menarini's meticulous introduction (which Belitt had translated into English). Belitt had begun with an unstable Spanish original and arrived at a translation that had aspired, paradoxically, both to be "creative," enduring, independent poetry (Glass, *Counterculture* 60) and to adapt itself to emergent textual history. Resigning himself to Martín's bifurcated edition of the New York poetry but emotionally invested in the unified *Poeta* of 1940—although it seemed, by the 1980s, "a Mesozoic relic"—Belitt assured publishers and friends that "there will now *always* be *two* versions of the *Poeta*, as there are two versions of Keats' *Hyperion*; that 40 years of worldwide diffusion of the 'old text' can never be reversed or undone, and the Bergamín-Humphries-Belitt mutations are a *fait accompli* divinized by translation into half a dozen (?) tongues, all over the world."[60] Belitt's ideas for the cover of the divided—and aborted—edition had tried to emphasize the country/city, earth/moon fissure in *Poeta*: a "bold diagonal dividing the author's face into two colors" or a "space-shot of earth as seen from the moon's curve, a natural in 1982."[61] Gone was the elegant geometry of Roy Kuhlman, whose covers had ushered the 1955 *Poeta*—and its reprintings—into the visual and verbal orbit of abstract expressionism.[62] Amused by a Spanish editor's inclusion of the entire Bergamín edition as an appendix to a bipartite *Poet in New York / Earth and Moon*, Belitt joked that *Poeta* might "have to be read synoptically before the 'good news' of the total vision of Lorca's New York is ever revealed to the Faithful!"[63] He later wrote, "We cannot *force* a tidiness on the canon of The New York Poems that never existed—least of all, for Lorca: the world of the *Poeta* is getting to look more and more like an expanding universe—from a city, to an earth and a moon, to appendices like galactic nebulae and black holes in space!"[64]

Despite the withdrawal of support from the Lorca estate, Belitt's translation— the 1955 edition and its numerous reprintings—was a commercial success.

Decades after its initial publication, it was still (in Belitt's own account) far from "extinct" and had sold close to sixty thousand copies in the United States and in England, where it had been published by Thames and Hudson.[65] With its appendices of prose poems and Lorca's lectures on Góngora and on *duende*,[66] it was "something of a classic in translation," Belitt reminded his publisher, Barney Rosset; and he was proud to recall that Theodore Roethke, writing to Howard Nemerov, had been one of its divinizers: "Say, tell Ben Belitt some time that his translation of Lorca has become practically a holy text with my kids: god it is a beautiful job, if my old tin ear is still functioning—better than Humphries' even."[67] Above all, Belitt's book had helped shift American perceptions of Lorca. By 1982, Belitt gushed, a book "meant to ... supplant the ethnic baroqueries of [Lorca's] '*canciones*,' '*casidas*,' '*gacelas*,' '*coplas*,' '*peteneras*,' gypsy '*romances*'" had "come to be regarded as a masterwork of the twentieth century idiom," and scholarly attention had shifted from country to city: "from a poet in Andalusia to a poet in New York."[68] Or almost. Even for Belitt, there would *always* be *two* poets: the urban one and the residual rustic. In his "Conferencia-recital" on *Poet in New York*, Lorca tells of his—literal—return to the city after a week with Cummings in Vermont. On returning to Manhattan, Lorca writes, "Penetro un poco más en la vida social y la denuncio. La denuncio porque vengo del campo." "I denounce it," Belitt translates. "I denounce it because I'm a hillbilly myself."

A "hillbilly" read by hippies. To Belitt's amusement, there were rumors that his 1955 translation of *Poeta* had "launched a whole generation of California poets," lighting up "the whole Western coast like a switchboard." Weren't there echoes of Belitt's Lorca in Ginsberg's *Howl*, asked a graduate student at Berkeley who was writing a thesis on the Bay Area poets. "I find so many similarities between [*Poet in New York*] and *Howl*," he wrote Belitt, "that I am almost certain that Ginsberg knew it, that the words were ringing in his head, that you and Lorca were sitting on his shoulder and moving his pen around while he was writing."[69] The two howls of protest had been published one after the other: Belitt's Lorca in 1955, Ginsberg the following year. Ginsberg's homage to Whitman, "A Supermarket in California," in which he spots Lorca "down by the watermelons," dates from 1955. Had Ginsberg and Belitt been in touch? Had the former seen Belitt's translations prepublished in poetry journals? In his response, Belitt distances himself from Ginsberg, pleads innocence of anything "Californian," and takes the story back to 1952, to the offices of Donald Allen. The 1955 *Poet in New York* was really Allen's idea, Belitt wrote:[70] "His nose for vogue was infallible." It was his idea

> to resurrect a book derogated and refuted by lorquistas in Spain and long out of print in this country, precisely because he could sniff its contemporaneity in the

flying pollen. I thought the idea decidedly strange, and held out little hope of any sale for such a book, but fortunately I went ahead with it and was proven wrong. In the same way, Donald was aware of subterranean thrashings and rumblings in the San Francisco Bay Area. He knew a San Andreas fault or an O'Leary lantern when he saw one, and he set about annexing that to Grove Press, too. He had, and no doubt still has, a genius for the coming wave, the nouvelle vogue, the antepenultimate moment pushing its way toward the ultimate, and attacked it like a prophesying dowser. When the stick went down, there was water, and when he panned a handful of gravel, there was gold.[71]

As for *Howl*: "Sometime in 1954 or 1955 ... while *Poet in New York* was still in the press, I visited Donald in New York. He pointed to a stash of manuscript by one Allen Ginsberg, who I believe was identified with the New York scene. Here, he said ... is a poem called *Howl* which everybody in the Bay Area thinks is the All-American answer to Auden and the legitimate heir to Whitman."[72] "Here," Allen added, "is another *Poet in New York*." In the offices of Grove Press, Lorca had finally lost his country manners.

NOTES

1. This chapter, an expanded version of a lecture given at the City University of New York (CUNY) Graduate Center in April 2013, is part of a book in progress, *Surviving Lorca*. I am grateful for the help of Laura García Lorca, Philip Noonan, Andrew A. Anderson, Patricia C. Billingsley, Christopher Ricks of Boston University's Editorial Institute, John O'Neill of the Hispanic Society of America, and Sean Noel of Boston University's Howard Gotlieb Archival Research Center.
2. Reviewing Lorca's poems (1939) in the *New York Times Book Review* (September 3, 1939), Peter Monro Jack finds Lorca's poetry "a curious blend of folk song and sophisticated speech," with qualities found also in "the Scots ballad and the Elizabethan lyric and the Greek Anthology." For other reactions to the first edition, see Andrew Anderson, "La trayectoria de *Poeta en Nueva York* a través de sus traductores estadounidenses: Humphries, Belitt, Simon/White y después," in *El impacto de la metrópolis: La experiencia americana en Lorca, Dalí y Buñuel*, ed. José M. del Pino (Frankfurt: Vervuert, 2018), 93–115; and Andrew Samuel Walsh, "Lorca's *Poet in New York* as a Paradigm of Poetic Retranslation," in *Literary Retranslation in Context*, ed. Susanne Cadera and Andrew Samuel Walsh (Oxford, UK: Peter Lang, 2017), 21–51.
3. Roy Campbell, *Lorca: An Appreciation of His Poetry* (New Haven, Conn.: Yale University Press, 1952), 51.
4. On translations of the first line of "Romance sonámbulo," see Christopher Maurer, "Shades of Green," in Federico García Lorca, *Gypsy Ballads*, trans. Jane Duran and Gloria García Lorca (London: Enitharmon Press, 2011), 36–37.
5. Edwin Honig, *The Poet's Other Voice: Conversations on Literary Translation* (Amherst, Mass.: University of Massachusetts Press, 1985), 68.
6. Jonathan Mayhew, *Apocryphal Lorca: Translation, Parody, Kitsch* (Chicago: University of Chicago Press, 2009), 164.

7. Quoted in Efraín Kristal, "Philosophical/Theoretical Approaches to Translation," in *A Companion to Translation Studies*, ed. Sandra Berman and Catherine Porter (Cambridge, Mass.: Wiley Blackwell, 2014), 28–40, 33.
8. Francisco García Lorca, *Federico y su mundo*, ed. Mario Hernández (Madrid: Alianza, 1980), 342.
9. Anderson, "La trayectoria," 95–98.
10. R. Humphries to Edmund Wilson, December 4, 1936, in Richard Gillman and Michael Paul Novak, eds., *Poets, Poetics, and Politics: America's Literary Community Viewed from the Letters of Rolfe Humphries, 1910–1969* (Lawrence: University Press of Kansas, 1992), 134. See also his letters of July 6 and July 15, 1938, to Louise Bogan, on his liking for the "early" Lorca (142, 147).
11. Brickell wrote a reader's report for the publisher and a biographical evocation of Lorca for Humphries's translation. Humphries corrected and revised the translation with the help of Mildred Adams (who hoped to interest William Warder Norton in a biography of García Lorca), Guerra Da Cal, and his wife, Margarita Ucelay, recent exiles to the United States. On December 31, 1939, Humphries sent Adams the manuscript of his translation and explained, "Mssrs. Norton and Brickell have urged me to take advantage of your courtesy in connection with my forthcoming book translating *The Poet in New York and Other Poems* by García Lorca. There is practically no limit to the amount of profitable advice I can receive" (R. H. to M. A., December 31, 1939). On January 12, 1940, Humphries wrote to Adams, "Taking advantage of your kind invitation I am sending you another batch of stuff, about equal in length to what we went over last time. I understand that Sr. Daqual—I do not know the spelling—can not be available until after the 19th of the month; but I can come any time at his convenience.... This ... is the most constructive help I have ever had; and makes me feel as if the proper combination had been achieved. Thank you very much indeed; and do not let me become a nuisance." Both letters are in the Papers of Mildred Adams, Hispanic Society of America, New York City (hereafter abbreviated HSA).
12. Ángel del Río, introduction to Federico García Lorca, *Poet in New York*, trans. Ben Belitt (New York: Grove Press, 1955), x. Del Río is referring to critics like R. W. Short, Eugene Jolas, John Gould Fletcher, and Dudley Fitts. For a more complete account of the book's reception, see Anderson, "La trayectoria"; and Young.
13. R. H. to Louise Bogan, October 4, 1938, in Gillman and Novak, *Poets, Poetics, and Politics*, 152. Cf. the letter to Bogan of September 17, 1938, en route to Mexico (149). Humphries's comments to Bogan are quoted and studied by Anderson ("La trayectoria," 100), who notes the irony of Humphries's distaste for the book he was translating, and by Daniel Eisenberg, *"Poeta en Nueva York": Historia y problemas de un texto de Lorca* (Barcelona: Editorial Ariel, 1976), 58–59.
14. Gillman and Novak, *Poets, Poetics, and Politics*, 149.
15. Roy Campbell, too, believed it had taken Lorca "quite a long time" after returning to Spain "to recover his poetical eyesight and insight," in *Appreciation of His Poetry*, 94–95.
16. Mildred Adams to fellow translator Richard O'Connell, July 10, 1941. Copy in Papers of Mildred Adams, HSA.
17. See his mockery of the translations of A. L. Lloyd and those of "Mssrs. [Rafael Martínez-] Nadal, [Stephen] Spender and [Joan] Gili," in "Banderillas de Fuego" (1953), reprinted in Campbell, *Collected Works*, vol. 4, ed. Peter Alexander, Michael Chapman, and Marcia Leveson (Craighall: Ad Donker, 1988), 418–420. For a sampling of Campbell's published translations of Lorca, see Campbell, *The Collected Poems*, vol. 3 (London: Bodley Head, 1960), 61–80; Campbell, *Collected Works*, vol. 2, 337–438; and his book about Lorca. In a

preface to the posthumous *Collected Poems*, Mary Campbell writes that her husband "translated nearly all the works of García Lorca" (13). Many of them appeared in British literary magazines between 1947 and 1952, and others are still unpublished. See Noël Valis, "Lorca's *Agonía republicana* and Its Aftermath," *Bulletin of Spanish Studies* 91, no. 1–2 (2014): 267–294, 290n86.

18. Campbell had met Rafael Martínez Nadal (who was serving informally as an English literary agent for the Lorca family) in Oxford in spring 1944. Martínez Nadal, who had written the introduction to Stephen Spender and J. L. Gili's translation of Lorca's *Poems* (London: Dolphin, 1939), proposed the new translation project to Poetry London, an imprint of Nicholson and Watson and, after Poetry London failed, to T. S. Eliot at Faber and Faber (1949), praising Campbell's work both to Eliot and to the family. The project came to an end when Faber was unable to resolve satisfactorily the question of North American rights to Lorca's work. Martínez Nadal withdrew his support for Campbell's translations, and in 1953, the two exchanged a series of angry letters in the *Times Literary Supplement*.

19. The poet's brother, Francisco García Lorca, signed the contract with Grove Press for *Poet in New York* on January 20, 1953, agreeing to royalties of 8 percent and an advance of $150. New Directions Publishing Corp. Records, Am. Ms. 2077, Houghton Library, Harvard University, Cambridge, Mass. (hereinafter abbreviated NDR).

20. In an illuminating article on Lorca's political "afterlife," Noël Valis studies Campbell's strange ideological and personal trajectory; see "Lorca's *Agonía republican*," 290, on Francisco García Lorca's and Arturo Barea's opposition to the publication of his translations.

21. See also Green's reply of May 13, 1952: "It is, of course, an undeniable fact that Roy Campbell did support Franco in the Spanish Civil War. It is also true that he is writing a history of the Civil War for Eyre and Spottiswoode. Campbell is a converted Catholic, and it is for this reason that he supported Franco. It can hardly be said that Campbell is in any sense a pro-Fascist, as at a late age he volunteered to serve in the last war as a sergeant and took a very active part indeed in fighting the Fascists. I am sure that Mr. Lorca will appreciate that Campbell's views on Spain are entirely religious, and non-political, and that he is considered to be probably the finest translator we have in this country, in fact he won the Foyle Prize of £250 last year for his translation of St. John of the Cross, the reviews of which book have been quite remarkably outstanding." NDR.

22. Robert M. McGregor to Roy Campbell, September 24, 1954, NDR.

23. Roy Campbell to Robert MacGregor, September 27, 1954, NDR. Gayle Rogers, *Modernism and the New Spain: Britain, Cosmopolitan Europe, and Literary History* (Oxford: Oxford University Press, 2012), 195, would agree: "Campbell's translations do not twist Lorca's poems toward any particular political end."

24. A friend of Campbell, Spanish poet José María Alonso Gamo, reported in 1949 that Campbell, with his "empaque de ganadero salmantino," liked to call himself a "chalán" (1021–1022). He also called himself a *vaquero* (Campbell, *Collected Works*, 323, 344–345) and was referred to in the British press as a "toreador," or "matador among poets," and in the British 1939 *Who's Who* as a "fisherman, editor, poet, bullfighter (both on foot and on horseback), 'professor' of equitation, farmer, cowboy—by turns"; see Justin O'Brien, "Poet on Horseback," *Kenyon Review* 4, no. 1 (1942): 75. Who better to identify with a poet from Fuente Vaqueros!

25. Philip H. Cummings, trans., *Lorca, Songs*, ed. Daniel Eisenberg (Pittsburgh, Pa.: Duquesne University Press, 1976), 173.

26. See Ramón Sender's review of *Poet in New York* in the *New York Times Book Review*, October 9, 1955, 7, where he finds that *Poet in New York* has "less resonance" than other works by Lorca; Ben Belitt's letter to the editor in the *New York Times*, November 13, 1955, 43; and

Juan Larrea's letter of October 28, 1955, to Francis Brown, editor of the *New York Times Book Review*, accusing Sender of "trying to dismiss his distinguished contemporary as a mere folklorist who should have remained singing gypsy ballads in Granada." The letter was apparently to have been signed also by Mildred Adams and Ernesto Guerra da Cal. John Crow, who met Lorca during the poet's stay in New York, told Mildred Adams that he and his roommate—Francis C. Hayes—agreed with Campbell on the "mephitic" nature of *Poeta en Nueva York*. Letter of John A. Crow to Mildred Adams, March 18, 1968, Papers of Mildred Adams, HSA. On reviews of Humphries's edition, see Anderson, "La trayectoria," 100–104.

27. Campbell, *An Appreciation*, 95. For Philip Cummings, author of the first English version of *Canciones*, Lorca's status as an Andalusian Robert Burns complicates the translation of his poems: "Just as Robert Burns needs interpretation for the non-Celt, so does Lorca require much explanation to the reader . . . the innate pattern of a people can only be fully comprehended by that folk [and] this is usually disaster for the translator" (Lorca, *Songs*, 171).

28. Ironically, the same charge would be leveled at Campbell. In a 1944 review of *Talking Bronco*, G. S. Fraser observes that "satire should be urban, and Mr. Campbell's attitude is nomadic or pastoral. He therefore often lacks adroitness in attacking a society which he does not fully understand." *Times Literary Supplement*, June 22, 1944, 297.

29. Mayte Gómez, "Soldier of Franco, Soldier of Christ: Roy Campbell and Spain in the 1930s," *English in Africa* 34, no. 1 (May 2007): 21–41; 25.

30. *OED Online*, s.v. "mephitic (*adj.* and *n.*)," accessed April 5, 2018, http://www.oed.com.silk.library.umass.edu/view/Entry/116591?redirectedFrom=mephitic.

31. Randall Jarrell, "A Literary Tornado," review of *Selected Poems*, *New York Times Book Review*, April 17, 1955, 4.

32. As he is in the Peter Sellars production of Osvaldo Golijov's oratorio *Ainadamar*, Elvira Lindo complained about the scene in which "Lorca, es decir, la *mezzosoprano* Kelly O'Connor, se agacha, se pone a cuatro patas, y el verdugo le dispara pueden imaginarse ustedes dónde. Así unas cinco veces, por si no nos habíamos enterado." "Lo lorquiano," *El País*, July 15, 2012, http://www.elviralindo.com/blog/don-de-gentes/lo-lorquiano/.

33. Roy Campbell, *Flowering Rifle: A Poem from the Battlefield of Spain* (London: Longmans, Green and Co, 1939), 93. Campbell may be alluding to a section ("Demonio") of Lorca's "Oda al Santísimo Sacramento del Altar" where he dwells on the beauty of Satan. To my knowledge, none of Lorca's poems refer directly to the Antichrist. Noël Valis has analyzed this passage and Campbell's association of Lorca—in the 1939 edition—with the torero Marcial Lalanda, known for his "lovely" passes called *mariposas*. That particular *quite* involves turning one's back to the bull: still another allusion to Lorca's homosexuality. Walsh studies Lorca's translators' struggle with the "sensitive racial and sexual language" of *Poet in New York*.

34. Campbell, *Collected Poems*, 199; Valis, "Lorca's *Agonía republicana*," 289. In an otherwise approving review of *Flowering Rifle*, Arthur Bryant writes that Campbell's poem is marred by "intolerance, arrogance, brutal contempt for the pervert, the criminal, the humanitarian." See "Crusade or Tragedy? Two Aspects of the Spanish War," *Observer*, March 19, 1939, 8. "Babooneries" is a Campbell codeword for "homosexual" acts; see Campbell, *Collected Poems*, 170, 175n1. Hugh MacDiarmid scoffs at Campbell's treatment of Lorca's death: "Bah! Any poet worth his salt would liefer die / With Lorca, Campbell, than survive with you" (917; cf. 991, where MacDiarmid plagiarizes at length from Rolfe Humphries's account of Lorca's death; see Rolfe Humphries, "The Life and Death of García Lorca," *Nation*, September 18, 1937, 293–294; see also Valis, 292.)

35. Quoted and commented upon by Valis (291) and by Rogers, *Modernism*, 194. Campbell is referring to the translations of A. L. Lloyd, Stephen Spender, and Joan Gili. In 1949, he

also roasted Ben Belitt's earliest translations, *Four Poems by Rimbaud* (*Collected Works*, vol. 4, 335–337).

36. Henry S. Sommerville, "Commerce and Culture in the Career of the Permanent Innovative Press: New Directions, Grove Press, and George Braziller, Inc." (PhD diss., University of Rochester, 2009), 253.

37. Among poets published by Grove in 1955 and earlier were Belitt (*Wilderness Stair*), Cavafy, Edwin Muir, Ruthven Todd, and Valéry Larbaud.

38. For a different understanding of exceptionalism, see Mayhew, 27.

39. Sommerville, 309; Loren Glass, *Counterculture Colophon: Grove Press, the Evergreen Review, and the Incorporation of the Avant-Garde* (Stanford, Calif.: Stanford University Press, 2013), 104.

40. Glass, 124.

41. Del Río to Belitt, December 6, 1954, Ben Belitt Collection, Howard Gotlieb Archival Research Center, Boston University, Boston, Mass. (hereafter abbreviated HGARC), box 6, folder 11.

42. Belitt to Del Río, n.d., Ángel del Río Papers, HSA.

43. Lorca, *Poet in New York*, xiv.

44. Ángel del Río to Philip Cummings, December 1, 1955, Ángel del Río Papers, HSA: "I was, indeed, glad to finally identify the person whose existence especially interested me, but who was, much against my own desires, fast becoming a fantasmal one. I do now clearly recall that Federico spoke frequently of Philip. / I trust that my brief reference to you and subsequent dismissal of the matter in that one paragraph of the Introduction did not appear unduly hasty. I had, of course, never had the pleasure of meeting you personally nor was I ever able to glean an iota of concrete evidence that 'Mr. Cummings' was a real live person. Ben Belitt, the translator of *Poet in New York* and a teacher at Bennington College, had tried on several occasions to trace you in that region but his search was totally unproductive." For information on Cummings, see the website by Patricia C. Billingsley, *Philip H. Cummings*, http://www.philipcummings.net/.

45. From an interview by the late William L. Sackett (d. 2012), who provided me with a copy. The interview with Belitt at his home in Bennington, Vermont, is undated but refers to Sackett's interview, perhaps the day before, with Cummings on November 8, 1972. Sackett, who later became a journalist and media consultant, was working on a student project on "Lorca in Vermont" at Castleton State College.

46. Belitt in Lorca, *Poet in New York*, 188.

47. For an overview, see Howard Young, "La primera recepción de Federico García Lorca en los Estados Unidos (1931–1941)," in *America en un poeta: Los viajes de Federico García Lorca al Nuevo Mundo y la repercusión de su obra en la literatura americana* (Seville, Spain: Universidad Internacional de Andalucía / Fundación Focus-Abengoa, 1999), 105–118; Perulero Pardo-Balmonte; and Anderson ("La trayectoria"). In a letter to Del Río, the critic Stanley Burnshaw writes that reading Belitt's translation "was an interesting, startling, and in some ways annoying experience, for I was extremely troubled by the 'falsity' of some of the translations. Since I know little Spanish, I cannot speak with any assurance—and yet I could not fail to see a marked difference between the words used by Lorca (in many places) and the libertarian words used by Belitt. Here and there his changes struck me as ruinous; but what was much worse, he introduced words and phrases that seemed to me to de-poeticize the poem." Stanley Burnshaw to Del Río, April 11, 1957, Ángel del Río Papers, HSA.

48. Eisenberg, *Poeta en Nueva York*, 87–88.

49. Humphries to James Dickey, October 2, 1957, in Gillman and Novak, *Poets, Poetics, and Politics*, 246: "I was never very fond of it, nor the kind of Lorca it represents. Belitt later

[1955] brought out a version which surely rests on a sounder text—I forget who published it—probably corrects a lot of my errors, also, though in spots (naturally!) I think I did better."
50. Letters of Rolfe Humphries to Donald M. Allen, ca. November 19, 1952, and February 7, 1953, Grove Press Records, Syracuse University, New York, reproduced in Antonio García Carpio, "Poeta en Nueva York de Federico García Lorca y las artes plásticas" (PhD diss., Universidad Politécnica de Valencia, 2004), chap. 10 ("Búsqueda de documentación en Estados Unidos y en Cuba").
51. Rolfe Humphries to Louise Bogan, October 4, 1938, in Gillman and Novak, *Poets, Poetics, and Politics*, 153, previously quoted by Eisenberg. See also Anderson, "La trayectoria," 100.
52. Federico García Lorca, *Poeta en Nueva York / Tierra y luna*, ed. Eutimio Martín (Barcelona: Ariel, 1981). On the partitioning of the book into two, see Andrew A. Anderson, "The Evolution of García Lorca's Poetic Projects 1929–1936 and the Textual Status of *Poeta en Nueva York*," *Bulletin of Hispanic Studies* 60 (1983): 221–246; and his 2013 critical edition.
53. Piero Menarini (alluding to comments by García Lorca himself), unpublished introduction, trans. Ben Belitt, Edwin Honig Papers, John Hay Library, Brown University, Providence, R.I. (hereinafter abbreviated EHP).
54. Belitt to Barney Rosset, February 13, 1981, EHP.
55. Belitt to Lisa Rosset, May 18, 1981, EHP. Belitt had thought of including specially commissioned photographs of Vermont; New York City; and Newburgh, New York, as well as photos he had taken in Granada in 1956 but later dropped the idea.
56. Manuel Fernández-Montesinos to Belitt, September 20, 1982, EHP.
57. Belitt to Lisa Rosset, June 16, 1982, EHP.
58. Thus setting the stage for the Farrar, Straus and Giroux edition of 1988, edited by Maurer and translated by Greg Simon and Steven F. White. This edition was able to draw on the scholarship of Anderson, Hernández, and Nigel Dennis and affirmed the authenticity of Bergamín's edition. It brought together for the first time the poems, Lorca's lecture on *Poet in New York*, and his letters from the United States. It was thoroughly revised and enlarged in 1998 and further revised in 2013. *Poet in New York* was followed in December 1991 by the bilingual *Collected Poems*, edited by Maurer and translated by a group of twelve. A revised second edition was published in 2002 with a different group of translators and reissued in 2013 to coincide with the celebration of the Lorca exhibition "Back Tomorrow: Federico García Lorca / *Poet in New York*."
59. Belitt to Lisa Rosset, February 15, 1982, sending copies of "some back correspondence" about *Poet in New York* (copy of letter to Rosset and envelope), EHP.
60. Belitt to Daniel Eisenberg, January 16, 1981, and to Lisa Rosset, January 19, 1981, EHP.
61. Belitt to Lisa Rosset, May 4 and June 16, 1982, EHP.
62. The cover design of the 1983 Evergreen Book (ISBN: 0-394-62413-0) by Carl Lehmann-Haupt is clearly urban, with the author name and the title in a typeface suggesting graffiti on a black-and-white photo of a brick wall.
63. Belitt to Piero Menarini, February 16, 1981, EHP.
64. Belitt to Menarini, January 27, 1981, EHP.
65. Grove's initial printing sold more than thirty-five thousand copies (Glass 59).
66. Belitt planned to eliminate these two lectures from the 1983 edition. On their influence, see Mayhew, 63.
67. Belitt to Barney Rosset, October 20, 1980 (the phrase was also used as a blurb on the back cover of the 1983 edition); Belitt to Menarini, October 12, 1976; Belitt to Tica Fernández-Montesinos, March 22, 1975, all from Ben Belitt Collection, HGARC, box 6, folder 11; and Honig, *Poet's Other Voice*, 66. I have quoted from Roethke's letter of January 21, 1959, written

when both Nemerov and Belitt were teaching at Bennington College and Roethke was teaching at the University of Washington. Theodore Roethke, *Selected Letters of Theodore Roethke*, ed. Ralph J. Mills (Seattle: University of Washington Press, 1968), 224.

68. Ben Belitt, preface to Lorca, *Poet in New York* (1983), xlvi.

69. Francis J. Cebulski Jr. to Belitt, March 14, 1973, Ben Belitt Collection, HGARC, box 6, folder 11; and Honig, *Poet's Other Voice*, 66. On García Lorca, Ginsberg, and Whitman, see María Cristina C. Mabrey, "Mapping Homoerotic Feelings and Contested Modernity: Whitman, Lorca, Ginsberg, and Hispanic Modernist Poets," *South Atlantic Review* 75, no. 1 (2010): 83–98. Belitt's unpublished translation of the lecture "A Poet in New York" (with the mistranslation of "vengo del campo") is found in the Edwin Honig Papers.

70. Allen inquires about Belitt's interest in translating the book in letters from May 9 and May 21, 1952, expressing admiration for his translations of Neruda and Rimbaud and informing him that Grove is in negotiations for translation rights; that the poet's brother, Francisco, will choose the best English version; and that he suspects Francisco "will prefer a fairly literal rendering" (Belitt's translation was anything *but*.) Allen was already worrying about a reliable source text: the Spanish would be "as published by Losada of Buenos Aires, checked against photostats of the manuscripts (if possible) and plus the several poems not included in either the Norton (Humphries) or Losada editions." Donald M. Allen to BB, Ben Belitt Collection, HGARC, box 6, folder 11. On Allen as a "pivotal figure" in the dissemination of Lorca's work, see Mayhew, 59; and Glass, 58–59.

71. Belitt to Cebulski Jr., Ben Belitt Collection, HGARC, June 20, 1973, box 6, folder 11. Cf. the account in Honig, *Poet's Other Voice*, 63 (on Allen) and 67 (on Cebulski).

72. Belitt to Cebulski Jr., Ben Belitt Collection, HGARC, June 20, 1973, box 6, folder 11.

4 · "HERE IS MY MONUMENT"
Martín Luis Guzmán and Pancho Villa in the Mexico City Landscape[1]

NICHOLAS CIFUENTES-GOODBODY

BENEATH THE STREETS, BEHIND THE MONUMENTS

Mexico City has a reputation for chaos and fragmentation, but walking through its streets can sometimes feel like strolling through the pages of a carefully crafted history book, one where events of the past have been thoughtfully assembled into a single, glorious narrative. One might begin at the imposing Monument of the Revolution, where the remains of four Mexican presidents lie next to those of General Francisco "Pancho" Villa (1878–1923), a man who rose from obscurity to become a prominent *caudillo* in the state of Chihuahua, a central player in the Mexican Revolution, and the leader of the formidable División del Norte. What the monument does not communicate, however, is that all but one of these figures were exiled or assassinated, each most likely by someone now buried next to him. Such divisions are not evident in the architecture of the monument itself. Instead, the Revolution of 1910 appears as a unified movement—a "Revolutionary Family" under the guardianship of the Institutional Revolutionary Party (PRI), which completed the structure in 1938 and still rules Mexico today. Next, one might take the metro south to the División del Norte stop, walk down an avenue of the same name, and find him- or herself before a statue of Pancho Villa. Gazing up at the twenty-foot "Centaur of the North" on horseback, it seems impossible that he and his troops were seen for decades as criminals by those who occupied the seat of power in Mexico City. Finally, one might walk along an unassuming side street just a few miles northeast of the statue and never guess that the man for whom the street is named, author and politician Martín

Luis Guzmán (1887–1976), helped transform Villa from an enemy of the state into a government icon by declaring himself the general's official translator.

With the monuments, statues, and hundreds of streets that now bear his name in Mexico City, it may come as a surprise that Pancho Villa's redemption as a revolutionary hero and his subsequent transformation into a fixture of the capital landscape was a process that took years and was full of stops and starts. To begin with, although the term *Mexican Revolution* suggests a single and unified movement, the actual armed conflict that erupted in Mexico in 1910 was a bitter war among multiple factions. In fact, this infighting left Villa and his once-powerful División del Norte defeated and isolated in the north of the country by 1915. In 1923, the handpicked successor to the presidency, Plutarco Elías Calles (1877–1945), conspired to have Villa assassinated, fearing that he would join a rebellion against him. It was also Calles who, assuming the presidency in the wake of this failed coup, turned Mexico's civil war into a source of state doctrine in order to legitimate his administration.[2] This initiative would eventually give birth to the Institutional Revolutionary Party, Mexico's "perfect dictatorship" that would rule the country uninterrupted through the end of the century. Calles even inaugurated the practice of fomenting this conception of *la Revolución* through monumental architecture, coauthoring a proposal for the Monument to the Revolution in the early 1930s.

Beyond his enmity with Calles, Villa was excluded from this first phase of political consolidation because he represented the "anticentrist politics that were irreconcilable with the goals of the centrist postrevolutionary regime."[3] The government's stance, however, began to change during the presidency of Lázaro Cárdenas (1895–1970), who himself sent Calles into exile in 1936. For Cárdenas, the Centaur of the North became a symbol of his administration's new populist orientation.[4] This shift opened the door for subsequent PRI presidents in the 1960s and 1970s to use Villa as a source of political legitimacy in moments of crisis. In 1969, President Díaz Ordaz inaugurated a statue of the general, a year after ordering the violent repression of student protests in Mexico City. In 1976, as his government faced an economic crisis, President Luis Echeverría ordered that Villa's remains be brought from Chihuahua and interred in the Monument of the Revolution, next to those of the now-deceased Calles and Cárdenas (McGee, *Body Politics* 434). Though they had been enemies at one time or another, all three men ended up part of the same symbol of *la Revolución*.

It may also come as a surprise that, although the Mexico City streets that now bear their names do not intersect, the lives of Pancho Villa and Martín Luis Guzmán were intricately intertwined. Guzmán began as a representative for the general in Mexico City, a post that he abandoned as the Revolution splintered into factionalism in 1914. He returned six years later but was forced to leave again in 1923, finding himself on the wrong side of the same rebellion that caused Villa's assassination. When President Cárdenas sent Calles into exile, Guzmán was able to return for good, and it was in this context that he undertook an ambitious biography of Villa. This was more than just a biography; the author claimed that his *Memorias de Pancho Villa* (first appearing in serialized form in 1937 and published as a single volume in 1951) was a translation of the general telling his own story in his own northern Mexican dialect. It was more than just a book; he also described it as a monument, telling one interviewer in 1958 that "mientras no se le levante, en la ciudad de México, el monumento que [Villa] merece . . . su monumento es mi libro" (until they erect the monument that Villa deserves in Mexico City, his monument is my book).[5] In fact, when that statue was finally erected in 1969, the role that the *Memorias* played in its inauguration speaks to the book's monumental character. What is more, Guzmán's use of the statue following the inauguration—as a setting to announce his nomination to the senate in 1970 and to commemorate the fiftieth anniversary of Villa's death in 1973—reveals his continued role as Villa's translator. The high-profile nature of all these events speaks to another parallel between the author and the general. Over the half century that separated Villa's assassination by one Mexican president and his ceremonial entombment by another, both he and Guzmán went from being enemies of the state to icons of the regime.

What most ties the *Memorias* to the statue of Villa that now stands in Mexico City is that both seem to share an underlying claim of restoration—the recapturing of the general's authentic voice and the rehabilitation of his tarnished revolutionary legacy to its true heroism. However, a closer inspection of both Guzmán's writings and the Mexican government's memorial challenges these claims of authenticity. On the one hand, while aspiring to recapture Villa's voice by translating previous biographies and other historical documents in the *Memorias*, Guzmán creates a domesticated version of the general that is amenable to the Cárdenas administration. In redeeming Villa, he also redeems himself after decades in exile. On the other hand, the PRI's monumental architecture in Mexico City is clearly an effort to cement its place as the legitimate heir to the Revolution while cutting off dissension and debate. What emerges when the *Memorias de Pancho Villa* is examined in tandem with the monuments of Mexico City is that, although translation and the construction of urban space often seem to aspire to the restoration of authenticity, the capturing of otherness, and even the empowerment of the masses, both are exercises in rewriting that actively engage in the dynamics of power. Taken together, Guzmán's textual monument and the government's physical ones are the same gesture of possession carried out over different dimensions, the biographical and the geographical.

Cities are often celebrated as spaces for diversity and polyglossia. Cronin and Simon put forward the idea that they are *translation zones*, places of interaction and exchange.[6] Simon shows how these zones can act as spaces resistant to "violent forms of political hegemony,"[7] how "ghost tongues" can reclaim their rights in the wake of suppression ("City as Translation Zone" 121). This text, in contrast, looks at translation and the city in relation to the imposition of hegemony. Also, whereas Cronin and Simon rightly note that scholarship on the city has focused disproportionately on its physical landscape to the detriment of its soundscape (120), my goal is to draw these two dimensions together, showing how translation can carry narratives created through language into the physical world—from book to monument and back again.

TRANSLATION AND DOMESTICATION IN THE *MEMORIAS DE PANCHO VILLA*

In order to understand Guzmán's claim of authenticity in the *Memorias de Pancho Villa*, it is important to first address the image that the author puts forward of himself as a translator and his conception of translation—both of which are linked to the perceived role of the intellectual in postrevolutionary Mexico. First, there is a certain linguistic ambiguity in the book's title that is indicative of the work itself. Is this memoir written *by* Villa, or is it merely *about* him, written by someone else? Beth Jörgenson beautifully encapsulates this duality when she notes that "Villa owns the title, but not the title page."[8] More than the title, though, the ambiguous authorship of the *Memorias* originates in the fact that the book is narrated in the first person, in the general's own voice. Guzmán explains this decision in a prologue that he largely dedicates to the one historical document that has most informed his writing: another first-person biography, supposedly dictated by Villa to newspaperman Manuel Bauche Alcalde in 1914. While he deems this book historically reliable, he sees it as linguistically inaccurate: "Bauche Alcalde se dedicó a traducir a su lengua de hombre salido de la ciudad de México lo que Villa había dicho a su modo" (Bauche Alcalde dedicated himself to translating into the language of a man from Mexico City what Villa had said in his own particular way).[9] Thus Guzmán's first task is to retranslate (*retraducir*) the text back into Villa's speech. His second task is to take the other historical documents at his disposal and weave them together into a single, literary narrative in the general's voice: "no apartarme del lenguaje que siempre le había oído a Villa, y, a la vez, mantenerme dentro de los límites de lo literario" (not straying from the language I had always heard from Villa and, at the same time, keeping myself within the limits of the literary; *Memorias* 29). In other words, Guzmán represents himself as Villa's translator, a role that he considers more complex than that of a historian or a biographer because it comprises both a literary sensibility and a deep understanding of Villa's character and dialect.

As proof of the scope of his work, Guzmán ends his prologue by citing one particular section of Bauche Alcalde's book that grows from 6,500 words to

10,700 in his own version, supposedly through the addition of the "frases pleonásticas ricamente expresivas ... paralelismos recurrentes y ... otras peculiaridades" (richly expressive pleonastic phrases, recurring parallelisms, and other peculiarities) that are characteristic of Villa (*Memorias* 29). However, Guzmán's additions clearly go beyond the mere restoration of the general's voice. For example, there is a passage from Bauche Alcalde in which a revolutionary leader tells Villa to muster his troops. Villa's answer is the following: "Será usted puntualmente obedecido ... y puede usted estar cierto que seremos leales a nuestra causa y lucharemos por ella hasta el último instante de nuestra vida" (You will be punctually obeyed, and you can be certain that we will be loyal to our cause and fight for it until the last moment of our lives).[10] This one sentence becomes the following declaration in the *Memorias*:

> Señor, viva usted seguro que siempre será obedecido, y esté usted cierto que nosotros vamos a la lucha como revolucionarios conscientes, como hombres que saben que se batirán por el bien del pueblo y de los pobres, contra los ricos y poderosos, y que por ser ignorantes, pues nadie los ha enseñado, necesitan que los que más saben los guíen. Le aseguro, don Abraham, que obedeceremos siempre las órdenes de Cástulo Herrera, y que nos mantendremos leales a nuestra causa, y que pelearemos por ella hasta el último instante de nuestra vida. (67)

> (Sir, rest assured that you will always be obeyed, and know that we go to war as conscious revolutionaries, as men who know that they will take up arms for the good of the nation and the good of the poor, against the rich and powerful, as men who, because they are ignorant and uneducated, need to be guided by those who know more. I assure you, don Abraham, that we will always obey the orders of Cástulo Herrera, that we will remain loyal to our cause, and that we will fight for that cause until the last moment of our lives.)

More than the genuineness of Villa's words, what shines through in this passage is the language of the Cárdenas administration. The general has decided to fight on behalf of the poor against the rich and powerful, but he acknowledges that his efforts must be guided by others. Simply put, Villa explains that he is part of a class mobilization that is taking place around a common cause—the Revolution—and that he nonetheless remains obedient to a benevolent, paternalistic authority.[11] So while Villa is pledging his allegiance here to a former Chihuahua revolutionary, Guzmán is positioning the general—and thus himself—as an intellectual ally of the current president and his populist agenda (Parra, *Writing* 129).

Given the liberties that Guzmán takes with Bauche Alcalde's text, this passage in particular points to a question that applies to the whole of the *Memorias de Pancho Villa*. Even though Guzmán characterizes his work as an intralingual "translation," can it really be considered one? To answer this question, it is necessary to look at the *Memorias* while taking into account the place that the figure of the intellectual occupies in the wake of the Mexican Revolution. For his part, Max Parra maintains that the *Memorias* marks a departure from the writings on the Revolution by Guzmán and his contemporaries, where literary authority is "sustained by ... the presence of an educated narrator." Instead, the book fosters "a new kind of authority based on the writer's ability to convincingly reproduce the voice of the people" (Parra, *Writing* 130–131). According to this characterization, the *Memorias* seems less a translation and almost a precursor to the Latin American *testimonio* literature of the 1960s.

However, given the clear paternalistic undertone in the passage discussed earlier, it is important to temper this interpretation. Rather than a break with tradition, Horacio Legrás characterizes the *Memorias* as a continuation of the intellectual project that Guzmán began with his earlier novel on the Revolution, *El águila y la serpiente* (*The Eagle and the Serpent*). This book is typical of the works that Parra describes, in that the narrator and protagonist is a university student from Mexico City. Legrás observes that this narrator constantly occupies "el rol del intelectual como intérprete, como traductor" (the role of the intellectual as interpreter, as translator),[12] one whose task is to incorporate the violence and chaos of the Revolution (often personified in the novel by Villa himself) into an intelligible work of narrative art. *Memorias de Pancho Villa* is the next step in the domestication of what Parra calls the voice of the people: "El lado oscuro de esta historia es—como la sustracción misma de la voz de Villa en las Memorias escritas por Guzmán vendrá a probar—que cuando el pueblo sea finalmente expresado en las palabras del intelectual ya no será su voz sino la del estado la que resonará en la literatura" (The dark side of this story is that—just as the theft of Villa's voice in the *Memorias* would come to prove—when the voice of the people is finally expressed in the words of an intellectual, it will not be their voice that will resonate in the literary world but that of the state; Legrás, "Martín" 453). By transforming various documents into a single narrative, unified under the "authentic" voice of the Centaur of the North but also firmly situated within "los límites de lo literario," Guzmán is performing what is an essential role for an intellectual of his generation: translating the voice of a bandit into a language that is both intelligible to and reinforcing of the "fantasía paternalista-educadora" (paternalist-educative fantasy) of the Mexican government.[13]

If this conception of the intellectual helps explain why Guzmán describes his work as translation, it still leaves open the question of whether it really is. After all, there is no single source text for the *Memorias*, and the author clearly takes great liberties with the historical documents at his disposal. Several scholars have shown the limitations of strict definitions of translation and have recast it instead as one form of *rewriting*.[14] Focusing on Latin America, Sylvia Molloy[15] has shown how translation is an exercise in the conscious and unconscious rewriting of texts as a means of identity construction. Similarly, Georges Bastin, Álvaro Echeverri, and Ángela Campo define Latin American translation as the practice of *appropriation*.[16] Gentzler characterizes it as a process of "remembering and rehistoricizing"[17]—"less something that happens between separate and distinct cultures and more something that is constitutive of those cultures" (5). In this context, Guzmán's *Memorias* is very much a process of translation, the rewriting of Villa's words and life in the service of constituting an institutional revolutionary culture.

Lawrence Venuti has shown that translation is frequently a violent political act, one whose aim is the "wholesale domestication of the foreign text, often in highly self-conscious projects, where translation serves an imperialist appropriation of foreign cultures for domestic agendas, cultural, economic, political."[18] Applying this description to the *Memorias de Pancho Villa* in the context of the postrevolutionary government's efforts to extend its hegemony over the entirety of Mexico, I would argue that Guzmán is indeed translating in the sense that he is bringing back "a cultural other as the same" (18), returning the once-maligned Centaur of the North to the good graces of the postrevolutionary state. While claiming to preserve the general's foreignness, his translation is clearly an act of "wholesale domestication" (18). What is more, this exercise of power by means of translation is not only a political act; there is a geographical dimension as well. In capturing the general's particular Spanish of the Durango and Chihuahua mountains, he is delivering a regional, anticentrist figure to the seat of the central government in Mexico City.

PANCHO VILLA AND THE MONUMENTS OF MEXICO CITY

The idea of delivering Pancho Villa from the north of Mexico to the nation's capital is useful in not only understanding Guzmán's *Memorias* but also the process of Villa's incorporation into the official pantheon of revolutionary heroes. It is also important to note that this is by no means an abstract idea. While Guzmán uses translation to bring the general into the heart of Mexico City, it was President Luis Echeverría (b. 1922) who ordered Villa's remains brought from Chihuahua to the capital in 1976 and interred in the Monument of the Mexican Revolution. Of course, with nearly forty years elapsing between the first installments of the *Memorias de Pancho Villa* and Echeverría's order, Villa's incorporation was a process that involved much more than just Guzmán. As mentioned earlier, from the 1930s to the 1970s, Mexico witnessed the creation of an institutionalized conception of the Revolution, the emergence of monumental architecture in Mexico City to foment that concept, and a shift in the political landscape. Together, these events led to Villa becoming a member of what would be called the Revolutionary Family. For that reason, it is necessary to look at these three issues separately before focusing on the role that Guzmán and his *Memorias* played in bringing the general to the capital.

Coming to power in a presidential succession crisis that led to Villa's assassination and Guzmán's exile, one way in which Plutarco Elías Calles looked to cement his leadership was in the creation of a monument that would bring a concrete form to his conception of the Revolution. The Monument of the Revolution did just that, extending the Revolution as a unifying concept across the whole of the nation's history. The events of 1910 now became just one of four stages in the "great Mexican Revolution," which spanned the whole of the nation's history.[19] In his book *Architecture as Revolution*, Luis Carranza shows the way that this and other monuments of the same period cordon off large empty spaces in order to "forge and maintain control through fixing the limits of what is permissible and correct" (213). It is for this reason that he sees the Monument of the Revolution both as an effort to fix a definition of what the Revolution was and as an attempt to cut off dissention and debate.

Given that Calles was complicit in Villa's death, it should come as no surprise that his remains were not included when the Monument of the Revolution was originally completed in 1938. In fact, in spite of the attempts to redeem Villa's legacy during the Cárdenas administration—Guzmán's *Memorias* among them—the general continued to be an outlaw in the eyes of the establishment. It would not be until 1966 that then-president Díaz Ordaz (1911–1979) would include Villa's name on the Wall of Honor in the Mexican Congress and finally erect an equestrian statue of him in the capital in 1969. While it is tempting to see this as the culmination of a gradual process set in motion by Cárdenas, historian Anne Marie McGee has pointed out that it was more an abrupt change motivated by the immediate needs of government to counter charges of authoritarianism: "By co-opting Villa, and claiming to be the heir of Villismo, the federal government could confront claims that it was no longer 'revolutionary'" (*Body Politics* 433). In fact, the statue's inauguration took place only a year after the violent repression of the student movement of 1968, when government forces surrounded and opened fire on a demonstration in Mexico City, in the event now known as the Tlatelolco Massacre.

While it is unlikely that the Díaz Ordaz government ordered the construction of Villa's statue in direct response to Tlatelolco, the juxtaposition of the statue and the events of 1968 is significant because it opens up a discussion into the power and politics at play in the shaping of the Mexico City landscape. The statue is a clear case of monumental architecture, another president marking his contribution to the consolidation and modernization of the country on the "evolving landscape of urban Mexico" through monumental architecture.[20] It is also the further rewriting of Villa's biography, the incorporation of his person and life into the grand narrative of *la Revolución*. In this sense, the statue is as much the narrative extension of Guzmán's book as it is the physical extension of the PRI's political hegemony—an intermediate step in the process would culminate in Villa's body being interred in the Monument of the Revolution in 1976.

Of course, Mexico City was just one of many sites around the world that witnessed violent urban upheaval in 1968. In fact, it was in the wake of similar clashes between students and authorities in France that the philosopher and sociologist Henri Lefebvre began to explore the role that the city itself played in political conflict, coming to conclusions that speak to the transfer of Villa to the capital—be it in a translation, in a tomb, or as a statue. It was in 1968 that Lefebvre began to see "the significance of urban conditions of daily life . . . as central in the evolution of revolutionary sentiments."[21] More than merely showing that monuments are embodiments of power, the innovation in this thinking is that it casts space much more as an active and integral part of human interaction than as a neutral stage upon which society unfolds. To put it in more direct terms, the underpinning of all social relationships is spatial and, for that reason, any analysis of social production must take into account the role of space as well as "those institutions, substitutions, transpositions, metaphorizations, anaphorizations . . . that have transformed the space under consideration."[22] As Edward Soja has pointed out, social study tends to favor history and biography when explaining events, and it thus subordinates "space to time."[23] Lefebvre's ideas invert this dynamic, placing the geographical on equal footing with the historical. Returning to the case of Villa with this in mind, the implication is that Guzmán's translation of the general and Díaz Ordaz's statue are, at base, the same political act. Moreover, putting these two categories on equal footing reveals the fluidity that exists between book and monument, the continued role that Guzmán played as translator in relationship to the monument, and the extent to which translation and the city converge in the case of Villa's incorporation into the Revolutionary Family.

"HERE IS MY MONUMENT"

When Martín Luis Guzmán tells an interviewer that his book will serve as a textual monument to Villa until a stone one can be put in place, implicit in this statement is the idea that one can stand in for the other. In fact, this is exactly what happened when the statue was unveiled in 1969 at the center of the Glorieta del Riviera in the Navarte neighborhood. At 6.2 meters high, it was the largest statue of its kind in Mexico City and, as Guzmán's own weekly news magazine *Tiempo* claimed, it perfectly captured "la fuerza y el atractivo viril del hombre del campo y del guerrillero que fue el Centauro del Norte" (the force and virile appeal of the countryman and warrior that was the Centaur of the North).[24] Guzmán did not speak at the inauguration, but his book did play a role in the ceremonies. The author's publishing house released a two-volume, illustrated edition of the *Memorias*, which Guzmán then sent as a present to nearly a hundred members of Mexico's political elite. Among the gifts he received in return was a small replica of the Villa statue from the head of the Federal District.[25] The gesture of Guzmán giving a monument of Villa and receiving one in return speaks to the correspondence between book and statue, both circulating in the service of political alliance and revolutionary unity. Following the inauguration, a Spanish reporter asked Guzmán if he thought that Villa deserved a monument in Mexico City, given that the decision to erect one had been somewhat controversial.[26] The reporter notes that Guzmán points to two thick volumes of the *Memorias de Pancho Villa* on his desk before answering, "Absolutamente. Y mire, aquí está mi monumento a Villa, mis 'Memorias'" (Absolutely. And look, here is my monument to Villa: my *Memorias*).[27]

While Guzmán is clearly referring to his own book here in a strict sense, his gesture of possession takes on a larger meaning when read with an eye to the fluidity between book and statue. In the wake of Tlatelolco, the author was one of the few public intellectuals who continued to staunchly support the state. When his loyalty was rewarded in 1970 with a nomination to represent Mexico City in the Senate, it only seemed fitting that he should announce his candidacy at the foot of Villa's monument. The author opens his acceptance speech by characterizing the statue's very presence as a tacit endorsement of his campaign, party, and revolutionary spirit: "No podemos menos de sentir en este instante cómo desde lo alto de aquel monumento [Pancho Villa] preside nuestra reunión, cual si estuviera ... sumándose con el brío de su caballo a nuestro júbilo revolucionario" (We cannot but feel in this moment how Villa presides over our gathering from up high on that monument, as if he were joining in our revolutionary elation with the wild spirit of his steed).[28] Just as he has done in the *Memorias* during the Cárdenas administration, Guzmán now aligns Villa's life—and untimely death—with the current priorities of the government:

> Sabemos de sobra que así como la trascendental presencia de Francisco Villa no desapareció en la emboscada que daría muerte al cuerpo ..., así también, igual que ha sucedido hasta hoy, la presencia de los valores revolucionarios no se oscurecerá a causa de la emboscada que a modo de campaña cívica andan poniéndole en estos días a la Revolución los agentes de la antirrevolución. ... La inmensa

mayoría de él [el pueblo de México] siente dónde está la Revolución, nuestra revolución, la Revolución Mexicana, y sabe quiénes son los que la representan inspirados en los héroes que la hicieron. (*Discurso ... senadores* 6)

(We know all too well that, just as the transcendental presence of Francisco Villa did not disappear in the ambush that put an end to his body, our revolutionary values will never be eclipsed by the ambush that antirevolutionary actors are now staging against the Revolution in the guise of a civic campaign. The great majority of the Mexican people sense where the Revolution is—our revolution, the Mexican Revolution—and they know who represents it, inspired by the heroes that made it.)

In this passage, Guzmán turns Villa's biography on its head. Whereas the founder the political party that would become the PRI had been complicit in the caudillo's death, now that party is heir to his legacy. In contrast, those who criticize the party and its centralized government—as Villa himself did—are now responsible for his death. At the same time, the author describes Villa's spirit as an unstoppable force, one that will continue to drive the institutionalized revolution forward. More than just an invocation of the general's legacy, it seems a warning to the opposition. As Guzmán remarks elsewhere in the speech, "Seguirá adelante ... y cualquier obstáculo que se le oponga, lo apartará o lo allanará" (It will continue on, pushing aside or leveling any obstacle that opposes it; *Discurso ... senadores* 5). It is in this ceremony that the gesture Guzmán makes in his interview—"here is my monument"—reappears, writ large. The author lays claim to Villa's statue and life story as a source of power and legitimation not only for the government in Mexico City but also for himself as the chosen political representative for that city.

While it is clear that Guzmán reassumes the role of Villa's biographer in this speech, he is not channeling the voice of the general in the same way he does in the *Memorias*. However, on the fiftieth anniversary of the general's assassination in 1973, the author would make one more speech in the shadow of Villa's statue in which he would again play the role of translator. The author and now senator delivered what was essentially a pastiche of other talks that he gave during the previous decade. What sets this one apart, though, are the numerous anecdotes that seemingly come from Villa himself. Telling the assembled crowd that Villa was the personification of "la voluntad popular ... de llevar la Revolución hasta el fin" (the public's will to carry the Revolution to the end),[29] Guzmán offers an anecdote as proof that Villa himself was aware of this during his life. "Yo protejo la Revolución" (I protect the Revolution), the general once told his fellow soldiers, "y como la Revolución es del pueblo, Dios, que tiene fuerza para gobernar los astros que nos alumbran, también la tiene para protegerme a mí" (and just as the Revolution belongs to the people, God, who has the power to govern the stars that shine on us, also has the power to protect me; *Discurso . . . Villa* 2). Describing the general's awareness of the risks that individual greed posed to the Revolution, Guzmán recalls how Villa once remarked that there was no inherent difference between the rich and the poor; rather, "cuando a los hombres les toca la riqueza, muchos se ciegan por las ansias de tener más y ya no se acuerdan de los sufrimientos del pobre" (when men find fortune, many are blinded by their urge to have more, and they no longer remember the plight of the poor; *Discurso . . . Villa* 6). The only issue with Guzmán's quotations here is that they do not come from Villa but instead from the *Memorias de Pancho Villa* (267 and 286, respectively; also see Parra, *Writing* 129), and Guzmán is quoting his own translation as if it were the general himself.

Guzmán's speech ends with the author congratulating President Luis Echeverría (also in attendance) for the revolutionary unity he has created with this ceremony and saying that "la Revolución debe perpetuar, uniéndolas en un solo recuerdo, las imágenes perdurables de todos cuantos la hicieron" (the Revolution should continue on, uniting in a single memory the enduring images of all those who made it; *Discurso . . . Villa* 12). Beyond this unity, though, it is the unity between Guzmán, his book, and the statue that I want to highlight. Here the author is next to the image of Villa, ostensibly repeating Villa's own words, giving voice to the statue. In doing so, he not only again brings together his textual monument and the stone monument but also lays claim to both of them, imposing a single narrative—one that originates with him as author—on both the textual and the physical representation of the Centaur of the North.

CONCLUSION: TRANSLATION, SPACE, AND POWER

While it is clear that there exists a relationship between Martín Luis Guzmán's *Memorias* and the monumental statue of Villa that now marks the Mexico City landscape, there remains a larger question as to where translation and space intersect as modes of critical inquiry. The case of Guzmán and Villa, book and monument, reveals that what underlies both the act of translation and the construction of urban space is the exercise of power. As Edwin Gentzler and Maria Tymoczko explain, translations are inevitably partial: partial in the sense that "the information in a source text is . . . always more extensive than a translation can convey" but also partial in the sense of partisan, a characteristic that enables translation to "participate in the dialectic of power, [and] the ongoing process of political discourse."[30] Guzmán's *Memorias* and the speeches that he later concocted from it are clearly political acts of rewriting meant to reposition both himself and Villa within the power structures of the postrevolutionary state and then to fortify that new position. Likewise, similar gestures occur in the making of a city and its monuments. Iain Chambers has argued that a city is "the material and technical appropriation of ground, history and memory," a site where power and politics manifest themselves "in the seemingly neutral grid lines of the survey, the plan and the project."[31] As Mexico's population gravitated to cities over the course of the twentieth century, the state began developing "a national patrimony founded on the imagery of visual culture rather than print" in order to appeal to both its literate and illiterate populations.[32] It is in this context that the government erected monuments in Mexico City in order to forward its own reading of history, to create a sense of "revolutionary unity" of which it is the benefactor. It dots the urban landscape with symbols that it then lays claim to—"here is my monument"—and thus takes possession of history and space.

However, if what translation and the city have in common is power, this raises another critical question: What is to be gained by exploring cases like that of Guzmán and Villa through the optic of translation and the city at the same time? First and foremost, this approach draws our attention to the fact that neither translation nor space is neutral or empty, even if they are sometimes characterized as such. As Venuti says, a translation can operate under the "illusion of transparency," presenting itself to the target audience "as true semantic equivalence when it in fact inscribes the foreign text with a partial interpretation ... reducing if not simply excluding the very difference that translation is called on to convey" (21). In the *Memorias*, Martín Luis Guzmán translates numerous historical documents (some written under Villa's supervision and some not) into a single, unified voice. Working from a position of extreme partiality, he is able to elaborate a revisionist biography that transforms the general into a state-celebrated hero, all in a work that seems to come directly from—or, at the very least, to be authorized by—Villa himself. And much as Venuti does in the case of translation, Edward Soja insists, when it comes to the city, "We must be insistently aware of how space can be made to hide consequences from us, how relations of power and discipline are inscribed into the apparently innocent spaciality of social life, how human geographies become filled with politics and ideology" (6). What the monuments of Mexico City hide is the fact that they serve to limit the very revolution they claim to celebrate. Carranza describes this phenomenon as a dialectic. While these structures ostensibly serve "to educate and empower the masses," they are also "used as a tool for the ideological reproduction of power" (8). Inscribing Villa's name on a wall in the Chamber of Deputies, raising a statue to him on the streets of Mexico City, and entombing his remains in the Monument to the Revolution all seem to be acts of redemption and empowerment for the marginalized Villa and those who followed him. In fact, they are all meant to undermine the PRI's political opposition by depriving it of a powerful symbol.[33] In the end, what emerges from the consideration of Guzmán's translation in tandem with the PRI's monuments is that, no matter how supposedly transparent or accurate, such representations always mask an inherent partiality.

The second benefit of looking at translation and the city together in the case of Guzmán and Villa is that the exploration of space in and of itself exposes the limitations of approaching Villa's redemption as solely a question of history or biography. As Soja rightly points out, a singular focus on historicism leads to a narrow interpretation of the individual, built solely on a temporal axis. The truth, however, is that "'life-stories' have a geography too; they have milieux, immediate locales, provocative emplacements which affect thought and action" (*Postmodern Geographies* 13–14). Villa's life, death, and official redemption are as much a story of geography as anything else. Born on the periphery of a nation-state, his political power rises in proportion to his ability to move himself toward Mexico City. When defeated, he retreats back to the periphery, where he is assassinated in order to prevent his return to the city. It only makes sense that, when transformed from bandit to hero, he again ends up in the capital.

Also speaking on the primacy of geography, Foucault points out that it is only through "the use of spatial, strategic metaphors" that one is able "to grasp precisely the points at which discourses are transformed in, through and on the basis of relations of power."[34] This becomes all too clear when looking at the geographical emplacement of Villa's body. A reporter who chronicled the exhumation of the general speaks to this when he declares that Villa's remains "ya no le pertenecen a un lugar o un grupo en particular sino a la Nación entera, a México considerado como un todo, fuerte, unido, sin vencidos ni vencedores" (no longer belong to a place or group in particular but rather to the whole Nation, to Mexico as a single entity—strong, united, without victors or vanquished).[35] That is, it is only in removing Villa's body from its regional resting place and entombing it in Mexico City that he can become a symbol of the unified revolution. And it is only in looking at the geographical that the relationships of power that govern the concept of the Revolutionary Family become clear.

Villa's final journey to Mexico City—"la última cabalgata" (the last cavalcade), as one reporter described it (*La última* 155)—took place in November 1976, when his remains were interred in the Monument of the Revolution, next to those of Plutarco Elías Calles and Lázaro Cárdenas. At eighty-nine years old, Guzmán attended the ceremony but did not speak. A month later, the author would pass away from a heart attack. At a memorial ceremony for the author, one attendee would say, "Las *Memorias de Pancho Villa* es un libro muy interesante que se leerá ahora y dentro de 100 años" (The *Memorias de Pancho Villa* is a very interesting book that will be read now and a hundred years from now).[36] The truth is, however, that the book has already faded into relative obscurity.[37] For its own part, the statue of Villa was moved from the Glorieta Riviera to the Parque de los Venados to make room for the División del Norte metro stop.

It is hard to read these facts as anything other than evidence of the dynamic nature of monuments and meaning within the city. As historian Miguel Angel Centeno beautifully phrases it, "Yesterday's beloved general is today's neglected pigeon roost, and may be tomorrow's kitsch icon."[38] While the statue of Villa and other monuments were put in place to anchor the postrevolutionary government, impose its interpretation of the Mexican Revolution, and limit dissension and debate, those symbols continue to be open to interpretation. As signifiers, they shift in meaning much in the same way that Villa's statue has moved around Mexico City. Beyond exercises in political power, they are also "points of reference, places to meet, and ideal spots for traffic accidents [...]; they have a place in the city and also in the image of the city we all have."[39] And because they act simultaneously as tools for political hegemony and landmarks of personal (perhaps subversive) significance, such symbols are always subject to further rewriting and translation. For Guzmán, the translation of Villa begins in the realm of text, where he domesticates the Centaur of the North to suit the needs of the Cárdenas administration. This eventually extends to the statue erected decades later, when he again lays claim to the general as a symbol of institutional and personal legitimacy in the wake of 1968. In the end, what unites the memoirs and the statue of Villa, bringing together translation and the city, is Guzmán's gesture of possession ("this is my monument"), the notion that the lives and acts of others can be and are translated, be it on the page or on the street.

NOTES

1. This chapter is an adapted and extended version of an article published previously in *The Translator*. Nicholas Cifuentes-Goodbody, "Translation, Space, and Power in Martín Luis Guzmán's *Memorias de Pancho Villa*," *Translator* 23, no. 3 (2017): 279–291.
2. Thomas Benjamin, *La Revolución: Mexico's Great Revolution as Memory, Myth, and History* (Austin: University of Texas Press, 2000), 73.
3. Anne Marie McGee, "Body Politics and the Figure of Pancho Villa: From National Exclusion to Regional Resurrection," *Anuario de Estudios Americanos* 67, no. 2 (2010): 425–444; 429. Available at http://biblioteca.ues.edu.sv/revistas/10800305-2.pdf.
4. Max Parra, *Writing Pancho Villa's Revolution: Rebels in the Literary Imagination of Mexico* (Austin: University of Texas Press, 2006), 127.
5. Emmanuel Carballo, "Martín Luis Guzmán" (1965), *Protagonistas de la literatura mexicana* (Mexico City: Porrúa, 1994), 53–93, 68.
6. Michael Cronin and Sherry Simon, "Introduction: The City as Translation Zone," *Translation Studies* 7, no. 2 (2014): 119–132; 121–122, doi:10.1080/14781700.2014.897641.
7. Sherry Simon, *Cities in Translation: Intersections of Language and Memory* (New York: Routledge, 2012), 160.
8. Beth E. Jörgensen, *Documents in Crisis: Nonfiction Literatures in Twentieth-Century Mexico* (Albany: SUNY Press, 2011), 54.
9. Martín Luis Guzmán, *Memorias de Pancho Villa*, 1951 (Mexico City: FCE and INEHRM, 2010), 3:25–908; 28 (quote). The translations provided of the *Memorias* here are my own,

although Virginia H. Taylor has completed a much-abridged translation; see Martín Luis Guzmán, *Memoirs of Pancho Villa*, trans. Virginia H. Taylor (Austin: University of Texas Press, 1975).

10. Guadalupe Villa and Rosa Helia Villa de Mebius, eds., *Pancho Villa: Retrato autobiográfico, 1894–1914* (Valle, Mexico: Santillana Ediciones Generales, 2004), 139.

11. This passage is based on my monograph (Nicholas Cifuentes-Goodbody, *The Man Who Wrote Pancho Villa: Martín Luis Guzmán and the Politics of Life Writing* [Nashville, Tex.: Vanderbilt University Press, 2016]), where I provide a more in-depth analysis of the *Memorias* and the way in which it fits into the whole of Guzmán's biographical and autobiographical writing.

12. Horacio Legrás, "Martín Luis Guzmán: El viaje de la revolución," *MLN* 118, no. 2 (March 2003): 427–454; 425, http://www.jstor.org/stable/3252014.

13. Horacio Legrás, "El Ateneo y los orígenes del estado ético en México," *Latin American Research Review* 38, no. 2 (January 2003): 34–60, 48, http://www.jstor.org/stable/1555419.

14. André Lefevere, *Translation/History/Culture: A Sourcebook* (New York: Routledge, 1992); and *Translation, Rewriting, and the Manipulation of Literary Fame* (New York: Routledge, 1992); Susan Bassnett and André Lefevere, eds., *Constructing Cultures: Essays on Literary Translation* (Bristol, UK: Multilingual Matters, 1998); Susan Bassnett and Peter Bush, eds., *The Translator as Writer* (New York: Continuum, 2007).

15. Sylvia Molloy, *At Face Value: Autobiographical Writing in Spanish America* (Cambridge: Cambridge University Press, 1991).

16. Georges L. Bastin, Álvaro Echeverri, and Ángela Campo, "La traducción en América Latina: Propia y apropiada," *Estudios* 24 (2004): 69–94; 70 (definition), http://www.revistaestudios.ll.usb.ve/es/node/61.

17. Edwin Gentzler, *Translation and Identity in the Americas: New Directions in Translation Theory* (New York: Routledge, 2007), 184.

18. Lawrence Venuti, *The Translator's Invisibility: A History of Translation* (New York: Routledge, 1995), 18–19.

19. Luis E. Carranza, *Architecture as Revolution: Episodes in the History of Modern Mexico* (Austin: University of Texas Press, 2010), 190.

20. Raúl Rodríguez-Hernández, *Mexico's Ruins: Juan García Ponce and the Writing of Modernity* (Albany: SUNY Press, 2007), 26.

21. David Harvey, afterword to *The Production of Space*, by Henri Lefebvre (Cambridge, Mass.: Blackwell, 1991), 426–432; 30.

22. Henri Lefebvre, *The Production of Space*, trans. Donald Nicholson-Smith (Cambridge, Mass.: Blackwell, 1991), 404.

23. Edward W. Soja, *Postmodern Geographies: The Reassertion of Space in Critical Social Theory* (New York: Verso, 1989), 10.

24. "Una Estatua," *Tiempo*, November 1969, 43–44; 43.

25. This observation is based on a document in the Martín Luis Guzmán Franco archive in Mexico City that lists all the birthday and Christmas presents sent and received by Guzmán.

26. Of course, after having been labeled as a violent outlaw for so many years, the decision to bestow official honors on Villa was a controversial one. For example, in his exhaustive biography of the Centaur of the North, Friedrich Katz gives an account of the debate that took place in the Chamber of Deputies in 1966 over the motion to have Villa's name inscribed on the Wall of Honor (790–791).

27. Marta Portal, "Conversación con Martín Luis Guzmán," *ABC*, October 29, 1971, 122–123; 122.

28. Martín Luis Guzmán, *Discurso pronunciado por el señor Martín Luis Guzmán en el mitin que el Partido Revolucionario Institucional llevo a cabo, para apoyar a sus candidatos a senadores por el Distrito federal* (speech, Glorieta del Riviera, Mexico City, June 5, 1970).
29. Martín Luis Guzmán, *Discurso en el 50 aniversario de la muerte de Villa* (speech, Mexico City, Glorieta del Riviera, Mexico City, June 20, 1973).
30. Maria Tymoczko and Edwin Gentzler, eds., *Translation and Power* (Amherst: University of Massachusetts Press, 2002), xviii.
31. Iain Chambers, "The Translated City," *Translation* 1, no. 1 (September 2011): 101–106; 102.
32. Néstor García Canclini, "From National Capital to Global Capital: Urban Change in Mexico City," trans. Paul Liffman, *Public Culture* 12, no. 1 (2000): 207–213; 208, https://muse.jhu.edu/article/26182.
33. Emmanuel Carballo, "Glorieta y no gloria: Pancho Villa convertido en estatua," *Excélsior*, November 22, 1969, 7.
34. Michel Foucault, *Power/Knowledge: Selected Interviews and Other Writings, 1972–1977*, ed. Colin Gordon, trans. Colin Gordon et al. (New York: Pantheon, 1980), 70; see also Jeremy W. Crampton and Stuart Elden, eds., *Space, Knowledge and Power: Foucault and Geography* (Surrey, UK: Ashgate, 2007).
35. Oscar W. Ching Vega, *La última cabalgata de Pancho Villa* (Chihuahua, Mexico: Centro Librero La Prensa, 1977), 155.
36. "La muerte de Axkaná," *Tiempo*, January 1977, 5–23.
37. José Joaquín Blanco, "¿Por qué nadie lee las *Memorias de Pancho Villa?*," in *Veinte aventuras de la literatura mexicana* (Mexico City: CONACULTA, 2006), 91–112.
38. Miguel Ángel Centeno, "War and Memories: Symbols of State Nationalism in Latin America," *Revista Europea de Estudios Latinoamericanos y del Caribe* 66 (June 1999): 75–105; 80, http://www.jstor.org/stable/25675821; see also Carlos Monsiváis, "El hastío es pavo real que se aburre de luz en la tarde: Notas del camp en México" (1965), in *Días de guardar* (Mexico City: Ediciones Era, 1991), 171–197.
39. Guillermo Sheridan, "Monuments," in *The Mexico City Reader*, ed. Rubén Gallo and Lorna Scott Fox (Madison: University of Wisconsin Press, 2004), 149–151; 151. In this sense, Villa's statue and the Monument of the Revolution could qualify as what Foucault would term a *heterotopia*, a "single real place" that juxtaposes "several sites that are in themselves incompatible." Michel Foucault, "Of Other Spaces," trans. Jay Miskowiec, *Diacritics* 16 (1986): 22–27; 25.

5 · ON LANGUAGES AND CITIES
Rethinking the Politics of Calvert Casey's "El regreso"

CHARLES HATFIELD

"El regreso" ("Homecoming"), the short story by the Cuban writer Calvert Casey, was first published in the journal *Casa de las Américas* in early 1961, and it is as much a story about cities—Havana and New York—as it is a story about language, translation, and identity. Its unnamed protagonist is a Cuban-born cosmopolitan who lives in New York, surrounded by "biombos orientales" (Oriental screens), "las abstracciones" (abstract paintings), and "las colecciones primitivas" (primitive art).[1] Possessing a "conocimiento de idiomas" (knowledge of foreign languages; 17), he listens to "discos de jazz y las quejumbrosas danzas de los israelitas del Yemen" (jazz records and the mournful dances of the Yemenite Jews; 16), reads "libros, los de naturalism, los de hinduismo" (books of naturalistic philosophy, books on Hinduism; 18); and he has borrowed "la renunciación hinduista" (a Hindu resignation) from an Argentinian friend that matches "un tono elegante de cinismo que él creía de moda en Santiago y que adoptara entusiasmado de una amante chilena" (the elegantly cynical tone that he thought was in vogue in Santiago and had enthusiastically adopted from a Chilean mistress; 10). In conversations, he speaks of such things as "Kirilov y los actos absurdos [y] la gratuidad" (Kirilov and the absurd act [and] the notion of the gratuitous) or of "la nueva crítica y al ser para la muerte" (New Criticism and Being-toward-death; 16). He senses, however, that "de los muchos actos que realizaba y que había realizado" (of the many actions he was taking and had taken), few were actually "actos auténticos" (authentic acts) and not merely the effects of "la última lectura apresurada de libros" (the last hasty reading of some book) or of a "conversación oída a medias, a la influencia del

69

último conocimiento que trabara, a la última película vista" (some half-followed conversation, or of the influence of his most recent acquaintance, or of the last movie he'd seen; 7).

The protagonist in "El regreso" had always dismissed Cuba—"su país" (his native country)—as "incorrigible y sin esperanzas" (incorrigible and hopeless), and "no se atrevía a dar el viaje" (he didn't dare to go there) because, we are told, "ni en sus ademanes ni en su manera de hablar ni de ser recordaba en lo más mínimo a sus compatriotas" (his way of acting, of talking, and of being had nothing in common with that of his countrymen; 14). But when he receives news of a death in his family, he returns and realizes that Cubans were "infinitamente más felices que las de la hosca ciudad donde él vivía" (infinitely happier than the inhabitants of the harsh city where he lived; 15). Returning to New York, the protagonist surrounds himself "de libros, de ropas, todos procedentes del lejano país" (with books and clothes from his distant homeland) and throws out "los de todas las patrias previas de adopción" (the books and clothes from all his previous adopted homelands; 17). Finally, he decides to live permanently in his homeland, even though he has read newspaper reports about "movimientos revolucionarios en Cuba, con su secuela de represalias" (revolutionary movements in Cuba and the resulting countermeasures)—the story is set in the years or months leading up to the 1959 revolution (17). He imagines that his "conocimiento de idiomas" (knowledge of foreign languages) might allow him to become a "mensajero de la concordia y la tolerancia entre sus compatriotas" (messenger of harmony and tolerance among his countrymen; 17). Once in Cuba, with the same rapidity and ease that he had adopted foreign "patrias, religiones, cultura, actitudes, ideas" (countries, religions, cultures, postures, ideas), he sets out to adopt "su cultura" (his own culture; 19). Sporting a newly purchased *guayabera*, one night, he goes to the beach, where Batista's police mistake him for someone else (who has assassinated two government officials), take him at gunpoint, interrogate and torture him, and beat him to death.

The irony, of course, is that the protagonist in "El regreso" so successfully adopts what he considers to be his identity that he is *mistaken* for someone else (19). What leads to the protagonist's death, in other words, is his desire "a ser él, él, a entrar en su cultura, en su ambiente, donde no tenía que explicarse nada, donde todo 'era' desde siempre" ([to] be wholly and exclusively himself, moving into *his* culture, *his* environment, where nothing had to be explained, where everything had always just *been*; 18). The text of "El regreso" seems to underscore the extent to which this desire involves exchanging his cosmopolitan linguistic and cultural heterogeneity for a kind of nationalist singularity. (As he leaves New York, we are told, he gives away his "heterogéneo mobiliario" [motley furniture] to his neighbors [18].) Thus it is tempting to read "El regreso" as a text that diagnoses what Doris Sommer has called "the messiness of late modernity," in which "mass movements of economic and human capital unhinge people from their native languages and unmoor even anchor words such as *nation* and *state, gender* and *mother tongue*."[2] It is equally tempting to read "El regreso" as a text that embraces the "messiness of late modernity" and gestures toward a politics and aesthetics of multiplicity, ambivalence, and difference—which, Sommer suggests, could not only accommodate those who are linguistically and culturally "more than one" but also upset the "coherence of romantic nationalism and ethnic essentialism" as well as the "dangerous dreams of single-minded loyalty" (11).[3]

Sustained analyses of "El regreso" tend to see the text as an exploration of these same issues, especially as they pertain to Casey's own lived experience. Gustavo Pérez Firmat, for example, suggests that in Casey's writings, we can find a "Latino moment," an "uneasy and muted cohabitation of Spanish and English" that results in "a linguistic family romance that pits against each other the competing claims and attractions of Spanish and English."[4] What is ultimately at work in Casey's texts, Pérez Firmat argues, involves the linguistic and cultural dualism that defined the author's life: Casey grew up speaking both Spanish and English and "realized that to speak a language was to occupy a place, to settle into a cultural habitat with its history and contours" (93). Moreover, Pérez Firmat argues, Casey's work evokes "the phenomenon that linguists term diglossia," which refers to "the use of different languages for different purposes" or "the conviction that objects, events, emotions, ideas 'speak' a particular language" (94). "In English," Pérez Firmat suggests, "Casey is a different writer, and perhaps a different man, than he is in Spanish" (104). Thus the opening lines of "El regreso," which Pérez Firmat suggests are a "reflection on the difficulty of translating from English to Spanish," underscore "the linguistic self-consciousness [that] runs through all of Casey's work" (94).

It is hard not to read "El regreso" as a window onto Calvert Casey's troubled and mysterious life. The protagonist, after all, resembles Casey in a number of obvious ways—for example, he stutters and has a name that is "impronunciable" (unpronounceable; 16) and "extranjero" (foreign; 21). Much of what we know about Casey comes from Guillermo Cabrera Infante's 1980 essay "Who Killed Calvert Casey?," which intensifies the mysteries surrounding his life even as it attempts to outline it: "Calvert Casey was born in Baltimore and grew up in Havana. Calvert Casey was born in Havana and grew up in Baltimore. American, Cuban—who cares? It cannot be said with precision what Calvert was since he always evaded classifications and dates. Was he really born in the USA in 1924? No one knows. What is irrefutable is that he was a writer. Above all and above everyone, almost in spite of himself, Calvert wrote or thought about writing or dreamed he was writing. The biographical uncertainty (when did he really return to Cuba?) permits nevertheless some certainties."[5] In addition to consolidating a cult-like interest in Casey's life, Cabrera Infante's essay in many ways established the terms and parameters for subsequent discussions of Casey and his work: the life lived as "a game of errors and of identities and shifts" (120); the *poète maudit* with a guilt-ridden death drive, persecuted for his homosexuality and resistance to categorizations and social norms; and the artist-as-outsider who resists Cuban literary bureaucratization in order to produce a pure body of "true literature" that continually rises from the dead to achieve immortality (137). María Zambrano's "Calvert Casey, el indenfenso, entre el ser y la vida," published in 1982, similarly suggests that one of the essential questions we can ask and begin to answer by reading Casey's texts is "¿Quién era, pues, Calvert Casey?" (Who was, then, Calvert Casey?).[6]

And in his introduction to the 1998 English-language edition of Casey's stories, Ilan Stavans casts Casey as "the freakish nonconformist we all nurture within" and suggests that he belongs to a long tradition of "renegade artists" who are the "scapegoats of a society that doesn't quite know how to react to them."[7] Thus according to Stavans, it is not only that in life, Casey was "an artist of the unreal and nightmarish, isolated from society, alone and lonely" but also that in his stories, we are confronted with "an inescapable feeling of alienation, of remoteness that is very much the product of modernity" (xviii–xix).

Because Casey's own life was marked by alienation and in-betweenness, the assumption seems to be that "El regreso" must also work primarily outside or against accounts of linguistic, cultural, or national identity and belonging that produce alienation and in-betweenness. The result is that it is hard to see the ways in which "El regreso" reproduces ideologies about language, culture, and identity that were prominent in early 1960s Cuba. In Seymour Menton's *Prose Fiction of the Cuban Revolution*, for example, there is an emphasis on how "El regreso" ultimately transcends the politics from which it emerged. Menton acknowledges the "strong...tendency" in Cuban literature of the early 1960s "to justify the socialization of the Cuban Revolution" by "portraying pre-1959 Cuba as the country plagued by corruption, devoid of ideals, and populated by alienated anguish-laden individuals."[8] However, he insists that "El regreso" achieves "a transcendent level because the torture scenes are presented in all their gruesome detail, while allusions to the Cuban political situation in 1959 are minimal," and thus the story "not only effectively denounces the Batista police brutality against an innocent Cuban but also symbolizes the senseless tortures to which the individual human being is submitted in the hostile world of the atomic age, and perhaps in all ages" (176). In a similar vein, Pérez Firmat notes that the popularity of "El regreso" is "in no small measure because of its indictment of the brutality of the Batista regime" but concludes that in the end, "the murky personal subtext is more intriguing than the transparent political message" (98). Here the implication is that the politics of "El regreso" exist in tension with, or independent of, the story's literariness; its politics, Pérez Firmat suggests, are a kind of facile surface that we should look beyond in order to see the subtext that makes the story worthwhile. But perhaps "El regreso" is worthwhile not because of its literariness in spite of its politics but rather because of its insistence on both literariness *and* politics. In other words, perhaps the importance of "El regreso" is not so much the particular content of the politics it advances and endorses but rather its commitment to the political potential for literature as such.

In Casey's writings for *Lunes de Revolución* between 1959 and 1961, what we find is not a resistance to Cuban revolutionary nationalism but rather a full-throated embrace of it. His 1959 essay entitled "Cuba: Nación y nacionalidad," for example, is a celebration of José Martí as "el expositor más eficaz de la existencia de la nación cubana, el diferenciador más audaz" (the most effective exponent of the existence of the Cuban nation, its most courageous differentiator).[9] In "El regreso," these politics can be found in part in the text's approach to language and translation—even though translation plays an important role in "El regreso," the text is not a celebration of translation but rather a refusal of it. We first encounter the protagonist struggling with translation: "¿Cómo se llamaban esas cosas? ¿Actos fallidos? ¿Alienación del yo?" (What was the right term for those things? Freudian slips? Alienation of the self?; 7). But even before we get to these questions in the text, "El regreso" begins with an untranslated French epigraph from the final scene of Jean-Paul Sartre's 1943 screenplay *Les Jeux sont faits* (*The Chips Are Down*). It is important to note that Casey begins his text by quoting Sartre less than a year after his celebrated visit to Cuba with Simone de Beauvoir in 1960, when he was still an enthusiastic supporter of the Cuban Revolution.[10] But Sartre's words are important not only for their being his but also for the fact that, in Casey's text, they confront us with the difficulty or impossibility of translation. "Les jeux sont faits" is an idiomatic expression in French that originates from roulette and literally means "the games are made" but that in its idiomatic usage means something more along the lines of "the die is cast." What the extreme idiomaticity of "les jeux sont faits" means in practical terms is both that abstracted lexical or grammatical knowledge of French *alone* will do little or nothing to get at its meaning and that what is required is knowledge of its use within a culturally specific context—in other words, both its relationship to the group that uses it and its contextual relationship to the language that surrounds it in usage.

We might say, then, that "les jeux sont faits" in its untranslated form in the epigraph of "El regreso" is precisely the kind of language the protagonist is poised to miss: we know that he has a "conocimiento de idiomas" (knowledge of foreign languages), but we also know that he approaches language in general in an atomized way, focusing exclusively on individual words and even individual letters (17). When he thinks of life in Cuba, he imagines Cubans to be "tan sosegados" (so peaceful and content) and then thinks, "¡Cómo le gustaba la palabra" [How he loved that word!] (17) Like the objects in his apartment or the cultural practices that he imitates, words for the protagonist do not exist within cultural matrices or even in relation to other words but rather as isolated fragments: he reads "durante horas con la mirada fija en una misma letra" (for hours with his eyes fixed on a single letter); when he is being beaten, the narrator notes that "apenas acertó a pronunciar palabra" (he could barely bring out a single word; 8); when he is in "periodos de arrobo produndo con cada nuevo ídolo ... sólo ellos y sus palabras tenían realidad" (periods of his most intense infatuation with his successive new darlings ... only they and their words were real; 9); when he is focused on a single person, "todo lo demás ... perdía contornos" (everything else ... became blurred; 9); he utters "palabras imprescindibles" (essential phrases) but not sentences (19); and he reads fragments of books (mostly the dust jackets) but never the whole texts.

The protagonist's fragmentary, atomized approach to language—his tendency to focus on single letters or on single words—only mirrors his atomized approach to life in New York and later in Havana. Indeed, his life is described as a series of "episodios" (episodes) that leave him "inviolado y entero, no consumado, no usado, dispuesto de nuevo a henchirse de posibilidades" (untouched, not consumed, not used, ready once more to be filled with possibilities; 7). In other words, the protagonist experiences "un vacío" (a vacuum) that exists "entre él y cada uno de los episodios de su vida" (between him and each of the episodes in his life; 7). In this sense, the predicament of Casey's protagonist seems to embody the characteristics of underdevelopment as defined by the protagonist in Edmundo Desnoes's 1965 *Memorias del subdesarrollo*, Sergio Malabre:

> Una de las cosas que más me desconcierta de la gente es su incapacidad para sostener un sentimiento, una idea, sin dispersarse. Elena demostró ser totalmente inconsecuente. Es pura alteración, como diría Ortega. Lo que sentía ayer no tiene nada que ver con su estado de ánimo actual. No relaciona las cosas. Esa es una de las señales del subdesarrollo: incapacidad para relacionar las cosas, para acumular experiencia y desarrollarse.[11]

> (One of the things that unsettles me most about people is their inability to sustain a feeling, an idea, without it getting lost. Elena showed herself to be inconsistent. She is always in a state of flux—pure alteration, as Ortega would say. What she felt yesterday has nothing to do with her present feelings. She does not relate

one thing to another. That is one of the signs of underdevelopment: an inability to relate things to one another, to accumulate experience and develop oneself.)

Casey's protagonist seems to embody not only the fragmentary, ungrounded self that is described in *Memorias del subdesarrollo* but also bourgeois individualism. Just as he cannot relate fragments to the whole of which they are part, he cannot see himself in relation to the social totality of which he is a part. "El regreso" not only refuses to provide the name of its protagonist but also insists on the irrelevance of individual identity in other key ways: when the protagonist is being beaten by his interrogators, he attempts to tell them his name—that is, to identify himself as a specific individual who is innocent. But just as he begins to think that "si le dejaran hablar, llamar a sus jóvenes amigos, les explicaría, se aclararía el monstruoso error" (if they'd let him speak, call his young friends, he'd explain everything to them, and the horrible mistake would be cleared up), he hears his captors say, "Si no es éste, es lo mismo" (If he's not the guy, it's all the same; 22). That is to say, the idea that it doesn't matter whether he is the person they were originally looking for suggests that in "El regreso," the protagonist is not cast as a victim of cultures or identities, or even of individual, internal conflict and turmoil regarding those terms, but rather as a victim of impersonal structures of power—and struggles over power. When his interrogators say, "Es lo mismo" (It's all the same), it is because they see him primarily in terms of his political relations to others and to them and not in terms of either his cultural identity or his individuality. Hence the protagonist's faith that calling "sus jóvenes amigos" (his young friends) would clear things up is only a sign of his misunderstanding of what's happening and, ultimately, a symptom of both his tendency to see the world exclusively in terms of isolated episodes and his inability to relate those episodes to the broader matrices in which they take place (22).

Christopher Winks has persuasively argued for, and explored, the importance of cities as real and imagined places in Casey's work, and although Winks does not deal with "El regreso," one has to wonder if cities perform a unique function within the politics of the story not accounted for in Winks's readings.[12] The protagonist in Casey's story has two ways of seeing cities and the social relations they contain. On the one hand, New York is a cultural sea of difference, where his neighbor is a woman who "había llegado soltera del centro de Europa en los remotos tiempos de Francisco José" (had come from Central Europe as a young woman in the long-gone days of the Emperor Franz Joseph; 12) and is friends with "una centenaria irlandesa, cubierta por muchas capas de tiempo y sangre" (an ancient Irishwoman enveloped in many a layer of time and dirt; 13). On the other hand, Havana is represented as a relatively homogeneous cultural space where all men are "hermanos" (brothers) who understand each other "en el gran lenguaje atávico y no hablado con que se entienden los hombres de una misma tierra" (in the great unspoken ancestral language in which men of one and the same land understand each other; 17). What the protagonist misses, however, is the extent to which the dynamics he either perceives or experiences in those cities are not functions of either language or culture, and as a fictional participant in the very real gentrification of Lower Manhattan that began in the 1950s, he is unable to recognize the differences between himself and his neighbors that cannot be accounted for along cultural or linguistic lines—in other words, economic ones. In Havana, even though he has read newspaper reports about "movimientos revolucionarios en Cuba, con su secuela de represalias" (revolutionary movements in Cuba and the resulting countermeasures), he cannot imagine the presence of differences—that is, ideological and political ones—that are not subsumed into culture and language (27). In fact, it might be said that the protagonist's death is the result of his view of identity and difference along purely cultural and linguistic lines: for him, language and culture are what make men *hermanos* or not. Moreover, the conflict between himself and his captors is in no way like the differences between Spanish and English—or New York and Havana—inasmuch as it in no way can be overcome by translation.

The refusal of translation that occurs at the start of the story is in part a refusal to let the foreign in, an attempt to leave it foreign and unassimilated. A similar effort is at work in Nicolás Guillén's 1964 "Tengo" ("I Have"), the poem that is perhaps most closely associated with the years immediately following the triumph of the Cuban Revolution in 1959. The speaker of Guillén's poem, who declares that he is not only a black man but also a "campesino, obrero, gente simple" (a peasant, a worker, a simple person) enumerates the ways in which he has benefitted, in a relatively short time, from the most prominent accomplishments of the Revolution. Whereas "no más ayer" (only yesterday), he was "Juan sin Nada" (John with Nothing), today he is "Juan con Todo" (John with Everything); he has "el gusto de andar por mi país, / dueño de cuanto hay en él, / mirando bien de cerca lo que antes / no tuve ni podía tener" (the pleasure of walking about my country, / master of all there is in it, / looking very closely at what before / I didn't and couldn't have).[13] The speaker then celebrates the elimination of racial discrimination; the elimination of the *guardia rural*, which had become synonymous with the repressive regime of Fulgencio Batista; the Literacy Campaign; and the elimination of private clubs and beaches. Amid the speaker's account of the social and political changes ushered in after 1959, however, is also his account of a specifically linguistic one: "tengo el gusto de ir / (es un ejemplo) / a un banco y hablar con el administrador, / no en inglés, / no en señor, / sino decirle compañero como se dice en español" (I have the pleasure of going / [here's an example] / to a bank to talk with the manager, / not in English, / not in sir, / but to say *compañero* to him as it's done in Spanish; 270).

In his illuminating account of the politics and aesthetics of English and Spanish in Guillén's poetry, Roberto Ignacio Díaz has underscored the extent to which English "reveals itself as a central signifying element in the Afro-Hispanic house of Cuban writing."[14] More broadly, Díaz argues, "Code switching, which in U.S. Hispanic literature is often read as a liberating break with the literary practices of the monolingual English-speaking mainstream, often retains in the Spanish American tradition the negative ideological underpinnings evident in Guillén's texts" (41–42). Indeed, that the speaker in Guillén's "Tengo" celebrates the fact that he can now interact with a bank manager "not in English" but in Spanish refers in part to the nationalization of the Cuban branches of U.S. banks such as Chase Manhattan and the First National Bank of Boston in 1960.[15] But it also refers to the fact that the use of English *writ large* was bound up with the United States' long history of cultural, political, and economic influence on the island as well as its imperialist designs. In 1899, an article in the *New York Tribune* reported that English would be taught in Cuba "in all grades for the purpose of its Americanizing effect," and by 1901, English was officially established in Cuba's elementary school curriculum.[16] Although English never became the main language of instruction in Cuban elementary or secondary education, during the 1910s through the 1930s, it became a requirement in various grade levels, and the University of Havana made English a requirement for degree programs in fields such as medicine, architecture, and diplomacy (Corona and García, 88–89). English not only became the language of business but also became fashionable among middle-class and elite Cubans, especially during the 1940s and 1950s, and English was the language of the ten thousand U.S. citizens who lived relatively affluent lives on the island, not to mention the three hundred thousand U.S. tourists who visited it annually, by the end of the 1950s (Corona and García, 90). Indeed, the three Anglicisms or pseudo-Anglicisms that appear in Guillén's poem invoke the world of Cuban elites who sought to emulate North American culture before it is replaced by a vision of nature that is infinite and democratic: "no country, / no jailáif, / no tenis y no yacht, / sino de playa en playa y ola en ola, / gigante azul abierto democrático: / en fin, el mar" (no exclusive residential compound, no high life, no tennis and yacht clubs, / but from beach to beach and wave to wave, / immense blue, open, democratic: / in short, the sea; Guillén, 273).

This is not to say, however, that "El regreso" merely reproduces the dominant political ideologies of Cuba in the early 1960s. For Juan Carlos Quintero-Herencia, Casey's text—and in particular, the ending of Casey's text—

demonstrates that "este *drive* identitario es una fantasía de pertenencia que solo puede recibir el acoso, la tortura policial allí donde ya es obligatoria una concepción guerrera del saber-estar en la historia patria" (this identitarian drive is a fantasy of belonging that can only be the victim of assault and police torture in a place where there is already a militant conception of *saber-estar* in national history).[17] In other words, for Quintero-Herencia, while Casey's protagonist can perhaps be understood as a victim of "los discursos de la cultura y del poder dentro y fuera de la isla" (the discourses of culture and power inside and outside of the island), the text of "El regreso" opens up a space in which to "paladear la experiencia heterogénea que también fue el comienzo revolucionario" (savor the heterogeneous experience that was also the beginning of the Revolution), and thus "la exposición de estas subjetividades literarias es la forma misma de una polémica, de una batalla con las moralizaciones, con las evidencias que consolidarían y naturalizarían un modo de concebir y habitar el espacio nacional" (the exposition of these literary subjectivities is the very form of a polemic, of a battle against moralizations, against the evidence that would consolidate and naturalize a mode of conceiving and inhabiting the space of the nation; 402). Ultimately, however, "El regreso" is less interested in creating a space for subjective pluralities and heterogeneities than it is in creating a space for literature as such in the realm of the political. "El regreso" begins with a literary reference—to Sartre's *Les Jeux sont faits*—and it also ends with one. The final lines of Casey's text produce an unusual image in which "hundió las tenazas el cangrejerío" (the horde of crabs sank their claws) between the protagonist's "labios delicados" (delicate lips; 23), which evokes Neruda's *Canto General*, where the poet calls on crabs to resist conquerors: "y púdreles toda la sangre / devorándoles los pulmones / y los labios con tus cangrejos" (and rot all their blood, / devour their lungs / and lips with your crabs).[18] The final lines of "El regreso" thus extend and complete the work begun by the Sartrean epigraph. To face the difficulties of translation is to face the inseparability of meaning and form; to begin and end a literary text with references to other literary texts is not only to literally circumscribe the text with literariness but also to privilege, in a way, its relationship to literature as such over (or instead of) its relationship to the world. This is not to say that "El regreso" is not political—it obviously is. Rather, it is to say that in "El regreso," literary form is not an impediment to the political. Almost forty years ago, Roberto González Echevarría observed "a corrosive, critical element to Latin American letters," by which he meant "the struggle to transcend, to go beyond or remain outside of the literary" in the Cuban literature of the Revolution.[19] Perhaps Casey's embrace of the literary in "El regreso" constitutes—then as much as now—the text's most important political work.

NOTES

1. Calvert Casey, *Calvert Casey: Tres relatos rituales*, ed. Alberto Ruy Sánchez (Mexico City: Coordinación de Difusión Cultural, Dirección de Literatura, Universidad Nacional Autónoma de México, 2008), 16–18. English-language translations following the quoted text are taken from Calvert Casey, *Calvert Casey: The Collected Stories*, ed. Ilan Stavans, trans. John H. R. Holt (Durham, N.C.: Duke University Press, 1998).
2. Doris Sommer, introduction to *Bilingual Games: Some Literary Investigations*, ed. Doris Sommer (New York: Palgrave Macmillan, 2003), 3.
3. For recent readings of "El regreso," see Jason Bartles, "Calvert Casey's Wasted Narratives," *Revista Hispánica Moderna* 70, no. 1 (2017): 19–35; Carina Fernanda González, "La odisea del retorno: Calvert Casey y el regreso que se repite," *Hispamérica* 45, no. 134 (2016): 3–12; and Celina Manzoni, "Poéticas del retorno: Tres pesadillas cubanas," *Hispamérica* 45, no. 134 (2016): 3–12. For an important recent account of Casey's work, see Rafael Rojas, *La vanguardia peregrina: El escritor cubano, la tradición y el exilio* (Mexico City: Fondo de Cultura Económica, 2013).
4. Gustavo Pérez Firmat, *Tongue Ties: Logo-Eroticism in Anglo-Hispanic Literature* (New York: Palgrave Macmillan, 2003), 5.
5. Guillermo Cabrera Infante, *Mea Cuba*, trans. Kenneth Hall with the author (New York: Farrar, Straus and Giroux, 1994), 119.
6. María Zambrano, *Islas*, ed. Jorge Luis Arcos (Madrid: Editorial Verbum, 2007), 225.
7. Ilan Stavans, introduction to Casey, *Collected Stories*, ix–x.
8. Seymour Menton, *Prose Fiction of the Cuban Revolution* (Austin: University of Texas Press, 1975), 174.
9. Calvert Casey, "Cuba: Nación y nacionalidad," *Lunes de Revolución* no. 28 (September 28, 1959): 2.
10. On Sartre in Cuba, see William Rowlandson, *Sartre in Cuba—Cuba in Sartre* (New York: Palgrave Macmillan, 2018).
11. Edmundo Desnoes, *Memorias del subdesarrollo* (Mexico City: Joaquín Mortiz, 1980), 44.
12. Christopher Winks, *Symbolic Cities in Caribbean Literature* (New York: Palgrave Macmillan, 2009), 1–24.
13. Nicolás Guillén, *Nicolás Guillén: A Bilingual Anthology*, ed. and trans. Keith Ellis (Havana: Editorial José Martí, 2003), 270. English-language translations following the quoted text are taken from Ellis's bilingual edition.
14. Roberto Ignacio Díaz, *Unhomely Rooms: Foreign Tongues and Spanish American Literature* (Lewisburg, Pa.: Bucknell University Press, 2002), 40. According to Díaz, interlingualism in Guillén's poetry is ultimately "less an act of eviction than ... a testament to accommodation" (41). In his analysis of Guillén's "Canta el sinsonte en el Turquino" (1964), Díaz suggests that the poem "belies its seeming apologia for Spanish monolingualism," since even as "its repression is declared, English, or interlingual forms thereof, breaks into the monolingual spaces of Guillén's text" (39).
15. Cole Blasier, *The Hovering Giant: U.S. Responses to Revolutionary Change in Latin America* (Pittsburgh, Pa.: University of Pittsburgh Press, 1985), 79; Helen Yaffe, *Che Guevara: The Economics of Revolution* (New York: Palgrave Macmillan, 2009), 27.
16. Dolores Corona and Ofelia García, "English in Cuba: From the Imperial Design to the Imperative Need," in *Post-Imperial English: Status Change in Former British and American Colonies, 1940–1990*, ed. Joshua A. Fishman, Andrew W. Conrad, and Alma Rubal-López (New York: Mouton de Gruyter, 1996), 88. On language politics in Cuba during the 1950s, see also Louis A. Pérez, *On Becoming Cuban: Identity, Nationality, and Culture* (Chapel Hill: University of North Carolina Press, 1999).

17. Juan Carlos Quintero-Herencia, "'El regreso' de Calvert Casey: Una exposición en la playa," *Cuadernos de literatura* 17, no. 33 (2013): 402.
18. Pablo Neruda, *Obras escogidas*, ed. Francisco Coloane (Santiago, Chile: Editorial Andrés Bello, 1972), 236. English-language translations following the quoted text are taken from Pablo Neruda, *Canto General*, trans. Jack Schmitt (Berkeley: University of California Press, 1991). English-language translations of passages from Neruda's *Canto General* are by Schmitt.
19. Roberto González Echevarría, "*Biografía de un cimarrón* and the Novel of the Cuban Revolution," *NOVEL* 13, no. 3 (1980): 249–263; 250.

6 · A PALIMPSESTUOUS ADAPTATION

Translating Barcelona in Benet i Jornet's *La Plaça del Diamant*

JENNIFER DUPREY

> I have reflected that it is permissible to see ... a kind of palimpsest, through which the traces—tenuous but not indecipherable—of our friend's "previous" writing should be translucently visible.
>
> —Jorge Luis Borges, *Labyrinths*[1]

One of "the marked achievements" of the ancient city was "the passage from ritual to drama."[2] Historically, the city and the theater have been intertwined, as they are spaces for the formation and representation of the daily experience of collective life.[3] Theater (or drama), thus, portrays the city's dialectic oppositions, since it is a place of dialogue and gestures, reflection and action. Greek tragedy, for instance, was political; its subject matter was primarily the political and ethical issues of the *polis*—that is, the city-state. Moreover, in the Greek idea of a democratic city, theater played a central part. The social contexts—past or present—referred to in theater are, thus, what bestow meaning to the city and the collective life performed in theater. In Barcelona, theater has historically been a means for representing and dissecting the city's urban life, its social and human circumstances, which are constituted by antagonistic forces and relations.

Indeed, the history of Barcelona's social formation is rather complex. It is a city profoundly marked by the tribulations and changes of history. Among these changes are industrialization and the impact of the first form of capitalism in the nineteenth century, the turn of the century and early twentieth-century

Barcelona's Universal Expositions, the Spanish Civil War and its subsequent dictatorship, and the transition to democracy and Spain's incursion to a new sociopolitical map after 1989—namely, the new world order of late capitalism and globalization. This later process has its high point in Barcelona with the celebration of the Olympic Games in 1992. Yet none of these sociopolitical events is isolated or unrelated from the others. On the contrary, they are as profoundly related as the engravings of a palimpsest: each of them carries visible traces of the earlier form.[4]

Barcelona is, thus, a palimpsest. It is a city of inscriptions and of the traces of such inscriptions, a city noticeably marked by the passage of time and history. The following pages tackle the translation, from telling to showing—from the genre of the novel to the theater—specifically, the adaptation for theater of the novel *La Plaça del Diamant* (1962) by the Catalan writer Mercè Rodoreda (1908–1983). Indeed, this literary text is one of the most significant novels of Catalan literature that depicts the years before and after the Spanish Civil War and its consequences for Barcelona and for Catalan people in general. Rodoreda's novel was praised by Gabriel García Márquez (1927–2014) in an article for *El País* on May 18, 1983: "*La Plaza del Diamante* es, a mi juicio, la más bella que se ha publicado en España después de la Guerra Civil. La razón de que se la conozca tan poco, aun dentro de España, no puede atribuirse a que se hubiera escrito en una lengua de ámbito reducido, ni a que sus dramas humanos transcurran en un rincón secreto de la muy secreta ciudad de Barcelona" (*La Plaza del Diamante* is, to my judgment, the most beautiful novel ever published in Spain after the Civil War. The reason for being seldom read, even within Spain, cannot be attributed to the fact that it is written in lesser-used language nor to the fact that its human drama takes place in a secret corner of the very secret city of Barcelona).[5]

Among the visual adaptations—or visual translations—of Rodoreda's novel, there are Francesc Betriu's film *The Time of the Doves* (1982), the theatrical adaptations of Joan Ollé in 2004, and Josep M. Benet i Jornet's adaptation of the novel. Benet i Jornet's dramatic text was published in October 2007. Under the direction of Toni Casares, the play was performed at the Sala Gran of the Teatre Nacional de Catalunya during November of the same year, as part of the celebration of the centenary of Rodoreda's birth.[6] Benet i Jornet's adaptation, I suggest, transposed the narrative identity of Rodoreda's novel into a theatrical code through an "intersemiotic transposition,"[7] using Hutcheon's vocabulary—that is, from words to images. Particularly, this was an act of adaptation—which of involves a process of creation, reinterpretation, and reception—to a medium (theater) that is an art of both time and space. My contention is that Benet i Jornet's theatrical adaptation materializes history and spatializes time in the very process of translation from the novel to the dramatic form and the stage. His adaptation of Rodoreda's novel presents the city of Barcelona in its specific historical dimension. It allows us to see the entwinements of history and memory, the historical events that marked the city during the years of the Second Republic (1931–1936) and the Spanish Civil War and Post-War (1936–1939) periods, and, therefore, the existential aspect of the city and its denizens.[8] Because of its representation of the Barcelona of the 1930s, and its recollection of a collective past, Benet i Jornet's theatrical adaptation is, I argue, the perfect illustration of the relationship between theater and the city in Catalan theater.

The significance of Benet i Jornet's adaptation of Rodoreda's novel should also be contextualized in relation to the fate of Catalan theater under the Francisco Franco regime (1939–1975). Indeed, the history of drama and performance in Catalonia is intimately related to the memory of a society that has been limited by a series of internal and external conditions such as Primo de Rivera (1923–1930) and Franco dictatorships, periods in which Catalan language and culture were proscribed, as the censorship of both regimes forbade almost any expression of Catalan culture. The Spanish Civil War was one of the events that most profoundly created a hiatus in the development of Catalan culture and its artistic expressions. Barcelona, a city that before the fall of the Second Spanish Republic already had a remarkable history in visual arts, came to a crashing halt with Franco's victory. For these reasons, among others, contemporary Catalan theater has been concerned with memory as a hermeneutic of the past—both in creative terms and in a historical approach—and of the cultural and political processes that have afflicted Catalonia for more than forty years.

FROM TELLING TO SHOWING

Theatrical images make visible instances of life that might not otherwise be perceived, for theater materializes time and history and, therefore, memory. Here memory is conceived as the representation of the past in the form of images. This materialization, however, manifests itself in the scenic space of the theatrical performance as traces, since it is not a materialization of time or history as such. Rather, the spectator grasps an understanding of these instances of life through symbols and signs, gestures and images. What spectators find on stage is thus an epistemological materialization of time and history, which requires the audience's involvement with what is being shown. Indeed, theater involves not only telling a story but also showing it. This relationship of interdependence between the "narrative identity" of the literary text and the spatial and visual identities of theater has the ability of representing what is conceived as unseen instances of life.[9]

Apropos of this entwinement of the narrative and the visual aspects in the space of theatrical representation, in *A Theory of Adaptation* (2006), Linda

Hutcheon has pointed out that "there are significant differences between being told a story and being shown a story, and especially between both of these and the physical act of participating in a story's world" (15). On stage, contrary to the novel, "a visual and aural world is shown" (39). This particular visual and aural world is "created from verbal and notational signs on the page" (39).[10] Actually, the Greek word *theatron* means "place for seeing" (Boyer, *City of Collective Memory* 74). As a "place for seeing," the theatrical space functions as a "cultural prism through which the spectator experiences social reality" (74).

To be able to read and fully see Barcelona as it is portrayed on the space of the theatrical performance, the audience is required "to look at the city not only in formal and functional terms but in figural and interpretive ways as well" (19). One of the noteworthy characteristics of this novel is that the story is narrated through the voice of the main character: Natàlia (Colometa). In this way, through Natàlia's interior monologue, one comes across, simultaneously, the visualization of a war landscape as well as another modality of time that is very much related to the experience of war. This different modality of time is memory. Memory manifests itself on the stage of *La Plaça del Diamant* by means of various elements that pertain to the practice of adaptation, such as point of view, interiority and exteriority, symbols, and silences and absences (Hutcheon, *Theory of Adaptation* xv). On stage comes to life the story of Barcelona's popular urban life, as well as the materialization of a time of losses both for Natàlia and Catalonia. At that moment, her story begins—namely, Natàlia's story but also the story of a city and a country. As Resina has suggested, "Natàlia permits Rodoreda to excavate the entrails of the symbolic life that frames a national community."[11] Benet i Jornet's portrayal of this past—that is, the materialization of time and history as traces—contributes to the density of the play as a place of cultural memory. It is a play that becomes what Hutcheon has called "a palimpsestuous adaptation," which is haunted at all times by the original text. If we know the original, we find it continuously shadowing the adaptation (6). This adaptation, hence, is "a derivation that is not derivative—a work that is second without being secondary. It is its own palimpsestic thing" (Hutcheon, *Theory of Adaptation* 9) or what Gerard Genette denominated a text in the "second degree,"[12] in the sense of an earlier text that both "imitates" (does not copy) and "transforms." The poetics of such transformation, therefore, concerns not only the literary text in itself but its "textual transcendence" (ix).

LA PLAÇA DEL DIAMANT TAKES THE STAGE

The scenography of Benet i Jornet's play, designed by Jordi Roig, is extremely complex. Since Rodoreda's novel is laden with pictorial descriptions of Barcelona's urban life, in this theatrical adaptation, the audience sees the square, the bakery, the drugstore, the shop of *la senyora* Enriqueta, and the Plaça del Diamant where Natàlia meets Quimet, a site that "founds Natàlia's adult memory" (Resina, *Barcelona's Reception* 120). On stage, there were interior and exterior spaces; the buildings around the square—of the same dimension of the actual Plaça in the Gràcia neighborhood of Barcelona—moved. The music by Oscar Roig was written specifically for this dramatic piece and was performed live. It was a musical composition that reinforced the emotional tensions and oppositions of the play's story.[13] The size and vividness of Gràcia's urban space were replicated on stage. Spectators saw the house of Natàlia/Colometa and Quimet, the Parc Güell, the house of Quimet's mother, Antoni's shop, and so on. A stage that changed and rotated continuously, marking the passing of time, materialized a landscape of life, war, and death. In Benet i Jornet's adaptation, Casares and Roig not merely showed the audience a famished and depleted family, but what one saw on stage was the materialization of such destruction through theatrical images.

La Plaça del Diamant is "a novel about Catalonia's tragedy" (7), affirms Resina. This tragic dimension, I would add, is, in fact, part of the portrayal of Barcelona in its historical dimension. In this sense, Resina further affirms, "This novel shows that, when defeat supervenes, the survivors' only hope is to withdraw to the no-man's land of hope to preserve an emotional link between the past and the future" (7). In fact, the project of transforming Barcelona into one of the epicenters of modern culture, which began in the mid-nineteenth century, came to a halt during the Spanish Civil War and postwar periods. Catalonia's cultural and political projects were shattered by a series of political practices that, as Resina has affirmed, "marked a new stage in the city's status" (7). To be precise, these practices were "defeat, the exodus of the intellectual and political elite, a ban on public use of the language, destruction (by fire and pulping) of a large part of the literary and historical legacy, confiscation of archives for use in the repression of Catalans, purges and discrimination, the constraints and fiscal depredation of the Catalan economy, and efforts to reduce Catalonia to a province (7)." The aforementioned practices characterized the political, cultural, and daily life of postwar Barcelona. Benet i Jornet's *La Plaça del Diamant* reminds readers and spectators about these practices not only by telling but also by showing on stage their effects on Barcelona's collective and cultural life. His translation to the stage of Rodoreda's novel shows "the story of survival," which is "told by the surviving character."[14] Natàlia, in fact, describes the end of the Civil War with these striking words directed specifically to the audience: "I no hi havia res a fer. La ciutat es trasbalsava i mentre els uns se n'anaven, esverats i plens de por, els altres entraven a la ciutat i cantaven, cantaven" (And there was nothing to do. The city was agitated, and while some were leaving, frightened and terrified, others came to town and sang, sang).[15] The stage lights up and gradually begins to play, every time higher, the "Royal March," which is the Spanish national anthem: "Arriba, España, alzad los brazos hijos del pueblo español, que vuelve a resurgir" (Long live Spain, raise your arms, sons of the Spanish people, who are rising again; 139).

This story of survival begins to materialize visually by the persistence of shadows in Natàlia and Quimet's house. These shadows indeed reflect a physical world; they are the continual aide-mémoire of that world as well as of the instances of life that compose it. They are shadows that, as traces of that physical world, suggest a liminal point between life and death, being and nonbeing, presence and absence. The persistence of shadows in the scene creates an aura of fragility, which functions as dramatic prolepsis of the devastation that will come with the war.

While in Rodoreda's novel, we read Natàlia's interior voice, on stage we see her gaze: Rodoreda tells us Natàlia's story, while Benet i Jornet shows it to us. In fact, for Benet i Jornet, one of the great challenges at the moment of adapting the novel was to translate Natàlia's particular language and interior monologues into theatrical dialogues, since these were two aspects that made up an interior space full of collective echoes.[16] The challenge was how to translate Natàlia's language, a language that more often than not is rammed up against silence, into an exteriority.[17] Saying it differently, the challenge was, in general, how to materialize Natàlia's emotional world. Accordingly, her interior voice appeared as a voice-over in Benet i Jornet's adaptation. In this way, the voice-over recuperates the monologue of the novel and, at the same time, it emerges to the audience as Natàlia's constant reflection on her life since the beginning of the Second Republic until the postwar period, a life she recuperates at the end of the war. Natàlia's language, which is in constant "stream of consciousness," is translated on stage into visual and acoustic imagery—this later particularly composed by echoes. "The performance mode," Hutcheon highlights, "teaches us that language is not the only way to express meaning and to relate stories. Visual and gestural representations are rich in complex associations; music offers aural 'equivalents' for characters' emotions and, in turn, provokes effective [and affective] responses in the audience" (*Theory of Adaptation* 23). On stage, the theatrical representations of the powerful images of the Civil War, of the city of Barcelona, and of the passage of time in Rodoreda's novel are embodied, rendered alive. Natàlia's interior voice, her perception of the events, and the images of destruction during wartime are materialized in the scene by voices, shadows, sounds, and the presence of doves—doves that, as symbolic of the novel's story, die little by little as the war advances and comes to an end—leaving the audience with a feeling of what exists and does not exist, what appears and disappears, what once was and ceased to be.

The second part of the play, which portrays the Civil War—a political event that I understood as both continuity and discontinuity in the historical constellation that formed the history of twentieth-century Spain—is the most powerful. The pain and ruin brought about by the war are materialized on stage through theatrical means: yellow and bright lights permeated the stage during the Second Republic, but blue, gray, and red lights pervaded the stage during the war and postwar periods. In a grippingly poetic fashion, the stage annotations on the lighting and the performance of its design created a sort of visual synesthesia in the fusion of images of the evening and the sun with a multiplicity of red tones, reminiscent of blood: "El sol, en apagar-se, s'anirà fent de sang" (The sun, as it stops shining, will become blood; Benet i Jornet, *La Plaça del Diamant* 135). Also visually arresting is the following stage annotation, which recreated the beginning of the war and the bombing of Barcelona: "L'ambient s'ha fet més de sang que mai. Quan Mateu desapareix Colometa s'avança cap a nosaltres. Sempre amb el color de sang que ho acapara tot" (The atmosphere has become bloodier than ever. When Mateu disappears, Colometa advances toward us. Always with the color of blood that captures everything; 138).

The lighting design materialized not only the dimension of Natàlia's inner life but also the existential dimension that Barcelona and its collective life acquired during the war. In the dramatic text, one reads the following *didascalia*: "La llum del vespre ja s'ha fet completament de sang" (The light of the evening has become completely bloodier; 137) and "La llum canvia mentre persisteix la música. Es fa de nit i Colometa queda il·luminada per un llum electric" (The light changes while the music continues. The night falls, and Colometa is illuminated by an electric light; 159). The lighting design created its own language and its own communication process with the spectator; the first stage direction about lighting created a visual aura of death and decay; the second one, along with the music, focused on portraying the character of Natàlia in the solitude brought about by the war. Certainly, by means of a continuous jeu of shadows on the scenic space, beauty degenerates to ugliness and sadness. In this part, the most poetic, profound, and moving images unfold: Quimet, Mateu, Cintent, and Julieta leave to the front; Natàlia (Colometa) is forced to abandon her son, Antoni; and the bombings begin:

ANTONI PETIT: No em deixi! Els nens són dolents i em pegaran i no em vull quedar!
COLOMETA: [*quieta*] Hi has d'anar. Hi has d'anar.
ANTONI PETIT: No em deixi, em moriré i em pegaran! Em moriré i em pegaran!

Natàlia, inexpressiva, separa les mans del nen i el passa a Julieta. El nen calla de cop. Natàlia potser pren aire, mira un instant Julieta, agafa de nou la Rita, i llavors mira el nen, que la mira a ella, ara sense plorar. Natàlia gira cua arrossegant la seva filla, que potser encara mira el seu germà, i se l'emporta cap a casa. Julieta i el nen, quiets un instant. Després Julieta passa la mà per l'esquena d'Antoni Petit i l'empeny amb suavitat. (130)

(ANTONI PETIT: Do not leave me! The kids are ill and I do not want to stay!
COLOMETA: [*still*] You have to go. You have to go.
ANTONI PETIT: Do not leave me, I will die and they will beat me! I will die and they will beat me!

Natàlia, expressionless, separates the child's hands and delivers him to Julieta. The boy suddenly remains silent. Natalia, perhaps, takes a deep breath, looks at Julieta for a moment, takes Rita again, and then watches the child who looks at her now without crying. Natàlia drags her daughter, who, maybe, is still watching his brother and takes her home. Julieta and the child stand still for a moment. Julieta then touches the back of Little Anthony and pushes him gently.)

By now, the happiness of the beginning—the years of the Second Republic—has become misery. Natàlia is fully portrayed in a state of desperation, as she is about to kill herself and her children.

Parts of the collective echoes that haunt Natàlia are Julieta's words of happiness and hope. Julieta is one of the *milicianas* who truly believes that another society is possible and, thus, another future. In Rodoreda's novel, the character disappears, and the reader is supposed to interpret that she has died in the war. In contrast, in Benet i Jornet's play, the spectator witnesses Julieta's death by a firing squad:

JULIETA: No! Ho sents? No, Natàlia! T'equivoques el món anirà millor, i tothom podrà ser feliç, perquè a la terra hi hem vingut per ser feliços i no per patir sense parar. Si no fos per la revolució jo no hauria tingut una nit d'amor com la que vaig tenir. [*Pausa.*] Per tant, passi el que passi, hauré tingut aquella nit! Passi el que passi, Natalia. [...] Serem feliços, Natàlia! Ho entens? Serem tan feliços ... ! Tan...!

I de sobte ... la descàrrega dels fusells i Julieta cau morta a terra (141).

(JULIETA: No! Do you hear? No, Natàlia! You are wrong; the world will be better, and everyone will be happy, because we have come to earth to be happy, not to suffer endlessly. If not for the revolution, I wouldn't have had the night of love I had. [*Pause.*] So whatever happens, I will have had that night!.... Whatever happens, Natalia. [...] We'll be happy, Natàlia! Do you understand it? We'll be so happy...! So...!

FIGURE 6.1. *La Plaça del Diamant* by Mercè Rodoreda. Adaptation for theater by Josep Maria Benet i Jornet, Teatre Nacional of Catalunya, Sala Gran, Barcelona, Spain. Season 2007/2008. Photograph by David Ruano / Teatre Nacional de Catalunya.

And suddenly... the firing of the rifles and Julieta falls dead to the ground.)

The previous passages show how the playwright materializes on the page as well as onstage in an event that exemplifies the perverted part of history. The teleological idea of social and human progress and happiness was the enlightened conception of history, its somber side, and the failure of this idea is marked by the social and human atrocities committed in the world in the name of such progress and happiness. By viewing Julieta's death by a firing squad, spectators made intelligible their recent history of accumulated suffering, especially since this character allegorizes the supreme utopian values of happiness and liberty. The scene, therefore, created a reflexive pact between the theater and spectators. It allowed spectators to have an interactive relationship between the past and the present.

In the last part of the play, after marrying Antoni, Natàlia and Antoni receive Vincenç's (Rita's fiancé) visit to ask for Rita's hand. As he enters the house, Natàlia confuses him with Mateu:

De sobte a la botiga hi entra un xicot vestit amb correció. . . . Natàlia queda desconcertada.

COLOMETA: Mateu!
VINCENÇ: Com? Em dic Vincenç, senyora. (165)

(Suddenly, a young man dressed properly enters into the store.... Natàlia remains baffled.

COLOMETA: Mateu!
VINCENÇ: What? My name is Vincenç, *senyora*.)

In transporting these characters from the pages of the novel to the theatrical space, Benet i Jornet deploys a creative strategy that fuses the characters of Mateu and Vincenç for the audience. Its intent, however, is to give Natàlia—at the moment in which she is recuperating her life (for after overcoming war, hunger, and death, Colometa is Natàlia again)—a vindication of her past as well as of the secret love she felt for Mateu.[18] This strategy had both rhetorical and aesthetic effects. The fusion of these two characters becomes crystallized in Rita's wedding day, at the moment of the dance:

L'adroguer s'ha acostat i enllaça Natàlia i es posen a ballar ... l'adroguer i Natàlia se'ns perdin de vista i mentre la música, encara que no pari, es va convertint en un vals, per fin distinguim de nou Natàlia, però en braços de Vincenç que encara porta parcialment el seu vestit de nuvi pero també vesteix alguna peça de les que duia Mateu. El vals s'omple de tranquilla melangia i la llum general comença a canviar... tot el món va desapareixent, tots els elements de la festa, i és de nit, i al final només tindrem davant nostre la parella.... El vals està acabant i Natàlia es deixa anar.

COLOMETA: Vés; ara, vés.

Vincenç/Mateu somriu, s'inclina i se'n va. Natàlia es gira cap a l'adroguer. (182)

(The grocer has approached Natàlia and embraces her, and they start dancing ... we lose sight of them, and while the music sounds, it becomes a waltz; finally, we distinguish Natàlia again but on Vincenç's arm, who still partially wears his wedding suit but also a piece of clothing that Mateu used to wear. The waltz is full of quiet melancholy, and the light begins to change ... everybody begins to disappear as well as any trace of the celebration, and it is night, and at the end, we only have in front of us our couple.... The waltz is coming to an end, and Natàlia let herself go.

COLOMETA: Go; now, go.

Vincenç/Mateu smiles, bows and leaves. Natalia turns to the shopkeeper. [182])

Benet i Jornet's adaptation is what Marvin Carlson denominates a "haunted stage" in two ways. First, it is a haunted stage in that it is full of presences—the presences of the characters that died in the war: Mateu, Quimet, Julieta—as they are constantly evoked by Natàlia. Her evocation is a way of calling the dead, and such an evocation is a form of creating memory.

Second, even though the spectator has in front of him or her a familiar landscape, Benet i Jornet's theatrical representation is a form of repetition without replication; his representation is composed of material that the spectator has read or seen before, and the memory of that recycled material, which reappears again, contributes to the density of the theatrical piece as a place of cultural memory. Hence this dramatic adaptation of Rodoreda's novel created a literary memory of both Catalan history and literature.

Additionally, the presence of Mèrce Rodoreda is evoked both at the end of the play, when an enormous picture of her appears at the back of the stage, and in an epigraph at the beginning of the dramatic text: "Mèrce Rodoreda, d'una manera o altra, creu en presèncias. Presències de morts. No puc dedicar aquesta obra a ningú, perquè no em pertany. Pero Mèrce, si us plau . . . acompanya'ns" (Mèrce Rodoreda, in one way or another, believed in presences. Presences of the dead. I cannot dedicate this play to anyone, because it does not belong to me. But Mèrce, please . . . join us; 33). Since the beginning of Benet i Jornet's dramatic adaptation, the audience has been in front of a theatrical topology that materializes the past and collective memory: the victory of the Second Republic, the political projects that were defended and lost in the war at the cost of many human lives, and the prolongation of an authoritarian regime in the postwar period. Moreover, at the end of the play, we, as spectators, find ourselves having participated in a story comprising a city under siege and a country at war while reflecting about the influence of collective life on the fate of individual existence.

If "adaptation," Hutcheon suggests, "is a transgenerational phenomenon" and "stories do get retold in different ways in new material and cultural environments" (32), why, then, does Benet i Jornet adapt Rodoreda's novel into 2007? Unquestionably, one reason that can be deduced is the novel's literary value as well as the collective significance of the story represented in the play. Its collective and political import is part of the renewed effort in Spain to rethink a common, silenced past. This effort began a year after Spain's Socialist Workers Party (PSOE) government had declared 2007 the Year of Historical Memory and submitted for congressional ratification a "law of historical memory." This law represents a turning point in relation to the way that the period that Rodoreda's novel depicts has been remembered. For the first time, the mass killings committed by General Francisco Franco's regime were described as "unjust." Indeed, this "law of historical memory" leads to a rethinking of received notions of justice. Is justice reducible to what constitutes positive law? Or is it constituted, also, by memory? Is history just a scientific inquiry about the past, or is it a way to remember, a form of remembrance? Once the past is considered to be the domain of historical knowledge, as well as part and parcel of remembrance, memory can open up and re-cognize anew traces of the past that historical knowledge had relegated to dusty archives as part of a pact of forgetting. If memory can be a form of justice, what then was the critical intent behind Benet i Jornet's adaptation of *La Plaça del Diamant*? Was his sole purpose to pay tribute to Mèrce Rodoreda's great novel? Or was he motivated to retrieve the memory of Catalonia's collective past by portraying the struggles of the vanquished of that war? If it is true, as Hutcheon affirms, that "the idea of fidelity should not frame any theorizing of adaptation" (*Theory of Adaptation* 7), it might also be true that a form of fidelity existed in Benet i Jornet's motivations for adapting for theater Rodoreda's novel within a particular historical and political juncture. I would suggest that it is a form of fidelity that considers the political predicaments of Catalonia's past. It tells and shows how Catalan culture was historically under siege for wanting to affirm its particularity in front of the Spanish state. It is thus a fidelity to a historical event that marked an entire country.

The theatrical adaptation of Rodoreda's novel plays a part in that process of rethinking the past. The linkage between history and memory, collective and individual life, that frames Rodoreda's novel materializes in Benet i Jornet's adaptation in striking images of change and movement: life, death, and rebirth—as are the movements and changes of history. Let us not forget the epigraph of Rodoreda's novel: "My dear, these things are life." In this stage adaptation, while Natàlia walks through the city to the house where she lived with Quimet—a place laden with memories—those characters who have died because of the war (Quimet, Cintet Mateu, and Julieta) begin to appear and are illuminated with a direct blue-grayish light, thus creating an indeterminate space with an aura of darkness and light, of death and life. This scene also produces a mnemonic effect, for not only is Natàlia remembering and seeing them again, but she is also parting from—although not forgetting—them.

Throughout the play, history, along with a memory that is a sort of drainage of Natàlia's wounds, becomes a scream. Indeed, history becomes materialized in Colometa's cry at the end of the play. As I have shown elsewhere, through a violent act of writing and effacing, Natàlia stops being Colometa forever. That name remained inscribed on the abandoned space of her past, which is not to say it is a completely abandoned past.[19]

At the end of the dramatic text and its performance, Benet i Jornet changes from the indirect discourse that characterizes Rodoreda's novel to a direct one.

FIGURE 6.2. *La Plaça del Diamant* by Merçe Rodoreda. Adaptation for theater by Josep Maria Benet i Jornet, Teatre Nacional of Catalunya, Sala Gran, Barcelona, Spain. Season 2007/2008. Photograph by David Ruano / Teatre Nacional de Catalunya.

The effect is the linkage of two passages of the novel that point to an idea of natality (as the promise of something new) and happiness: when Natàlia goes to bed after inscribing the name of Colometa on the door of the house where she lived with Quimet and her last interior monologue about the image of birds drinking and reflecting themselves on the puddles of water at the park, which also mirror the sky:

COLOMETA: No vull que te'm moris mai. [. . .] El teu ventre. . . . El meu esgarradet. . . . Tornaré als parcs. Demà, avui, hi aniré. Ja no deixaré d'anar-hi. Ahir, o avui ha plogut. Al parc hi haurà tolls d'aigua. I als tolls s'hi veurà el cel i baixaran a beure-hi els coloms. [. . . ; *lausa més llarga*] Els coloms estaran contents. (187)

(COLOMETA: I do not want you to die. . . . Your belly. . . . My navel. . . . I will return to the parks. Tomorrow, today, I will go. I will not stop going. Yesterday, or today, it has rained. At the park, there will be puddles of water. Puddles of water that will reflect the sky, and the pigeons will come down to drink. . . . [*longer pause*] The pigeons will be happy.)

Using Walter Benjamin's words, this theatrical adaptation of Rodoreda's novel had its specific "presence in time and space, its unique existence at the place where it happens to be,"[20] since it is not a reproduction but an adaptation. Its presence and unique existence are the result of a retrieving of the city of

FIGURE 6.3. *La Plaça del Diamant* by Mercè Rodoreda. Adaptation for theater by Josep Maria Benet i Jornet, Teatre Nacional of Catalunya, Sala Gran, Barcelona, Spain. Season 2007/2008. Photograph by David Ruano / Teatre Nacional de Catalunya.

collective memory—namely, Barcelona in its historical dimension, in a time and a space that are those of the city of the spectacle or of the globalized city. Yet as a "stereophony of echoes, citations [and] references,"[21] Benet i Jornet's dramatic piece is theater that not only forms part of Barcelona but also functions as the "visual prism" that materializes the struggles and the changes lived in it.[22] In the theatrical adaptation of *La Plaça del Diamant*, both narrative voice and theatrical images gave flesh to Barcelona's history. The play was the artistic conjunction of the subjective and interior aspect of individual memory with the collective memory of a city marked by the continuities and discontinuities of history.

NOTES

1. Jorge Luis Borges, "Pierre Menard, Author of the Quixote," in *Jorge Luis Borges Collected Fictions*, trans. Andrew Hurley (New York: Penguin, 1999), 88–95.
2. Lewis Mumford, *The City in History: Its Origins, Its Transformations, and Its Prospects* (New York: Harcourt, Brace and World, 1961), 114.
3. Christine Boyer, *The City of Collective Memory: Its Historical Imagery and Architectural Entertainment* (Cambridge, Mass.: MIT University Press, 1996), 74.
4. Narcís Oller's *La febre del oro* (The Gold Rush, 1892); Carmen Laforet's *Nada* (Nothing, 1945); Mercè Rodoreda's *La Plaça del Diamant* (The Time of the Doves, 1964); Manuel Vázquez-Montalbán's *Los mares del sur* (The Southern Seas, 1979); Eduardo

Mendoza's *La ciudad de los prodigios* (The City of Marvels, 1999); Josep Maria Benet i Jornet's theatrical trilogy *Una vella, coneguda olor* (An Old, Known Smell, 1963), *Baralla entre olors* (Battle of Smells, 1979), and *Olors* (Smells, 2000); and Lüisa Cunillé's *Barcelona, mapa d'ombres* (Barcelona, Map of Shadows, 2004) are among the literary and dramatic representations of the aforementioned sociohistorical tribulations and changes.

5. See Gabriel García Márquez, "¿Sabía usted quién era Mercè Rodoreda?," *El País*, May 30, 2009, http://elpais.com/diario/1983/05/18/opinion/422056813_850215.html. The translation is mine.

6. Sylvia Bel performed the character of Natàlia/Colometa.

7. Linda Hutcheon, *A Theory of Adaptation* (New York: Routledge, 2006), 16.

8. The social and cultural development of Barcelona, which began in the nineteenth century, came to a halt with the Spanish Civil War and the subsequent dictatorship.

9. For the notion of "narrative identity," see Paul Ricoeur, "L'Identité narrative," *L'Esprit* 7–8 (1988): 295–314.

10. Yet as Hutcheon also asserts, "The text of a play does not necessarily tell an actor about such matters as the gestures, expressions, and tones of voice . . . it is up to the director and actors to actualize and to interpret and then recreate it, thereby in a sense adapting it for the stage" (*Theory of Adaptation*, 39).

11. Joan Ramon Resina, *Barcelona's Vocation of Modernity: Rise and Decline of an Urban Image* (Stanford, Calif.: Stanford University Press, 2008), 121.

12. Gerard Genette, *Palimpsests: Literature in the Second Degree*, trans. Channa Newmand and Claude Doubinsky (Lincoln: University of Nebraska Press, 1997), 5.

13. The sound and lighting designs were by Pepe Bel and Albert Faura, respectively.

14. María Campillo, "La novel la *La Plaça del Diamant*," in *La Plaça del Diamant: Adaptació teatral de J. M. Benet i Jornet* (Barcelona: Editorial Proa, 2007), 9–25, 11 (quotes). Regarding Benet i Jornet's adaptation and the play's historical context, María Campillo has affirmed, "Els personatges que ocupen l'escenari ens traslladen a un temps històrics, a unes formes de vida, a un llenguatge i a uns espais ciutadans que, tal com eren, no tornaran mai més. Que els mals temps no tornin hem de considerar-ho una sort. Però que els bon temps, els de la República o el d'unes formes de vida de barri que ja no existeixen hagin quedat en el passat per sempre, forma part de les nostres moltes i irrecuperables pèrdues" (The characters that inhabit the stage take us back to a historical time, to ways of life, a language and public spaces that, as they were, will never return. If bad times do not return, we must consider ourselves lucky. But the good times, those of the Republic or of a neighborhood lifestyle that no longer exists, have remained in the past forever and are part of our many unrecoverable losses; 25). This translation is mine.

15. Josep Maria Benet i Jornet, *La Plaça del Diamant* (Barcelona: Proa, 2007), 139. All translations are mine.

16. Another perspective of the notion of the "gaze" in Benet i Jornet's plays is the one proposed by Feldman (Sharon G. Feldman, *In the Eye of the Storm* [Lewisburg, Pa.: Bucknell University Press, 2009]) and Cattaneo (Mariateresa Cattaneo, "La ciudad y el tiempo: Sobre una trilogía de Benet i Jornet," *Anales de la literatura española contemporánea* 27, no. 1: 7–22), which centers on the idea of the kaleidoscopic jeu (based on the kaleidoscopic mechanism) that the Catalan author re-creates in his plays.

17. In this process of adaptation, the Catalan playwright shifted from the indirect discourse that characterizes Rodoreda's novel to the direct discourse that characterizes theater.

18. This part, which portrays the new family context, develops mainly in Antoni's shop. Colometa has become old; Antoni and Rita have grown up.

19. See Jennifer Duprey, "*La Plaza del Diamante*: Memoria de lo innombrable," *Revista de Estudios Hispánicos* 21, no. 2 (2004): 91–101; 99.
20. Walter Benjamin, "The Work of Art in the Age of Mechanical Reproduction," in *Illuminations*, ed. Hannah Arendt, trans. Harry Zohn (New York: Schocken, 1969), 214, 217–251.
21. Roland Barthes, "From Work to Text," in *Image-Music-Text*, trans. S. Heath (New York: Hill and Wang, 1978), 155–164; 160.
22. For an extensive discussion of this part of the play, see Jennifer Duprey's *The Aesthetics of the Ephemeral: Memory Theaters in Contemporary Barcelona* (Albany: SUNY University Press, 2014).

7 · MONTREAL'S NEW *LATINITÉ*
Spanish-French Connections in a Trilingual City[1]

HUGH HAZELTON

Quebec and Latin America have a great many historical and cultural parallels, including literary and artistic currents, and have established a complex mutual relationship over the past fifty years. As lands of the Americas, they have both passed through the same stages of indigenous habitation, European conquest and colonization, the struggle for independence, industrialization, immigration, the eventual waning of the power of the Catholic Church, and the emergence of the modern state. As the center of French language and culture in North America, Quebec has always had a distinct trajectory from that of English Canada, yet it also forms part of a bilingual and bicultural—and now, increasingly multicultural—nation. After all, French-speaking Canadians not only are found in Quebec but constitute an archipelago in every province and territory in the country, with particularly large populations in the Maritime provinces (l'Acadie), Northern Ontario, and Manitoba.

Over the past forty years, as Quebec has become increasingly conscious of itself as "une nation" ("a nation" in the sense of a distinct people), it has made a concentrated effort to break out of its relative linguistic and cultural isolation and reach beyond the 350 million Anglophones that surround it in order to establish strong new ties with Latin America, thus reinforcing Quebec's own *Latinité* and also proclaiming its *Américanité*, its place in the Americas, in which the majority of inhabitants now speak languages other than English. Latin Americans have a keen interest in the originality and freshness of Quebec literature and art, and Quebec publishers have begun bringing out increasing numbers of translations of Latin American writing. Two major intermediaries

97

of this cross-cultural exchange have been the Hispanic community in Quebec, particularly in Montreal, which has served as a nexus between the two cultures, and, of course, translation.

The Iberian and Latin American presence in Quebec and Canada dates back to the very first visits by Basque fishermen and whalers to the North Shore of the Gulf of St. Lawrence in the sixteenth century (and possibly earlier), followed by explorers sailing under the Portuguese flag on the east coast, as places with names like Labrador and the islands of Baccalieu and Fogo in Newfoundland attest. Later, toward the end of the eighteenth century, the cartographical and scientific expeditions of the Peruvian Juan Francisco Bodega y Quadra (1743–1794), the Spaniard Alejandro Malaspina (1754–1810),[2] and others explored the Pacific coast as far north as Kodiak Island in Alaska, naming many islands, straits, mountains, and glaciers. The Bolivian Canadian poet Alejandro Saravia (1962–), who lives in Montreal, has written about this early Spanish presence in the country in the trilingual poems of his collection *Lettres de Nootka* (2008).

The French were also great explorers of Canada and the northern United States, whether navigating the Great Lakes with Jesuit fathers such as Père Jacques Marquette (1637–1675) in search of souls to save or working as *coureurs des bois*, independent trappers and fur traders who fanned out ever farther to the north and west and often had Indian wives. Pierre Gaultier de la Vérendrye (1685–1749) explored the Canadian and American prairies in the 1700s, making contact with several Spanish forts, and his son Louis-Joseph (1717–1761) is credited with reaching the Rocky Mountains in 1743. When the young Scottish fur trader and explorer Alexander Mackenzie (1764–1820) traversed the continent from Montreal to the Arctic Ocean in 1789, and then to the Pacific in 1793, his expeditions were carried out by seasoned *voyageurs* from Quebec. French topographical names abound across the North American prairies and boreal forests, as far north as the Yukon and as far south as Colorado, and French surnames are very common among First Nations and *Métis* peoples.

With the fall of Quebec City and the advent of British rule after 1763, however, the French Canadian[3] people turned inward. The French state was now absent, and the Catholic Church took over the key cultural role, prioritizing farming, large families, the commemoration of a glorious past, and devotion to ecclesiastical culture. French-language literature reflected these themes, though, occasionally, extraordinary writers such as the Symbolist poet Émile Nelligan (1879–1941) burst through with a more turbulent spirit. France was often eulogized, as in the epic poem *La légende d'un peuple* by Louis Fréchette (1839–1908), but also criticized for having neglected the colony and, in the view of the Church, for later having followed the heresies of the revolution. References to the world outside of Canada, Europe, and the United States were limited; the Quebec people were simply searching for the strength to survive. British and English Canadian commercial interests dominated the growing urban economies of Montreal and Quebec City, and English became the language of business. Many of the immigrants who poured into Canada from Europe in the late nineteenth and early twentieth centuries settled in Montreal, which would remain the economic and financial heart of the country till the 1970s, but new patterns of linguistic adaptation began to develop. Most immigrants learned English, the better to advance in the world of commerce, marginalizing French as the language of rural areas and of the new Quebec working class that was migrating from the countryside to urban centers. Some groups, such as the Irish Catholics, however, integrated more into the French side, due to shared religious beliefs. Since Quebec culture, especially in Montreal, was split linguistically, there was little pressure on immigrants to assimilate, and many continued to speak their native languages for several generations, even developing independent literary worlds of their own. During the 1930s, for instance, Yiddish was the third language of Montreal, with a particularly rich and varied literature. Later on, most second- or third-generation immigrant writers, some of whom, such as Mordecai Richler and Leonard Cohen, were to become internationally known, would work in English.

By the end of the Second World War, however, cracks were beginning to appear in the monolithic edifice of church and state in Quebec. In 1948, a prominent group of young Quebec artists, including the abstract-expressionist painters Paul-Émile Borduas (1931–2001) and Jean-Paul Riopelle (1923–2002), together with the *automatiste* author Claude Gauvreau (1925–1971) and the avant-garde dancer and artist Françoise Sullivan (1925–), drew up a manifesto titled *Refus global*, in which they affirmed their complete artistic freedom to pursue their own individual forms of expression. By the 1960s, the movement had generalized in Quebec society, and the *Révolution tranquille* was under way, in which the state was modernized, the church was sidelined, and the French language and Quebec culture were celebrated and reinvigorated. Quebec nationalism was now proclaimed, and the survival of the Quebec people was seen to depend on the adoption of French as the working language of the province. After coming to power in 1976, the Parti Québécois passed Bill 101, the Charter of the French Language, declaring French the official language of the province and ensuring that immigrant children would have to attend French schools. The avant-garde novelist and political theorist Hubert Aquin (1929–1977) foresaw a new culture of the Americas, one that followed the hemispheric pattern of immigration and renewal but within the framework of Quebec culture and the French language,[4] similar to the assimilation of immigrants from all over the world into the Spanish-speaking countries of Latin America, such as Argentina and Chile, or into Portuguese-speaking Brazil. Immigration to Quebec no longer meant becoming Anglophone: there was a new French-speaking land in the Americas.

At the same time, Quebec writers, stimulated by the intense artistic renaissance and breakthrough that their culture was experiencing, turned outward in search of new directions in which to search for inspiration and experiments in artistic form. Many young revolutionaries of the 1960s, such as the poet Paul Chamberland (1939–), were inspired by revolutionary authors such as Aimé Césaire (1913–2008) and Frantz Fanon (1925–1961) from the French-speaking Caribbean. Moreover, as the tyrannical regime of "Papa Doc" Duvalier tightened its grasp on Haiti during the same period, Montreal became the preferred destination of exile for Haitian writers and artists, further enriching Quebec culture and bringing it into contact with the vitality of other Francophone cultures of the Americas. Indeed, this extraordinarily talented nucleus of Haitian writers in Quebec was to serve as a link to Latin America, both in terms of a cultural gateway to Central and South America and as a model for Hispano-Québécois writers for the creation of their own diasporic literature. In the 1950s, just prior to this time, the first Spanish- and Portuguese-speaking writers began to arrive, most of them driven out of the fascist regimes in Franco's Spain and Salazar's Portugal by a combination of political repression and economic hardship. Like the Haitians, many of them were intellectuals, and a number became university professors across Canada. One of the most prescient among them—and a true precursor of multilingualism in the city—was Manuel Betanzos Santos (1933–1995), a Galician poet, critic, and journalist who settled in Montreal in 1959 and later taught at both McGill and the Université de Sherbrooke. Perhaps because he himself was a native speaker of a minority language, Galician, Betanzos Santos viewed the linguistic situation in Montreal as a source of inspiration and cultural enrichment rather than division. In the 1960s, he founded the trilingual literary review *Boreal*, which would appear intermittently for the next quarter century and circulated in both Canada and the Americas, bridging the isolation of the so-called "two solitudes" (the title of a famous novel by Hugh MacLennan [1907–1990] set in Montreal) of French and English Canadian culture and linking them with Spain and Latin America. Betanzos Santos also read at cafés in the city with English- and French-speaking writers and published a selection of Canadian and Quebec poetry in the Argentine literary review *Cormorán y Delfín* in 1969 and a short anthology of Canadian writers in Mexico a few years later, as well as a key article giving an overview of contemporary Quebec and Canadian poetry in the *Revista de la Universidad Complutense* in Madrid in 1974.

Major interest in the Spanish-speaking world in Canada, and vice versa, began with the large numbers of Latin Americans who started to arrive in the country in the 1970s, eventually numbering over almost half a million, of which a large proportion settled in Quebec, mainly in the Montreal metropolitan area, which now has a population of over four million people.[5] A majority of the immigrants came for economic reasons, often due to the restructuring of the economies of their home countries, but many were also exiles and refugees from military regimes that hunted down, tortured, disappeared, and eliminated sectors of the population that opposed them. These military takeovers began in Brazil in 1964, continued on to Uruguay and Chile in 1973, and befell Argentina in 1976. By the end of the decade, most of South America was under military rule, a trend that was to continue in Central America during the 1980s. In some cases, the choice of coming to Canada or another country was simply a matter of which embassy was accepting refugees on a given day. A large proportion of Latin American immigrants were artists, musicians, and writers from the most progressive sectors of their societies: some had already begun to publish or produce their works before they left their home countries, while others, often younger, began to write or work in other artistic endeavors once they arrived in Canada. These authors eventually created a parallel Spanish-speaking literature that included all genres of writing, from novels, poetry, essays, and journalism to children's books, history, and political science.[6] The majority wrote in Spanish, though a few preferred to work directly in English or French as well. Most of those who settled in Quebec adopted French as their second language and moved into Quebec culture, though a few felt more at home in English. After the French Revolution and the wars of independence in Latin America, French culture had taken ascendancy over that of Spain; Paris rather than Madrid was the European lodestar of Latin American culture throughout the periods of romanticism and symbolism of the nineteenth century and right through the artistic revolts of Dadaism and surrealism in the first half of the twentieth century. Many incoming Latin Americans therefore felt more of an affinity with Quebec culture than with that of English Canada or the United States. While English was often considered the language of the empire against which they had struggled and that had largely caused their oppression, French was perceived as that of a kindred culture, and Quebec was a generally welcoming environment. A number of Latin Americans were sympathetic to the cause of Quebec nationalism, and some joined the Parti Québécois and were elected to the Quebec National Assembly. Quebec's immigration policy is semi-independent, and its patterns are quite different from those of English Canada. Quebec promotes and favors the immigration of peoples from French-speaking cultures or countries, as well as from areas where there is an affinity with Quebec culture. Besides being one of the principal immigrant languages in the province, Spanish is also the most widely taught second language (after English) in Quebec, making it *de facto* the province's third-most important language.

As Latin American writers who settled in Quebec became increasingly active, they began to move beyond unilingual publication in Spanish and search for translation and publication in French or English. Their first translators were often their friends, partners, wives, or husbands, a number of whom would go on to become professionals and would ultimately constitute much of the first major wave of Spanish-language literary translators in Canada. In Montreal, a variety of bilingual editions of individual books of poetry began to appear, most often published by small Hispanic presses, and by the 1980s included works by the Colombian poet Yvonne América Truque (1955–2001); the illustrated *livre d'artiste, Juglario/Jongleries*, by Chilean poet and filmmaker Jorge Cancino (1930–); and the illustrated Zen children's book *Cuentos de la cabeza y la cola / Contes de la tête et de la queue*, by the Chilean playwright Rodrigo González (1948–). In the early 1990s, following in the footsteps of Manuel Betanzos Santos, another Montreal publication, *Ruptures: La revue des Trois Amériques*, under the direction of Edgard Gousse (1950–), a Haitian Canadian who had studied in Buenos Aires, reached a type of apotheosis of multilingualism, publishing works from the Americas and other parts of the world in the four principal (European) languages of the Western Hemisphere: French, English, Spanish, and Portuguese. This attractively produced review, which included drawings, designs, and full-color paintings on its covers, published fourteen issues between 1993 and 1998, enriching and cross-fertilizing cultures of the Americas through a flood of translated works, many of them done by other writers. It also included five thematic issues, dedicated to the literatures of Mexico, Quebec, the Caribbean, the Southern Cone (some six hundred pages), and Venezuela, which constituted, in effect, quadrilingual anthologies of contemporary works from each country or region. *Ruptures* served as an exchange between translators and authors from different languages and countries and was enthusiastically received abroad. Many of the translations into Spanish, in fact, were done by Hispanic authors living in Montreal, who thus came full circle, translating the works of Quebec writers for diffusion in Latin America. The principal translator into Portuguese, Álvaro Faleiros (1972–), who was finishing a master's degree in linguistics at the Université du Québec à Montréal (UQAM) at the time, eventually returned to Brazil, where he continued translating and publishing Quebec poetry (as well as that of Apollinaire), and is now a well-known poet and figure in translation studies as well as a professor of French literature at the Universidade de São Paulo. The fact that *Ruptures* published writers from outside Canada, however, made it largely ineligible for government grants, and virtually all translation and revision was done on a volunteer basis. In a similar way, Hispanic Canadian poetry readings evolved into trilingual or multilingual events attended by a wider public at which poets read their works in Spanish, French or English, thus again uniting the two official languages via a third. Lapalabrava, for instance, a trilingual series of poetry readings in French, Spanish, and English that is held five to six times annually, is now a major venue for poets from the three languages and is celebrating its tenth year of events. Its success has been paralleled by that of the biannual Hispano-Québécois literary journal *The Apostles Review*, founded in the late 1970s by the Argentine writer Ramón de Elía, who gave it an English name in order to avoid scrutiny by the military regime and then reestablished it in Montreal, where it has published works in Spanish, French, and English in both online and print editions for over ten years.

As Spanish-speaking authors began to receive heightened recognition in the English- and French-speaking literary worlds, small trade presses began to take increasing interest in their works. In the 1980s, a number of both French- and English-language publishers in the Montreal area brought out bilingual and unilingual French and English editions of works by Latino Canadian authors. Humanitas published *Dieuseries et odieuseries / Dioserías y odioserías*, by the Salvadoran poet Salvador Torres (translated by his friend Laure Palin), and awarded it their annual prize in 1989. André Goulet, of Les Éditions d'Orphée, which had published early works by many of Quebec's most noted authors—including Nicole Brossard (1943–), Jacques Ferron (1921–1985), and Claude Gauvreau (1925–1971) in the 1950s and '60s—brought out ten books of poetry by the Chilean author Alfredo Lavergne (1951–), many of them translated by his *compañera* Sylvie Perron and several others by the Chilean activist Tito Alvarado. Mainstream Quebec presses such as Éditions Fides and Éditions du Boréal both brought out works by the accomplished Mexican novelist and short-story writer Gilberto Flores Patiño (1941–), who writes in Spanish but publishes chiefly in French, thanks to the translations of his wife, Ginette Hardy. Some Quebec publishers even published works by Hispanic Canadian writers living outside of Quebec, such as the Argentine Canadian novelist Pablo Urbanyi (1939–) and the Chilean author Leandro Urbina (1948–), both of whom lived in Ottawa. Urbina received Chile's national book award in 1993 for his novel *Cobro revertido*, which was set in Montreal. Canada Council grants for translation into French, English, and First Nations languages are available to Canadian translators and publishers of works by Canadian citizens and permanent residents written in third languages. Nevertheless, the essential axis of translation in Canada remains between English and French, as might be expected in a bilingual country. Canada has been a world leader in the establishment of literary-translation programs in its universities, yet only now are these programs beginning to include other languages, particularly Spanish. All literary-translation awards in the country, with the exception of the yearly John Glassco prize for a first published book-length translation, awarded by the Literary Translators' Association of Canada (LTAC/ATTLC), are only for works translated between the two official languages or, in the case of the Governor General's award, from or into First

Nations languages. Canada Council funding for translation is not available to Canadian publishers for the work of authors or translators from abroad that are not Canadian citizens or permanent residents.

One of the most linguistically unique bodies of work of the period was that of the noted Chilean playwright, poet, and singer/songwriter Alberto Kurapel (1946–), whose experimental multimedia theater, produced by his troupe La Compagnie des Arts Exilio, was well received in Montreal and in Canadian literary circles. The seven plays that Kurapel wrote and produced in Quebec, in which dialogue and stage instructions are given in succession in both Spanish and French, are always essentially bilingual, but only two of them are actually translations. The other five plays are, in reality, hybrid texts in which some passages are fully translated by the author and others only partially so or not even at all. In this way, Kurapel fuses the two languages into a single metalanguage, writing his plays in Spanish and French at once for what is essentially a bilingual audience. Kurapel and his theater company returned to Chile in the late 1990s, and his Quebec works are now widely known in Latin America.[7]

The Canada Council and Heritage Canada have also aided the diffusion of Canadian works by making grants available for their translation abroad. Canadian publishers, however, have been slower to translate the works of Spanish- and Portuguese-speaking authors from outside the country, owing to both the concentration of resources on domestic translation and the long-established dominance of British, American, and French publishing houses in the translation of international literature. Nevertheless, over the past fifteen years, two Quebec presses have established themselves as major publishers of writers from Latin America. The first to do so was Les Écrits des Forges, which, under the leadership of Gaston Bellemare and Bernard Pozier, has published over sixty translations of Latin American poetry into French over the past decade. Most of these are of Mexican authors, ranging from the high-profile (Jaime Sabines [1926–1999], Elsa Cross [1946–], and Homero Aridjis [1940–]) to the newly published, but there are also books by Brazilian, Colombian, Venezuelan, Uruguayan, and Argentine authors (including Juan Gelman [1930–2014]). The majority of works have been published in bilingual format, and Nicole and Émile Martel have translated over thirty of them. In tandem, Les Écrits des Forges has also brought out some forty bilingual French-Spanish translations of works by Québécois poets, ranging from Saint-Denys Garneau (1912–1943) to Yolande Villemaire (1949–). All these translations, now totaling over a hundred works, are copublished with Latin American presses, thus circumventing the need for government subsidies, and distributed in Mexico and other parts of Latin America as well as in Canada and France. The size of the exchange, the range of authors involved, and the extensive, unprecedented involvement of a Canadian publisher in Latin American poetry have caused the initiative to have a major literary impact, especially in Mexico, where Quebec was the culture of honor at the Guadalajara Book Fair, the largest in the Spanish-speaking world, in 2003 (Canada had been the country of honor in 1996). The second publisher to move ahead on her own was Brigitte Bouchard, whose Éditions Les Allusifs specialized in the translation of fiction from other countries to such an extent that three-quarters of the press's titles were translations. Les Allusifs, which was recently taken over by Leméac Éditeur, a much larger press with an impressive list of translations of its own, was also prescient in choosing prominent writers at an early stage in their careers, garnering translation rights for a number of works by the Chilean writer Roberto Bolaño (1953–2003) and the Salvadoran novelist Horacio Castellanos Moya (1957–) before they achieved widespread recognition in North America. In the past few years, two new sources of funding have appeared: both Brazil and Argentina have established subsidies for the translation and publication of works by their national authors in other countries. Interest in Quebec literature has also grown in Spain and Latin America. Nicole Brossard, Hélène Dorion (1958–), and other Quebec poets have been translated into both Spanish and Catalan, an indication of the close cultural and artistic ties between Quebec and Catalonia, and Quebec fiction by authors such as Jacques Godbout (1933–), Gérard Étienne (1936–2008), and Réjean Ducharme (1941–2017) has been published in Brazil.[8] Anthologies such as *Literatura francófona II: América* (1996), edited and translated by the Mexican scholar Laura López Morales and published by Fondo de Cultura Económica, which includes Quebec as part of world Francophone literature, and *Vozes do Quebec: Antologia* (1991), edited by Zilá Bernd and Joseph Melançon and published by the Universidade Federal de Rio Grande do Sul in Porto Alegre, Brazil, have been foundational in introducing Latin Americans to Quebec literature.

Quebec governmental and cultural agencies have also had the long-term goal of creating and reinforcing artistic contacts between the province and Latin America, especially Mexico, providing energy and focus that have no federal government counterpart on the English-Canadian side. The Centre des auteurs dramatiques (CEAD), the Union des écrivaines et écrivains québécois (UNEQ), and the Conseil des arts et des lettres du Québec (CALQ), working with the Consejo Nacional para la Cultura y las Artes (CONACULTA) in Mexico, have initiated exchange programs, reciprocal artist's residencies, and special events, such as the Festival de Théâtre des Amériques (now known as the Festival TransAmériques), that have drawn the two regions together. A number of plays by Quebec writers, including Michel Tremblay (1942–), Robert Lepage (1957–), and Évelyne de la Chenelière (1975–), have also been translated for production and publication in Spanish. At the moment, more Quebec plays are staged in Latin America than in English Canada, and one Mexican theater group and publisher, the Teatro de la Capilla, has translated and produced over two dozen Quebec plays, which have then toured across Central and South America. Its director, Boris Schoemann (1964–), a French actor and dramaturge who has settled in Mexico, prefers to translate theater from Quebec, which he considers highly original and more open than that of France, which he finds too ensconced in traditional patterns.[9] Moreover, some works of Quebec theater have been translated by Hispanic authors from Montreal. The Mexican novelist Gilberto Flores Patiño has been especially active in translating plays by authors such as Michel Marc Bouchard, which have gone on to win awards in Mexico City. One of the most interesting examples of cultural exchange between the two regions through theater is that of the Quebec actor and playwright Julie Vincent (1954–), who has written several plays set simultaneously in Montreal and either Montevideo or Buenos Aires that have then been translated and produced in all three cities. Vincent and her theater company Singulier Pluriel also toured Uruguay, Argentina, Paraguay, and Brazil with a French version of *Jocasta*, a play by the Uruguayan author Mariana Percovich (1963–) and translated into French by Guy Lavigerie, which Vincent presented in French with surtitles in Spanish and Portuguese.

Literary festivals have also played an important role in the exchange. The Festival International de la Poésie, held for ten days every fall in Trois-Rivières, was founded in conjunction with Les Écrits des Forges in 1985 and is now the largest in Canada, with 350 activities and thousands of visitors, and includes authors from thirty different countries, many of them from Latin America. In 2013, the weeklong Festival de la poésie in Montreal, held every spring, chose Mexico as the first country to be invited as the guest of honor and, in the following two years, included roundtable discussions on the links between Quebec and Latin American poetry, as well as the participation of poets from Argentina, Catalonia, and Scotland. The multilingual literary festival Blue Metropolis / Métropolis bleu, founded in 1999 and held over a ten-day period, also includes authors from around the world and has a yearly series of events in Spanish and Portuguese that is held in conjunction with Montreal's Spanish-language bookstore, the Librería las Américas, the largest in Canada. The festival also gives out an award, el Premio Azul, in recognition of an author whose work deals with the culture or history of the Spanish-language diaspora. Winners have included Junot Díaz and Francisco Goldman.

Canadian Studies programs have grown steadily throughout Latin America over the past quarter century and have had a major impact not only on cultural and literary exchanges but also on the development of a new dynamic and framework within comparative literary studies of the Americas. Almost forty institutions and universities are members of Canadian-studies programs, which are particularly strong in Brazil, Mexico, Argentina, Venezuela, and Cuba. The Brazilian Association of Canadian Studies, ABECAN, publishes a review,

Interfaces Brasil/Canadá, that includes comparative articles, as does the Mexican *Revista Mexicana de Estudios Canadienses*. These publications have served as the basis for comparativist research that runs to well over forty books and theses in Brazil alone. *Confluences littéraires Brésil-Québec: les bases d'une comparaison* (Montreal, 1992), a collection of essays compiled by Michel Peterson and Zilá Bernd, laid the basis for a theoretical structure for studying Brazilian and Quebec literatures. At times, it seems as if Brazil's fascination with Quebec might actually represent a displacement of its long interest in France by the younger, more fluid culture of its sister people from its own hemisphere. At the same time, Quebec literary reviews such as *Dérives*, *Vice Versa*, *Ruptures*, and *Exit* have been highly instrumental in the translation and diffusion of Latin American literature to the Quebec public. Canada's best-known review of literary translation, *Ellipse: Canadian Writing in Translation / Textes littéraires canadiens en traduction*, founded at the Université de Sherbrooke in 1969 and relocated to Fredericton, New Brunswick, in 2001, has brought out four special issues on Latin American writing, including a trilingual edition of contemporary poetry from Argentina and a follow-up collection of Canadian and Quebec prose and poetry translated into Spanish in Buenos Aires. In 2010, the review published a trilingual double issue (nos. 84/85) dedicated to present-day Brazilian literature, with all works translated from Portuguese into English or French. The Banff International Literary Translation Centre, a program founded jointly by Canada, Mexico, and the United States in 2003 and based at the Banff Centre in Alberta, has also done much to foster literary translation to and from French in the Western Hemisphere. Over the years, some two hundred translators from thirty countries have participated, working among over forty different languages, including indigenous languages of the Americas.

In addition, Hispanic writing from Quebec and English Canada has become increasingly integrated into courses in Hispanic studies, comparative literature and translation studies in Canadian universities. A number of master's and doctoral dissertations have appeared on Hispanic writers, and academic conferences and journals in Canada, Mexico, Chile, the United States, Britain, and Germany now include articles on their themes and works, working to define and analyze the development of this new field of literature and establish a corpus of Hispanic Canadian literary criticism. Luis Torres, a Chilean Canadian poet and professor at the University of Calgary, published his incisive study "Writings of the Latin-Canadian Exile" in the prestigious journal *Revista de Estudios Canadienses* in 2001–2002, expanding the definition of exile from a topos into an analysis of the pain and trauma of displacement and uprootal and working with Hispanic Canadian writers from the Southern Cone. In 2007, my own book, *Latinocanadá: A Critical Study of Ten Latin American Writers of Canada*, appeared, giving both an overview of the literature and a detailed analysis of the work of writers from six different countries who had settled both in Quebec and in various regions of English Canada. The collection of essays *Canadian Cultural Exchange / Échanges culturels au Canada: Translation and Transculturation / Traduction et transculturation*, edited by Norman Cheadle and Lucien Pelletier and published in 2007 by Wilfrid Laurier University Press, included a number of timely contributions, particularly an analysis of the depth of interest in and identification with Latin America in Quebec society by the Argentine Canadian sociologist Víctor Armony, as well as a study by Norman Cheadle of how the protagonist of Leandro Urbina's novel *Cobro revertido* is drawn to both the Anglophone and the Francophone worlds of Montreal, each associated with specific women and experiences in his life. Cheadle's 2013 essay "Emerging from a Cloud: The Inter-American Discursive Position of Hispano-Canadian Literature" also offers an excellent analysis of the differences between Hispanic writing in the United States and Canada, especially in its comparison of the degree of groundedness felt by Hispanics in the two countries and their very different attitudes toward the societies in which they live.

As the interchange between Quebec and Latin American writing continues, a certain maturation in the cross-fertilization is now taking place. A large number of Quebec authors, ranging from Jean-Paul Daoust (1946–) to Claire Varin (1954–) and Pierre Samson (1958–), have set their fiction and poetry in Latin America, incorporating the area into their own culture and vision, and several Latin American writers have returned the favor. The prolific Brazilian author, painter, and psychologist Sergio Kokis (1944–), who now lives in Quebec (and who is undoubtedly the best-known Latin American writer in the province), writes exclusively in French, and several of his novels have been translated into Portuguese for Brazilian audiences. Some Montreal Hispanic authors now prefer to write books in multiple languages, often self-translating from one language to another; others, such as Salvador Torres (1957–), continue to bring a hispanicized, baroque style and sensibility to the poetry they compose in French, enriching their texts with the echoing strangeness of the other tongue. The Uruguayan Québécoise writer Gloria Escomel (1941–) often sets her fiction in both Quebec and the Río de la Plata region, incorporating both cultures and realities into a single plot. In his search to reflect linguistic hybridity, Alejandro Saravia has brought out a new trilingual collection of poems, without translation, called *L'homme polyphonique* (2014). In an echo of Hubert Aquin, his fiction as well speaks of the new multilingual, multicultural reality that international migration has brought to Montreal, with its uniquely polyglot culture, bridged increasingly by French. Recently, a new wave of second-generation Latin American authors, such as the Chilean Québécois novelist Mauricio Segura (1969–) and the Guatemalan Québécois poet Hector Ruiz (1976–), carry the Latin American fervor for writing into French, often dealing with themes of transculturation. Latin

America has come to Quebec, bringing with it new linguistic, literary, and cultural relationships that continue to increase Québécois awareness of the north as being part of the Americas. At the same time, Quebec literature, in a French from the Americas, is receiving vastly greater interest in the Spanish- and Portuguese-speaking worlds. Montreal, a nexus of languages and cultures in which literature and art develop in unique and surprising ways, is moving along with Quebec toward a new *latinité*.

NOTES

1. Portions of this study have previously appeared in Hugh Hazelton, "Traduzir o Latino-Canadá: Translation Strategies of Spanish- and Portuguese-Speaking Authors in Canada," *Interfaces Brasil-Canadá* 11 (2010): 29–42; and in Hugh Hazelton, "11 September 1973: Latin America comes to Canada," in *Translation Effects: The Shaping of Modern Canadian Culture*, ed. Kathy Mezei, Sherry Simon, and Luise von Flotow (Montreal: McGill-Queen's University Press, 2014), 182–196.
2. See John Kendrick, *Alejandro Malaspina: Portrait of a Visionary* (Montreal: McGill-Queen's University Press, 1999), for an excellent recounting of the scientific voyages of discovery of one of the three great European circumnavigators of the Age of Enlightenment (along with James Cook and Louis-Antoine de Bougainville). Juan Francisco Bodega y Quadra's colorful and insightful account of his voyage up the west coast, *El descubrimiento del fin del mundo, 1775–1792* (Madrid: Alianza, 1990) is also of interest.
3. The names of what is now the province of Quebec and of its people changed several times during the hundred years following the conquest. After the Treaty of Paris (1763), which ended the Seven Years' War, the British administration named the territory Quebec, and its people were called Canadians. In 1791, the provinces of Upper Canada (southern Ontario) and Lower Canada (southern Quebec) were created, and French-speakers were referred to as French Canadians. Finally, in 1867, the Dominion of Canada was formed, consisting of the four provinces of Quebec, Ontario, New Brunswick, and Nova Scotia, after which the term *Québécois* came to be used mainly with reference to French-speaking inhabitants of the province, though it officially includes all residents of Quebec.
4. Aquin, Hubert, "La fatigue culturelle du Canada français," in *Blocs erratiques* (Montreal: Les Quinzes, 1982), 81–82.
5. As of the 2016 Canadian National Household Survey census, some 28,570 Chilean immigrants were living in Canada, the third-largest Spanish-speaking nationality in the country, after Mexicans (95,410) and Salvadorans (40,445). Portuguese immigrants numbered 143,160 and Spaniards 13,580; Brazilians accounted for 40,445 immigrants. "Immigrant Status and Period of Immigration," Statistics Canada, http://www12.statcan.gc.ca/census-recensement/2016/dp-pd/dt-td/Rp-eng.cfm?TABID=2&LANG=E&A=R&APATH=3&DETAIL=0&DIM=0&FL=A&FREE=0&GC=01&GL=-1&GID=1257309&GK=1&GRP=1&O=D&PID=110526&PRID=10&PTYPE=109445&S=0&SHOWALL=0&SUB=0&Temporal=2017&THEME=120&VID=0&VNAMEE=&VNAMEF=&D1=0&D2=0&D3=0&D4=0&D5=0&D6=0.
6. The Chilean Canadian writer Jorge Etcheverry has commented that "the more optimistic among us believe that a Spanish-speaking literature is now beginning to arise that is increasingly autonomous in relation to the English and French-speaking hegemonic literatures"

(my translation). "Notas para situar la literatura chilena en Canadá," *Escritores*, Winter 2012, http://www.escritores.cl/base.php?fi-articulos/texto/congreso.htm.
7. See Hugh Hazelton, "The Bilingual Performance Theatre of Alberto Kurapel," in *Latin@ Canadian Theatre and Performance*, ed. Natalie Alvarez (Toronto: Playwrights Canada Press, 2013), 109–132; and Mayté Gómez, "Infinite Signs: Alberto Kurapel and the Semiotics of Exile," *Canadian Literature / Littérature canadienne*, no. 142–143 (1994): 38–48.
8. "Autores Canadenses com Publicações em Português," *Canada International*, August 15, 2013, http://www.canadainternational.gc.ca/brazil-bresil/cultural_relations_culturelles/authors-auteurs.aspx?lang=por.
9. Boris Schoemann, personal conversation with author, October 5, 2013.

WORKS CITED

Aquin, Hubert. "La fatigue culturelle du Canada français." In *Blocs erratiques*. Montreal: Les Éditions Quinze, 1982.
Armony, Víctor. "La 'latinité' des Québécois à l'épreuve." In *Canadian Cultural Exchange / Échanges culturels au Canada: Translation and Transculturation / Traduction et transculturation*, edited by Norman Cheadle and Lucien Pelletier, 247–267. Waterloo, Ontario: Wilfrid Laurier University Press, 2007.
Borduas, Paul. *Refus global et autres écrits*. Montreal: Typo, 1991.
Cheadle, Norman. "Canadian Counterpoint: Don Latino and Doña Canadiense in José Leandro Urbina's *Collect Call* (1992) and Ann Ireland's *Exile* (2002)." *Canadian Cultural Exchange / Échanges culturels au Canada: Translation and Transculturation / Traduction et transculturation*, edited by Norman Cheadle and Lucien Pelletier, 269–304. Waterloo, Ontario: Wilfrid Laurier University Press, 2007.
———. "Emerging from a Cloud: The Inter-American Discursive Position of Hispano-Canadian Literature." *Interfaces Brasil/Canada* 13, no. 17 (2013): 17–55.
Hazelton, Hugh. *Latinocanadá: A Critical Study of Ten Latin American Writers of Canada*. Montreal: McGill-Queen's University Press, 2007.
Torres, Luis. "Writings of the Latin American Exile." *Revista Canadiense de Estudios Hispánicos* 26, no. 1–2 (October 2001 / Winter 2002): 179–198.

SECONDARY CRITICISM

Armony, Víctor. *Le Québec expliqué aux immigrants*. Montreal: VLB, 2007.
García Canclini, Néstor. *L'Amérique latine au XXIe siècle*, translated by Emmanuelle Tremblay. Quebec City: Les Presses de l'Université Laval, 2007.
Giménez Micó, José Antonio. "Latin-Americanizing Canada." In *Canadian Cultural Exchange / Échanges culturels au Canada: Translation and Transculturation / Traduction et transculturation*, translated by Kate Alvo, edited by Norman Cheadle and Lucien Pelletier, 59–74. Waterloo, Ontario: Wilfrid Laurier University Press, 2007.
Harel, Simon. *Le voleur de parcours: Identité et cosmopolitisme dans la littérature québécoise contemporaine*. Montreal: Éditions XYZ, 1999.
Hazelton, Hugh. "Polylingual Identities: Writing in Multiple Languages." In *Canadian Cultural Exchange / Échanges culturels au Canada: Translation and Transculturation / Traduction et transculturation*, edited by Norman Cheadle and Lucien Pelletier, 225–245. Waterloo, Ontario: Wilfrid Laurier University Press, 2007.

———. "Québec Hispánico: Themes of Exile and Integration in the Writing of Latin Americans Living in Quebec." *Canadian Literature / Littérature canadienne* 142, no. 43 (1994): 120–135.

———. "Transculturation and National Identity in the Novel *Rojo, amarillo y verde* by Alejandro Saravia." In *Canada and Its Americas: Transnational Navigations*, edited by Winfried Siemerling and Sarah Phillips Casteel, 219–230. Montreal: McGill-Queen's University Press, 2010.

Palmero González, Elena. "Desplazamiento cultural y procesos literarios en las letras hispanoamericanas contemporáneas: La literatura hispano-canadiense." *Contexto* 15, no. 17 (2011): 57–81.

Simon, Sherry. "Translating in the Multilingual City: Montreal as a City of the Americas." In *Canada and Its Americas: Transnational Navigations*, edited by Winfried Siemerling and Sarah Phillips Casteel, 171–185. Montreal: McGill-Queen's University Press, 2010.

———. *Translating Montreal: Episodes in the Life of a Divided City*. Montreal: McGill-Queen's University Press, 2006.

8 · TRANSLATING THE LOCAL
New York's Micro-Cosmopolitan Media, from José Martí to the Hyperlocal Hub

ESTHER ALLEN

> Miriadas cuentan estas columnas de papel, que como alas de la memoria, ahora revuelvo.
>
> (These columns of paper, opening and closing in my hands like the wings of memory, speak myriads.)
>
> —José Martí, May 1883

New York City has always been polyglot. The Lenape natives who first peopled the island they called Manahatta (hilly island); the Italian explorer Giovanni da Verrazzano and his crew who, almost five hundred years ago, were the first Europeans to describe it; and the Dutch fur traders who were its first European settlers all spoke and—in the unlikely event they happened to be literate—wrote in languages the city's largest present-day media would characterize as foreign or ethnic. After it became known as New York, in 1664, the city's multilingualism only increased, especially during the great waves of immigration of the mid- to late nineteenth and early twentieth centuries. Some publications founded then—the Swedish biweekly *Nordstjernan*, launched in 1872, and the *Amerikai Népszava*, a Hungarian weekly that first appeared in 1891—still serve local readers.[1]

Never in its history, though, has New York City been more polyglot than it is today. Census Bureau figures indicate that in 2014, 49 percent of the city's population of 8.5 million spoke a language other than English at home. The population-facts page on the city government's website (nyc.gov) boasts that residents speak more than two hundred languages.[2] When a near-majority of city inhabitants are in a position to get their news, information, and culture—local and global—in languages other than English, it may be time to interrogate the term *ethnic media*, as well as the notion of marginality that attaches to it.

Relations between languages and linguistic communities are rapidly evolving, both in global cities and in academic fields. The media sphere of *any* contemporary global city (or of any place that has internet access) is a complex, polyglot entity that cannot be subsumed within the long-hallowed binary of translation studies: foreignization and domestication. These opposing approaches to literary translation, formulated by the German theologian Friedrich Schleiermacher in 1813, have their parallel in what was long the immigrant's stark choice: between retention of the old language and culture of the home country or abandonment of both for assimilation to the new. In an era of rapid travel, instantaneous digital communication, and vastly polyglot urban areas, such binary oppositions have long since diversified into a broad range of readily available options that include multilingual education, multiple national affiliations, multilingual media serving local communities in a variety of languages, and constant, immediate access to local digital, television, and radio media in every language and almost every place across the globe. When ways of being present exist that are not captured by the physically defined either/or of home and away,[3] it is no longer useful to view translation as a summoning forth of a remote and absent other. Translation is, rather, a continual, vital part of everyday life.

Accordingly, the academic discipline of translation studies has also been undergoing a process of reframing, shifting its focus toward the study of what Michael Cronin has dubbed the microcosmopolitan: "What microcosmopolitan transnationalism is arguing for is not that place or identity be dissolved into a rootless geography of free-floating diasporic fragments, but rather that we take transnational phenomena like translation . . . to reinvest place with the full complexity of micro-cosmopolitan connectedness."[4] This new focus is variously exemplified in works such as Cronin's own *Translation and Identity* (2006) and *Translation in the Digital Age* (2013) and Sherry Simon's *Cities in Translation* (2011). In *Is That a Fish in Your Ear? Translation and the Meaning of Everything* (2012), David Bellos, for his part, urges translation studies to look beyond not only the conventional focus on relations between monolithically separate national languages but also the literary texts that have long been its central subject matter. Bellos addresses the translation of legal, political, commercial, and diplomatic texts and devotes an entire chapter to journalism, detailing the complex networks of translation and rewriting that are an essential, unacknowledged component of the global coverage provided by news agencies such as Reuters, the Associated Press, and Agence France-Press.[5] During a 2005 panel at the PEN World Voices festival in New York, the late, great Polish journalist Ryszard Kapuscinski proudly announced, "I am a translator." But U.S. news consumers don't see journalists that way or acknowledge a relationship between journalism and translation—largely because the news industry doesn't want them to. Bellos notes that the language operations performed in news-agency work are of particular interest because they are predicated not only on the total invisibility of translation but also on anonymity and impersonality.[6]

At the same time, a growing number of translators and translation-studies scholars have begun protesting the prevailing tendency of the Anglophone book-publishing industry to translate—when it translates at all—primarily fiction and poetry to the neglect of the vast category known by the problematic and uniquely Anglophone catch-all of nonfiction,[7] which covers journalism and literary *reportage*, as well as biography, history, memoir, scholarly and philosophical work, cookbooks, self-help, how-to, and other, still-more-uncategorizable areas, such as the work of the 2015 Nobel Prize winner Svetlana Alexievich.[8] The book editor and programming curator Sal Robinson has noted that *most* published books, in general, fall into the nonfiction category, which further problematizes the dearth of nonfiction in translation into English. "I find it disturbing," she writes, "that American publishers and readers seem to favor fiction as the way to see the rest of the world."[9]

The relationship between periodical media and the book-publishing industry is tight: newspapers and magazines often function as seedbeds for books, particularly nonfiction books, so Robinson's point is just as pertinent with respect to the nonfiction industry of journalism and to the role of translation in local media spheres. It's true, of course, that the kind of multilingual local media that constitute this paper's main object of study do not exclusively publish nonfiction: a good reminder of that is another Nobel Prize winner, Isaac Bashevis Singer, who first published much of his fiction in Yiddish in New York's *Jewish Daily Forward*. But most local media are fact-based and rarely translated. The bias against the translation of nonfiction not only makes much important non-English writing—be it in book, magazine, newspaper, or digital form—unavailable to Anglophones (except insofar as the work of local reporters is anonymously subsumed into the information translated and packaged by global media conglomerates) but also risks giving Anglophone readers the erroneous impression that the English language has some sort of monopoly on fact.

A fledgling digital phenomenon known as the hyperlocal media hub sits at the confluence between the increasing interest in translation as a local, urban phenomenon and the push for more translation of nonfiction. The origins and practices of New York City's hyperlocal media hub can provide a glimpse of what all translation, local or transnational, of nonfiction, fiction, and poetry may come to look like or, in some cases, may already look like, when the one-way paradigm of foreign versus domestic is discarded in favor of a paradigm of connectedness, in which translation and the original text are in constant dialogue:

mutually aware, mutually impacted, and serving as extensions of each other. The focus on New York here is not only because it's where the first hyperlocal media hub originated but also for the context offered by a key media figure from the city's history, José Martí, whose story may offer new insight into the possibilities of the digital present and future.

JOSÉ MARTÍ AND NEW YORK'S NINETEENTH-CENTURY MULTILINGUALISM

Both of the tendencies just limned—the neglect or marginalization of ethnic communities and their media and the neglect of journalism in particular, and much nonfiction in general, as a discourse that does not merit translation or is translated only as anonymously authored, commercially packaged information—are at play in the reception in English of the work of Martí, a leader of the Cuban independence movement who lived in New York from 1880 to 1895, where he worked, among other things, as a journalist and newspaper publisher. One of the most significant figures in the history of New York City itself, and of its non-Anglophone media, Martí remains unknown to most New Yorkers not of Hispanic descent. His life and work are not taught in the city's schools (though they are widely studied in, for example, Miami), nor is his office on Front Street or the various places across the city where he lived marked with historic plaques, though such plaques are in place in virtually every other city he passed through during his peripatetic life, including Havana, Madrid, Zaragoza, Mexico City, Guatemala, and Tampa, Florida.

The quest for freedom of speech was decisive for Martí. Born to Spanish parents in Cuba in 1853, he was jailed at the age of sixteen for his criticism of Spanish colonial rule. After nine months of hard labor, he was deported in 1871 to Spain and then moved to Mexico in 1875, with a two-week stopover in New York along the way, his first visit to the city. Once established in Mexico City, he began publishing extensively as a journalist. When his objections to military dictatorship began to stir trouble with Mexican President Porfirio Díaz, he accepted a teaching position in Guatemala, arriving there in 1877. After a little over a year, the Guatemalan authorities' displeasure with his strongly expressed views—as well as the surrender of the Cuban insurgency that brought Cuba's first, ten-year-long war of independence against Spain to an end—sent him back to the island in August of 1878. By September of the following year, his participation in revolutionary activities had led to his second deportation from Cuba to Spain.

From Spain, he made his way back to New York, where he arrived in 1880. Within a year, he'd left for Venezuela, where he lasted barely six months before President Guzmán Blanco had him thrown out. At that point, he resolved to make New York his home base and did so until his tragic death in 1895, in Cuba, in a skirmish with Spanish forces during the early weeks of Cuba's third revolution of independence, the necessary war he had worked toward all his life, which culminated three years later in the events known to historians in the United States as the Spanish-American War.

New York was a global center of the cigar industry during the late nineteenth century and thus had stronger ties to Havana, source of the finest tobacco, than to almost any other city. New York was already home to the wealthiest and most powerful community of Cubans outside the island by the time Martí first visited in 1875. As such, it offered many advantages to the principal organizer of the Cuban independence movement. Nevertheless, he repeatedly sought to establish himself in Latin America and only abandoned that goal after being thrown out of Mexico, Guatemala, Cuba, and Venezuela within the span of five years. These thwarted attempts can perhaps best be understood from a linguistic perspective. In Mexico City and Caracas, Martí was read and celebrated by mainstream local society, politicians, and leading cultural figures, as well as by Cuban communities on the island and in exile, and by international audiences across Latin America. To write in Spanish in New York, on the other hand, was to express himself in a marginal language, read locally only by members of the city's tiny Hispanic community—only 5,294 people in a total population of 1.2 million[10]—while remaining isolated from, unread by, and largely unknown to the major local power structures, social, cultural, and political.

Finally, it was freedom of speech itself that led him to settle in the city. And true to form, Martí exercised that right, retaining a clear and critical eye and an independent perspective throughout the thousands of pages of coverage of the United States he would produce over the next fifteen years, coverage that applauds some aspects of the U.S. system and criticizes others—up to and including freedom of speech itself. In a searing 1887 *crónica* on the execution of the Haymarket anarchists in Chicago, Martí objected to a fetishization of free speech that accorded legal protection even to the publication of specifications for bomb making:

> Pero todo era verba, juntas por los rincones, ejercicios de armas en uno que otro sótano, circulación de tres periódicos rivales entre dos mil lectores desesperados, y propaganda de los modos novísimos de matar—¡de que son más culpables los que por vanagloria de libertad la permitían que los que por violenta generosidad la ejercitaban![11]

(It was all words, backstreet meetings, drilling with weapons in some cellar, three rival newspapers circulating among two thousand desperate readers and propagandizing the latest methods of killing—and those who permitted that, boastful of their liberty, are more at fault than those who, out of violent generosity, exercised their right!)

Among the Chicago anarchists' newspapers were the *Arbeiter-Zeitung* and the *Farheit*, both published in German. Martí was acutely aware that the Anglophone press constituted only one dimension of a far more complex media sphere, and his reporting depicted many other communities and their media, whether or not he spoke their languages. While he sometimes sourced these pieces from Anglophone media coverage, in other cases, such as his story about the 1888 funeral of Chinese general Li-In-Du in New York City's Chinatown, he relied on the lingua franca of English to communicate with local Chinese sources who clarified aspects of the funeral and their meaning to him.[12] In an earlier article, published only a year after the Chinese Exclusion Act of 1882 prohibited the immigration of all Chinese laborers, Martí mentions the importance for New York's Chinatown of the Chinese newspaper produced by Fom Ling-Cho, a dedicated and highly lettered fellow who earned much of his living as a typesetter for the Anglophone papers:

> y leen cada sábado, detrás de las cortinas rojas que ponen como de muestra a sus lavanderías, el periódico chino que en papel amarillo saca a la luz de las prensas el diestro Fom Ling-Cho, mozo de letras, que suele tener mesa y paga buena en los diarios cristianos.[13]

> (and every Saturday, behind the red curtains they put up as a kind of signal in their laundries, [the Chinese community] reads the Chinese newspapers, brought out from the presses on yellow paper by the dexterous Fom Ling-Cho, a lettered fellow who has a place at the table in the Christian dailies, and good pay.)

Martí was among the earliest local writers to understand New York City as a microcosm of the globe and report on it accordingly. He covered African American communities along Manhattan's Sixth Avenue and in Brooklyn, Irish families taking a holiday on Coney Island, Russian and Jewish communities on the Lower East Side, and giant celebrations—the opening of the Brooklyn Bridge, the inauguration of the Statue of Liberty—attended by the city's whole gorgeous mosaic (to adopt the term used by New York Mayor David Dinkins a century later, as the city began to officially foreground its own multiculturalism).

Martí had a gift for languages and readily conversed in French, Italian, and English. During his first year in New York, he formed a strong connection with Charles Anderson Dana, publisher of the New York daily *Sun*, and soon began contributing both to the *Sun* and to Dana's cultural magazine, the *Hour*. Writing in

English did not come easily; most of his initial articles for Dana were penned in French, then translated. Some months into the job, Martí did experiment with writing a three-part series titled *Impressions of America (By a Very Fresh Spaniard)* in English.[14] From the first, he understood the need to reach out to the Anglophone U.S. public, address its prejudices, and try to shape its views. Like many a Cuban political figure since, Martí was well aware that U.S. public opinion could have a determinative impact on Cuba's national aspirations. But he also recognized the risk that the writing he was doing for Dana posed to his own political aims. In his work for the *Hour* and the *Sun*, he was forced to portray himself as a European, a Spaniard—precisely the identity he sought to eschew—and to write almost entirely about European painting and literature. In all, twenty-three articles appeared in English under his byline in the *Hour*, and thirteen more in the *Sun*, but after October of 1881, he wrote nothing more for either publication, though his friendship with Dana lasted until the end of his life.[15] A writer's choice of language constitutes a statement about the audience he or she is writing for. Martí did not want to become an assimilated *yanqui*; his priority was not to make a name for himself with Anglophone readers but to promote the cause of Latin American unity and lead Cuba to independence from Spain. Writing extensively in any language but Spanish could only undermine that goal.

During 1880, that first year in New York, Martí also began making himself available to the Anglophone media as a source on Cuban affairs and would continue to do so until his death. In the final weeks of his life, while encamped with the Cuban insurgency in the rugged *manigua* of Cuba's Oriente province, he gave long interviews to Manuel Fuentes of the *New York World* and Eugene Bryson of the *New York Herald*. But after the initial experiment with Dana's *Sun* and *Hour*, he would publish his own writing in New York's Anglophone media only on occasions of urgency.

One such occasion came up in 1889. Responding to rumors that the U.S. government was again contemplating an annexation of Cuba, the *Philadelphia Manufacturer* and the *New York Evening Post* published editorials that opposed annexation and derided the entire population of Cuba as unfit for the exercise of democracy: "To the faults of the men of the parent race [the native Cubans] add effeminacy and a distaste for exertion which amounts really to disease. They are helpless, idle, of defective morals, and unfitted by nature and experience for discharging the obligations of citizenship in a great and free republic."[16] While sharing their opposition to a U.S. annexation of Cuba, Martí was appalled by the editorialists' rhetoric. In a powerful letter, he refuted it by drawing attention to the connectedness of local Cuban communities in Philadelphia and New York: "[In the United States] Cubans are found everywhere, working as farmers, surveyors, engineers, mechanics, teachers, journalists. In Philadelphia, the

Manufacturer has a daily opportunity to see a hundred Cubans, some of them of heroic history and powerful build, who live by their work in easy comfort. In New York, the Cubans are directors of prominent banks, substantial merchants, popular brokers, clerks of recognized ability, physicians with a large practice, engineers of world-wide repute, electricians, journalists, tradesmen, cigarmakers."[17] After the letter appeared in the *Post*, Martí had it published under the title "Vindicación de Cuba," with an accompanying translation of the offensive editorials, as a supplement to *El Avisador Hispano-Americano*, a paper based on Vesey Street in Manhattan.[18] His argument against a depiction of Cubans as the degenerate inhabitants of a distant sphere relied on the local in several ways: he not only gestured toward the achievements of the local Cubans but included their community in the dialogue by publishing the entire exchange in a local Spanish paper. Standard models of translation adopt a one-way paradigm within which a translation moves from the source into the target language, from the foreign into the domestic. Martí's tactic establishes the two-way connectedness required for coexistence within an urban microcosmopolitan sphere.

During his New York years, Martí earned part of his living as a foreign correspondent. His coverage of the United States appeared in major newspapers across Latin America: *La Nación* in Buenos Aires, *El Partido Liberal* in Mexico City, *La Opinion Nacional* in Caracas, and several others. But he also published locally, and founded or ran a number of local papers, in the tradition of New York's history of Spanish-language media, which goes back at least to 1825, when exiled Cuban patriot priest Félix Varela published *El Habanero* in Manhattan. Enrique Lopez Mesa has established a list of eighty Spanish-language publications that were founded or edited by Cubans in New York prior to 1898.[19] Among them are *El Economista Americano* (1886–1888), directed by Martí; *La América* (1882–1893), which Martí edited in 1883–1884; and the magazine for children, *La Edad de Oro*, which he founded, edited, and wrote almost all of in 1889. Most significant of all was *Patria*, the voice of the Cuban Revolutionary Party, launched in 1892 and published out of Martí's office at 120 Front Street in Lower Manhattan.

Martí's 1895 death was covered on the front pages of Anglophone publications across the United States in articles that assumed their readers knew who he was: the leader of Cuba's revolution of independence from Spain. But though he reached the height of his fame during the years after *Patria*'s first publication, *Patria* itself remained as marginal to Anglophone New York as any of the city's other ethnic media. However freely it circulated, it wasn't considered an element of the city's own history, to be saved and passed on. To what is now the chagrin of local librarians, no copy of *Patria* was preserved in any New York City archive. To see a complete volume of its pages, the researcher must visit the

Centro de Estudios Martianos in Havana, where, during most of the years of its publication, to be found in possession of *Patria* was to risk severe reprisal from the Spanish colonial authorities.

Likewise, the first translation of Martí's New York journalism into English, aside from those he himself created or supervised during his lifetime, only appeared in 1954, half a century after his death.[20] By then, six separate editions of his voluminous complete works had already been compiled and published in Spanish.[21]

The case of Martí is of particular interest because it conjoins the issue of linguistic alterity with that of the cultural status of journalism. Though in the wake of groundbreaking work by Susana Rotker (1992), Julio Ramos (2003), and others, Martí's journalism is now widely acknowledged as one of the most essential components of his vast and varied *obra*, the *crónicas*—and, indeed, the entire genre of the *crónica* in general—were for many decades after his death largely ignored by scholars. However fervently Martí's writings on the United States were hailed by contemporaries such as Argentinian president Domingo Faustino Sarmiento, who said Martí's only rival for thunderous prose was Victor Hugo himself,[22] during much of the century that followed his death, scholarly focus remained on the high-status genres he practiced: the poetry, the essays, the political manifestos (in particular, the obsessively cited 1891 "Nuestra América"), and even his sole novel, *Lucía Jérez*, written in less than a week and dismissed by Martí himself as trivial. Relatively little attention was given to the journalism, except insofar as the *crónicas* could be mined for pithy, decontextualized epigrams.[23] We must be grateful that, in accordance with his expressly stated wishes, Martí's journalistic work has always been included in the various editions of his *Obras completas* and, indeed, constitutes the bulk of those editions.

Most editions of the *Obras* also include another genre generally accorded even less status than journalism: translation. Martí occasionally earned extra income working as a translator for the publishing house of D. Appleton & Company; between 1883 and 1886, he translated three scholarly nonfiction works and a novel for the company's Latin American export business. Out of passionate conviction and without pay of any kind, he also translated Victor Hugo's agonized 1874 memoir, *Mes fils*, and *Ramona*, Helen Hunt Jackson's 1884 novel about the plight of California's Hispanic and indigenous peoples.

The Spanish-language *Ramona* that Martí published and distributed in Mexico at his own expense was a classic one-way translation, which warned Mexicans of the danger of U.S. invasion and annexation by making astute tactical use of a highly emotional narrative composed by a *norteamericana*. The Hispanic and indigenous *californios* Jackson's novel portrays were never her intended readers; instead, her novel was meant to rouse Anglophones emotionally about their plight, much as Harriet Beecher Stowe's *Uncle Tom's Cabin* had roused emotions against slavery. Those same *californios* and their Mexican compatriots *were* the intended readers of Martí's translation, but in its turn, it had no impact on Anglophone readers except an ironic one, insofar as it made Anglos who learned of it view Martí as an ambassador of their culture. (The brief entry on Martí in the 1903 *Encyclopedia Americana* lists the following accomplishments: his political activity and death, the founding of *Patria*, his poetry, and the fact that he translated *Ramona*.) A long while later, however, some dialogue and connectedness began to be established between Martí's translation, Jackson's *Ramona*, and the communities the novel portrays. A 2005 Modern Library edition of *Ramona* includes both an English translation of the preface Martí wrote for his translation of the novel into Spanish and a newly commissioned introduction by New Mexico playwright Denise Chávez.

All editions of the *Obras* place the categories of journalism and translation under different headings—and rightly so. Nevertheless, it's clear that the two categories overlap and that translation played a large role in Martí's journalism. Whenever a journalist covers events that transpire largely or entirely in a different language, there is, as Bellos notes, an often-unacknowledged relationship between journalism and translation. In Martí's case, that connection is particularly intricate. While he witnessed a number of the events he covered for himself, he had little budget or time for extensive travel to report on faraway news such as an earthquake in Charleston, South Carolina, or the lynching of a group of Italians in New Orleans. Thus he was often called upon to write about things he knew of only from whatever coverage was available in the Anglophone press. As he moved that information into Spanish, he imprinted it with his sensibility and wove in contextual information to make it intelligible to its new audience.[24]

In a recent essay, Spanish journalist Pablo Sanguinetti provides a good example of how this process works, as well as how it tends to create what he calls a double invisibility for the person who performs it. He gives a paragraph from a German news item on the resignation of an official whose job title is *Der Präsident des Verfassungsschutzes* and offers three translations: Google's, a translator's, and a journalist's. Google's mechanical translation service gives the title as "El presidente de la protección constitucional," while the professional translator gives it as "El Presidente de la Oficina de Protección de la Constitución." The journalist-translator, however, provides readers with what they need in order to understand the information, translating the title as "El jefe del espionage alemán" (The man in charge of German espionage).[25] Martí performed similar adjustments for his readers and also imbued the material he reworked with his own literary style and political perspective and objectives, in a process that involved linguistic erudition, investigative smarts, political discipline and foresight, and literary skill. In nineteenth-century Latin America, this work did not leave him in anonymity but instead contributed to his fame.

Hispanic journalists in the United States today are so well aware of José Martí that the award given out annually by the National Association of Hispanic Publications is called the José Martí. The same cannot be said for their Anglophone counterparts. In the spring of 2016, President Barack Obama visited Havana and placed a wreath at the base of the giant monument to Martí that stands at the heart of the city. In its coverage, the Anglophone U.S. media—assuming readers would not know who Martí was—generally described him as Cuba's national hero, sometimes adding that he was a poet. The fact that he was a journalist was less frequently mentioned; the fact that as a journalist he reported extensively on New York City and the United States was hardly mentioned at all.[26] The nonconnectedness of New York's nineteenth-century microcosmopolitan media impacted twenty-first-century reporting.

THE HYPERLOCAL MEDIA HUB

The Independent Press Association (IPA) was launched in San Francisco in 1996 to help small, nonprofit, and independent magazines survive in a world increasingly dominated by deep-pocketed, corporate-controlled media.[27] The publications it assisted through grants and enhanced distribution were mainly or entirely Anglophone—*Harper's*, *Mother Jones*, the New York arts interview magazine *Bomb*, the Oakland quarterly of feminist responses to pop culture *Bitch*, and so forth. In 2000, sociologist and journalist Abby Scher founded a linked Independent Press Association in New York City, with many of the same goals.

In response to the September 11, 2001, attacks, however, the New York IPA began to view its concern with small, local, and independent media from a new angle: linguistic diversity. In November of 2001, the IPA launched a website, *Voices That Must Be Heard*, which—like Martí's 1889 letter to the editor of the *Evening Post*—gave voice and drew attention to local communities as a counterattack against hatred. The site's earliest posts, now part of the September 11 Digital Archive, were translations from the publications of New York City's Muslim communities.[28] As Scher later described it, the initiative sought to make the grief of these communities available to Anglophone readers at a moment when Muslims were the objects of growing fear and suspicion. In the face of a terrorist attack and an agonized response to it that was all too often marked by racism and religious intolerance, *Voices That Must Be Heard* offered the possibility of dialogue and connectedness. By March of 2002, the site had become a chorus of ethnic news from the Irish, Chinese, Polish, Caribbean, and Spanish-language presses.[29] Thus was the first hyperlocal media hub born.

The IPA's initial focus on small, independent community media emerged from the economic philosophy known as localism—most familiar for its impact on food consumption habits—which Scher defines as a largely middle-class movement, often of small business owners, which challenges the inevitability of globalization by promoting small, local enterprises, municipal ownership, and sustainable local economies.[30] The media localism that the IPA espoused, in combination with its new emphasis on multilingualism, led to various efforts to support these linguistically diverse media businesses economically. A complete catalog of New York's community and ethnic media titled *Many Voices, One City* was developed and published, and in 2002, the IPA established the All Communities Advertising Service to enable mainstream advertisers such as telephone companies and large department stores to place ads in many ethnic publications with one phone call.[31]

Economic localism should not be confused with the global translation industry's practice of localization, which, in many cases, is its exact opposite. Localization takes the products of global corporations and adapts them linguistically and culturally to enhance their appeal and salability within national markets. The quickest glance at McDonald's websites for France, Chile, Japan, and India reveals localization at work in the different languages and currencies employed, as well as the different color schemes, graphic design elements, marketing campaigns (pegged to local celebrities and holidays), and menu items designed to suit local tastes and religious beliefs.[32] While its practices vary when what's for sale is a media product rather than a sandwich, localization is also a key component in the way global news media conglomerates reach their many audiences.

When it established a digital space where New York City's multilingual communities could interact with each other and with the Anglophone mainstream, the IPA discovered that it had to alter its initial stance on economic localism, for in fact, many non-English media outlets in New York are the properties of global enterprises. The *Sing Tao Daily*, for example—one of six dailies Chinese readers in New York can choose among—is one of the largest Cantonese newspapers in the world. Founded in Hong Kong in 1938, it has published a New York edition since 1965 and offers local editions in several other U.S. cities as well. Another example is *El Diario / La Prensa*, New York's largest and oldest Spanish-language newspaper. Founded in 1913 as a local, independent business, it was, after a long series of mergers and acquisitions, purchased in 2012 by the Argentinian corporation S. A. La Nación—by coincidence, the media conglomerate that emerged from and still publishes the very newspaper where Martí published many of his *crónicas* from New York in the 1880s. However local much of their content and history may be, these papers have more to do with localization than with localism: they are manifestations of alternate, non-Anglophone forms of globalization. In the end, however, the new website that aimed at establishing links between New York's communities across language barriers clearly could not exclude them.

More recently, the city's paper of record, the *New York Times,* has begun publishing editions in Spanish and Chinese. *Voices* does not include these among the local ethnic media it draws upon. The logic is simple: both new editions of the *Times* are aimed at global audiences. Unlike the global Chinese newspapers that are localized for New York City, the *Times*'s Chinese and Spanish editions include only limited coverage of local Spanish- and Chinese-speaking communities in New York City itself.

The All Communities Advertising Service did not last beyond 2003, and by 2010, both the San Francisco and New York branches of the Independent Press Association had shut down. But the media hub once known as *Voices That Must Be Heard* still exists today, its name changed, in 2011, to *Voices of New York* (voicesofny.org) when ownership of the site was assumed by the Center for Community and Ethnic Media (CCEM) at the City University of New York's (CUNY) Graduate School of Journalism, now known as the Craig Newmark Graduate School of Journalism. (By another curious coincidence, this new ownership means *Voices* is housed at an address on West Fortieth Street that was for many decades the headquarters of the *New York Herald,* a paper Martí read and cited assiduously and whose correspondent he met with in Cuba in the weeks before his death.) The site's mission is to curate the best journalistic work being produced by scores of community and ethnic publications and, where necessary, translate that work into English. In addition, *Voices* continues to publish a catalog of New York's community and ethnic media and even carries forward the IPA's mission to enhance advertising revenues for these media, though now by urging city government to devote more of its advertising budget to them. The CCEM also continues to give out the Ippies, a set of awards first established by the IPA that are the only journalism awards in New York City to honor reporting in English and in languages other than English by the ethnic and community press. That sector has only expanded since the initial *Many Voices, One City* catalog came out in 2000, listing 198 ethnic and community media outlets. A new edition published in 2013 included 270 outlets. As of July 2016, the digital catalog of the New York media on the CCEM website includes a total of 276 media businesses, working in forty languages, from Albanian to Yiddish.[33]

Voices of New York has become an extraordinary space for open-ended and inclusive community dialogue via translation—that is, for microcosmopolitan connectedness. For example, *Voices* has covered many local ripples of the story of the comfort women—Korean women forced into sexual slavery by Japanese forces during World War II. The first such article, "Korean 'Comfort Women' Demand Apology," posted December 21, 2011, was a translation (credited to Heesook Choi) of a piece by Dongchan Shin about a public forum in Queens featuring Holocaust survivors and two former comfort women, all now living in the New York area. The English version on *Voices* links to the original piece in the *Korea Daily*.³⁴ Though the *Korea Daily* did not, in that instance, link back to *Voices*, many of the non-English papers *Voices* links to do provide their readers, in turn, with links to the site's English translations (which would, for example, have enabled *Korea Daily* readers to share the comfort-women article with friends and neighbors who do not speak Korean). Karen Pennar, *Voices*'s current editor, notes that the journalists who write the original articles generally promote *Voices*'s translations, even when their papers don't link back to *Voices*.

The story heated up when the nearby town of Palisades Park, New Jersey, erected a small monument to the comfort women. A group of visiting Japanese legislators then tried to persuade the town's mayor to take it down. The *Voices* piece about that situation, which gives both writing and translation credit to Chloe B. Park, was sourced from the Palisades Park local paper, *The Record*, as well as from three local Korean papers, the *Korea Daily*, *New York Ilbo*, and *Korea Times*, and links to all of them (along with an additional link to contextual material in the *New York Times*). The invisible translation work of the global wire services as described by Bellos is, on *Voices of New York*, made visible. Writers and translators are named, and links are provided to all sources in multiple languages.

This multilingualism carries over—sometimes heatedly—into the comments sections. A May 21, 2012, piece headlined "'Comfort Women' Monument Controversy Comes to Queens," sourced from the Anglophone *Queens Chronicle* and *Queens Tribune*, generated twelve comments over the following eighteen months. Most are in English, but two are entirely in Japanese, while another defends the comfort women by alluding to a Korean-language report whose title appears in both Korean and Chinese. The *Voices* coverage of the comfort women story is a local, contemporary layer in a palimpsest of longstanding international controversy. As such, it is of potential interest and concern to a wide array of intersectional communities, in this case, Koreans, the Japanese, World War II survivors, feminists, historians, and residents of Queens and Palisades Park, New Jersey, to name but a few. These communities are both local and global. Several of the aforementioned comments speak of the general public in America or people in the United States in a way that suggests their authors are not U.S.-based. *Voices of New York* user stats indicate that its content is viewed in more than two hundred countries.

The degree of connectedness that *Voices* can provide should not be overstated. Representing the city's entire range of linguistic communities is an impossible task. Both Pennar and her predecessor as *Voices*'s editor, Maite Junco, are multilingual, but New York has media in forty languages, far more than the most hyperpolyglot among us could manage. *Voices* offers coverage of media in thirteen of those languages: English, Spanish, French, Portuguese, Russian, Ukrainian, Polish, Chinese, Nepali, Arabic, Hindi, Urdu, and Bangla. Pennar's staff includes only three journalist-translators under contract—two in Spanish and the other in Chinese—who regularly pitch stories to her for translation. Otherwise, *Voices* depends on a loose network of contacts, including past and present students and interns at the Newmark Graduate School of Journalism, and their multilingual acquaintances. Coverage of languages beyond Spanish and Chinese is inevitably scattershot. A Nepalese journalist newly enrolled at the school had brought new vibrancy to the site's coverage of the city's Nepalese community, but "I wish we could do a better job with the West African and the Arab communities," Pennar confessed when I interviewed her in August of 2016. And even where good contacts with journalist-translators in established media exist, Pennar has sometimes encountered reluctance to translate news items that may reflect badly on a community, however extensively the item may have been covered in the community's own media.

Time is also an issue. *Voices of New York* is in the news business in the era of instantaneous information; all too often, a story may feel hopelessly outdated by the time it has been reported on and published in one language, then pitched, translated, and published in English on *Voices*. Slowing things down even further is the fact that translation is a complex process, and the translated articles often require a good deal of additional investigation, clarification, and polish. The question of how to maintain quality without knowledge of the original language is always a major concern for Pennar, as it would be for the editor of any publication. (It's the same concern that leads the *New York Times* to reject all foreign-language comments on the stories in its English edition and to accept no comments whatsoever on its Spanish and Chinese editions.) Yet such concerns inevitably limit the extent to which *Voices* can be multidirectionally connected.

In February of 2016, the site published an original piece by Zaira Cortes, a reporter for *El Diario*, about Francisco Guachiac Ambrocio, an immigrant from Guatemala who speaks K'iche', no English, and very little Spanish. After he was arrested in Brooklyn in 2015, his family was unable to locate him for months. In the course of reporting the story, for which she later won the Carlos Vélez Journalism Prize, Cortes found Guachiac Ambrocio in the Rikers Island jail and reunited him with his family. Cortes's piece originally appeared on *Voices* in English and was translated into Spanish when it won the Vélez prize. She hoped it could appear on *Voices* in Guachiac's own language, K'iché, as well, but it proved difficult for Pennar to find a reliable K'iche' translator on short notice. Still, the story did eventually connect with another local community that also fears for those of its members who speak minority languages that the city bureaucracy has difficulty interpreting: Rong Xiaoqing translated Cortes's article into Chinese for publication on *Voices*.

Voices doesn't just practice translation but also covers it as a major city issue, reporting on such matters as the outcry over a flawed translation of a Flushing park sign into Korean[35] and the language services the public school system offers parents. In spring 2016, a new section of the site called "Translating NYC" was launched, offering firsthand accounts of what it's like to volunteer as an interpreter, in-depth investigation of city government spending on translation services, and other coverage.

On the whiteboard at the back of the *Voices* office, Pennar has written a list of words to "AVOID": *first, last, biggest/largest, only, best, everywhere,* and *everyone*. And she's right: such claims are eye-catching but perilous and difficult to substantiate. Even so, I'm going to go out on a limb and say that although there are several bilingual Spanish-English local news hubs in operation across the country, *Voices* is the only multilingual hyperlocal media hub still active in the United States today.[36]

INVISIBLE DUALITIES

In launching her exploration of linguistically dual cities such as Montreal (French-English) and Barcelona (Catalan-Spanish), the critic and theorist Sherry Simon digresses for a moment to reject the idea that New York might be one. New York is exuberantly multilingual, she asserts, but no one would contest the fact that English is the dominant language, the single gateway to social promotion. Drawing on Doris Sommer's 2004 *Bilingual Aesthetics,* Simon maintains that New York is riven by a home-host, insider-outsider divide that is far simpler than the situation of the dual cities she describes, where there is more than one strong "home" language.[37]

By 2010, however, the small local community that José Martí once knew had grown to 2.4 million and constituted 28.6 percent of New York's total population. In its Latino category, the CCEM's guide to local media includes forty-four outlets in 2017, an increase of almost 30 percent since the 2013 survey, which listed thirty-one. New York is now—according to the population facts on the nyc.gov site—the largest Hispanic city in the United States. Furthermore, as Simon notes, a city can be dual—linguistically, racially, and religiously—in many overlapping and intersectional ways. New York, as we've seen, has not only English-Spanish and English-Chinese linguistic dualities but also Chinese-Spanish. *Voices* seeks to reflect and connect as many of these intersections as it can, thereby rendering all of them visible to local Anglophones. *Voices* thereby invites the city it serves to acquire a different sense of itself, a new awareness of its own linguistic being.

In 2016, the CUNY Graduate School of Journalism took a large step in underscoring New York's English-Spanish duality by launching a subject concentration in Spanish-language journalism, headed by noted Argentinian journalist

Graciela Mochkofsky—the first such program in the nation. (New York University has, since 2007, offered an MFA in creative writing in Spanish.) The new program proposes that journalists following in Martí's footsteps can have flourishing careers in Spanish in New York without pressure to write primarily in English, and that is proving to be the case. And the program itself, alongside the history of Martí's life and work and that of the generations of Spanish-language journalists who preceded him in New York, constitutes compelling evidence—if any further evidence were required—that New York *is* a dual city, where at least two strong home languages have deep, historical roots.

Each of the dual cities Simon analyzes in *Cities in Translation* turns out to have its own distinctive way of *being* dual. In Montreal, a translator class formed to negotiate between the city's French and English cultural spheres and lead them toward a heightened awareness of each other and of the practice of translation. In Barcelona, by contrast, there's been a marked tendency toward self-translation; a tradition has emerged of writers who work first in Catalan and then translate themselves into Spanish. In New York, the extreme degree to which the city is polyglot—two hundred languages!—seems to many New Yorkers, as it does to Simon, to confirm the natural and inevitable hegemony of English, the language that—or so the Anglophones tell themselves—all the emigrés, exiles, and immigrant strivers must adopt if they want to get ahead. Meanwhile, a significant part of the city's current population is empowered within linguistic spheres that are bilingual or non-English monolingual. I would argue that the peculiarly distinctive feature of New York is that although the city's Hispanic community—rooted, demographically powerful, and wielding increasing political power—experiences the English-Spanish duality as one of the central features of daily life, it remains, like Martí himself, persistently, weirdly invisible to the city's Anglophone sphere. This invisibility is highly visible to the Hispanic community and was the central premise of a 2017 one-man show (in English) by the Colombian American actor and comedian John Leguizamo, a premise apparent in its title: *Latin History for Morons*.

Simon identifies two opposing tendencies that translation serves among microcosmopolitan urban communities, both equally important, both equally necessary. The first, distancing, uses translation to separate a given community off and bolster its distinctive identity. Distancing leads each community to require its own publications, which translate events in the city into its own language, through its own cultural perspective. The other tendency, furthering, uses translation to bring communities closer to one other and create understanding and connectedness between them. *Voices of New York* is a small-scale effort at furthering, still fragile and tentative. It might wither away in the coming years, or it might thrive, flourish, become an increasingly central feature of the New York City mediascape, and give rise to other hyperlocal media hubs in other cities across an increasingly multilingual nation. How much of a difference would that make?

The literate Anglophone *norteamericanos* of Martí's time were eager to know what their country looked like when viewed through foreign eyes. Martí himself, as part of his coverage, read and commented on works about the United States published here (in English) by the Englishman James Bryce, the Frenchman Max O'Rell, and, of course, that earlier Frenchman Alexis de Tocqueville.[38] But his Anglophone contemporaries, obsessed with how Europe saw them, remained almost wholly unaware of Martí's own insightful description of and commentary on their country.

When, as often happens, a literary writer gains great prominence in his or her country but isn't translated into our language until much later, we may regret the missed connections, the influences that could have shaped our own literature if the reception had occurred earlier. In the case of Martí, however, the *desencuentro*, to use Julio Ramos's term, has larger consequences. Let's imagine a late nineteenth-century New York where, by some peculiar twist of history, cultural leaders and ordinary citizens alike had been intensely curious to see their city from the perspective not of visiting European dignitaries but *of its own minority communities* and had therefore established some print version of *Voices of New York*, bringing journalism from those communities, including Martí's, into English and making it available to a wide readership. How different might Martí's story, and Cuba's, have been?

His vast body of *crónicas*—rather than just a letter to the editor or two—would have been a visible refutation of the accusations of ignorance, laziness, and unfitness for democracy that the city's Cuban and Latin American communities were continually subjected to. More crucially, the United States would have had an opportunity, in a determinative era, to *see itself* (and not only Cuban affairs) in the complex and insightful portrayal of a brilliant Cuban who, like many of his Anglophone contemporaries, saw the United States as a sometimes inspiring history lesson, a laboratory of democracy, and a beacon for the twin causes of abolition and political independence—and, at the same time, as a nation beset with racism, violence, corruption, and greed, which represented the single greatest threat, after the Spanish empire itself, to the cause of Cuban independence.

Given the geopolitical interests in play, it may seem naïve to suggest that an urban linguistic infrastructure such as *Voices*, granting readers access to the full spectrum of local media, might have changed the course of late nineteenth-century U.S. and Cuban history. But what might the development and reinforcement of such an infrastructure change in twenty-first-century history?

NOTES

1. See http://www.nordstjernan.com and http://nepszava.us for digital versions of the two publications, which both continue to appear in print as well.
2. See "New York City Population: Population Facts," NYC.gov, http://www1.nyc.gov/site/planning/data-maps/nyc-population/population-facts.page. The city's website responds to the multilingualism of which it boasts, and users may consult it in 102 languages, from Afrikaans to Zulu, with options such as Esperanto and Latin. However, most of the languages are simply Google Translate versions of the English.
3. Michael Cronin, "Digital Dublin," in *Speaking Memory: How Translation Shapes City Life*, ed. Sherry Simon (Montreal: McGill-Queen's University Press, 2016), 105.
4. Michael Cronin, *Translation and Identity* (New York: Routledge, 2006), 24.
5. Another important study of translation and the media industry is Esperança Bielsa and Susan Bassnett's *Translation in Global News* (Routledge, 2008).
6. David Bellos, *Is That a Fish in Your Ear? Translation and the Meaning of Everything* (New York: Farrar, Straus and Giroux, 2011), 243.
7. For more on the problem of the term *nonfiction*, see, for example, Richard Lea, "Fiction v. Nonfiction: English Literature's Made-Up Divide," *Guardian*, March 24, 2016.
8. Precisely because nonfiction is such a baggy, difficult-to-track category, ranging from literary works to technical manuals, *Three Percent*, the University of Rochester–based database of translated books, does not include it. For the sake of our sanity, we've limited our data gathering to original translations of fiction and poetry published or distributed here in the United States. See http://www.rochester.edu/College/translation/threepercent/index.php?s=database.
9. "The Nonfiction Gap," *Three Percent*, September 19, 2011, http://www.rochester.edu/College/translation/threepercent/index.php?id=3613. One of the works Robinson singled out as particularly deserving of translation was a nonfiction book by Peter Fröberg Idling about a group of Swedish observers who visited Cambodia in 1978 during the worst of Pol Pot's massacres and noticed nothing. That book, excerpted on the website http://wordswithoutborders.org in 2009, never found a publisher in English. In 2014, however, Fröberg's first novel, also about Cambodia, was published in English as *Song for an Approaching Storm* (London: Pushkin Press, 2014).
10. Based on US census figures cited by Gabriel Haslip-Viera, "The Evolution of the Latino Community," in *Hispanic New York: A Sourcebook*, ed. Claudio Remeseira (New York: Columbia University Press, 2010), 34, 35–56.
11. José Martí, "Un drama terrible," *La Nación* (Buenos Aires), January 1, 1888, in José Martí, *Obras completas* (La Habana: Editorial de Ciencias Sociales, 1975), 11:338–339; José Martí, "Translation, Class War in Chicago: A Terrible Drama," in *José Martí: Selected Writings*, trans. Esther Allen (New York: Penguin Classics, 2002), 201.
12. José Martí, "Un funeral chino," *La Nación*, October 29, 1888, in Martí, *Obras completas*, 12:75–83.
13. José Martí, "Cartas de Martí," *La Nación*, June 20, 1883, in Martí, *Obras completes*, 9:412.
14. Published in three installments in the *Hour*, between July 10 and October 23, 1880. See Martí, *Obras completas*, 19:101–126.
15. Volume 7 of the *Edición Crítica* of the *Obras completas* (La Habana: Centro de estudios martianos, 2003), gathers together all the material written for Dana in 1880–1881.
16. José Martí, "A Protectionist View of Cuban Annexation," *New York Evening Post*, March 21, 1889, in Martí, *Selected Writings*, 262.
17. Letter to the editor, *New York Evening Post*, March 25, 1889, in Martí, *Selected Writings*, 265.

18. José Martí, "Vindicación de Cuba," in Martí, *Obras completas* 1:229–241.
19. Enrique Lopez Mesa, *La comunidad cubana de New York: Siglo XIX* (La Habana: Centro de estudios martianos, 2002), 104–107.
20. José Martí, *The America of José Martí*, trans. Juan de Onís, ed. and with a preface by Federico de Onís (New York: Noonday Press, 1953).
21. By my count, there are now eleven editions of the *Obras completas*, including the *Edición crítica* compiled by the Centro de Estudios Martianos, which, at twenty-four volumes, remains incomplete.
22. "En español, nada hay que se parezca a la salida de bramidos de Martí, y después de Victor Hugo, nada presenta la Francia de esta resonancia de metal," Sarmiento wrote in a letter to Paul Groussac published in *La Nacion* on January 4, 1887, cited by Julio Ramos, *Desencuentros de la modernidad en America Latina* (Santiago, Chile: Ediciones Callejon, 2003), 143.
23. It should be noted that far from inhabiting a sphere of pure aestheticism, Martí's poetry intersects with both his journalism and his political activity. It rails against the horrors of slavery ("El rayo surca, sangriento"), describes the rush and angst of New York City life ("Amor de ciudad grande"), and even interprets a major news story out of Little Rock, Arkansas, where a Swiss father threw his three children down a well and then threw himself after them ("El padre suizo").
24. See Anne Fountain, *José Martí and U.S. Writers* (Gainesville: University Press of Florida, 2003), for a detailed description of Martí's use of Anglophone press sources in several of the *crónicas*.
25. Pablo Sanguinetti, "La doble invisibilidad del periodista-traductor," in *Hijos de Babel* (Madrid: Fórcola Ediciones, 2013), 141–142.
26. See, for example, David Brooks, "José Martí, the National Poet," *New York Times*, April 22, 2016.
27. Dan Fost, "S.F. Nonprofit Helps Small Magazines Stay Alive," *SFGate*, December 12, 2002, https://www.sfgate.com/business/article/S-F-nonprofit-helps-small-magazines-stay-alive-2711854.php.
28. See http://911digitalarchive.org/collections/show/10.
29. Bernard L. Stein, "A New 'Voices' for a New Decade," *Voices of New York*, September 7, 2011, https://voicesofny.org/2011/09/411/.
30. Abby Scher, "Reading, PA," *Dissent*, Winter 2015, http://www.dissentmagazine.org/article/reading-pa-solidarity-economy.
31. Aaron Donovan, "Connecting Large Advertisers and Ethnic Newspapers," *New York Times*, May 22, 2002.
32. See http://www.mcdonalds.fr, http://www.mcdonalds.cl, http://www.mcdonalds.co.jp, http://www.mcdonaldsindia.net, and so on.
33. *Many Voices, One City: The Guide to the Community and Ethnic Media of Metropolitan New York* (New York: Center for Community and Ethnic Media, City University of New York Graduate School of Journalism, 2013).
34. Dongchan Shin, "Korean 'Comfort Women' Demand Apology," trans. Heesook Choi, *Voices of New York*, December 21, 2011, http://voicesofny.org/2011/12/korean-comfort-women-meet-with-holocaust-survivors/. Originally published in the *Korea Daily*.
35. Jinwoo Cho, "All in the Tone: A Korean Translation in Queens Strikes Wrong Note," *Korea Times*, trans. Hyemi Lee for *Voices of New York*, June 7, 2012.
36. New America Media, a multimedia ethnic news agency and coalition of ethnic media founded by the Pacific News Service in 1996, once maintained a network of ethnic media hubs for hyperlocal news. However, many of the sites it listed had gone dormant when I checked

on them in 2016, while others were rarely updated blogs or business alliances among local ethnic media companies that offered no news content. Then, in November of 2017, New America Media itself shut down.

37. Sherry Simon, *Cities in Translation* (New York: Routledge, 2012), 2.

38. See, for example, the review of O'Rell's *Jonathan et son continent*, published in the Mexico City paper *El Partido Liberal* in March of 1889, in Martí, *Obras completas* 12:149–163.

9 · LITORAL TRANSLATION
TRADUCCIÓN LITORAL
URAYOÁN NOEL

(oral improvisation   South Bronx   Bronx Kill   Randalls Island **improvisación oral**

http://tinyurl.com/h48wwvn   based on the WOKITOKITEKI project **basada en el proyecto WOKITOKITEKI**   http://www.wokitokiteki.com/)

1

I'm improvising a poem   **estoy improvisando un poema**   actually a self-translation   **en realidad una auto-traducción**   next to the BorinCuba Unisex   **junto al BorinCuba Unisex**   the closed tattoo shop   **el negocio de tatuajes clausurado**   y el Caridad Express   and the Caridad Express   express is what I do   **expresar es lo que hago**   along Cypress Avenue   **por la avenida Cypress**   y a punto de cruzar el Bruckner Boulevard   about to cross the Bruckner Expressway   a way to express   **una manera de expresar**   the legacy of Robert Moses   **el legado de Robert Moses**   en mi voz vasta y devastada   in my vast and devastated voice   **de colonizador y colonizado**   equal parts colonizer and colonized   as you can see   my translations are nonequivalent   **como ven mis traducciones son no-equivalentes**   y por aquí va lenta la voz   the voice slows down here   **toda traducción es no equivalente**   all translation is nonequivalent   this particular translation   **esta traducción en específico**   is litoral   **es litoral**

2

Litoral como la extraña novela de Palés o como el Williams de Kora in Hell también improvisando Litoral like Palés Matos's strange novel or like the Williams of Kora in Hell who was also improvising Caribbean langscapes **lenguapaisajes caribeños en el fruncido ceño de la crisis** in the furrowed brow of these crisis days did I mention I've crossed over to Port Morris? **acaso dije que ahora estoy en Port Morris?** nineteenth-century factory buildings rapidly gentrifying **fábricas decimonónicas en rápidos procesos de blanqueamiento y especulación de bienes raíces** and real estate speculation new zones **nuevas zonas** new laws **nuevas leyes** to ensure financial interests **para salvaguardar intereses económicos** welcome to the city in 2016 **bienvenido a la ciudad del 2016 pero mi ciudad es también y siempre** but my city is also and always its littorals **sus litorales** its diasporas **sus diásporas sus revoluciones improvisadas** its improvised...

3

as I was saying its improvised revolutions its street art **su arte urbano** even when brought to you by sponsors **si bien auspiciado por intereses económicos bienvenido de nuevo a la ciudad del 2016** once again welcome to the 2016 city but there's a history here **pero hay historia aquí también** migrant history **historia migrante** embodied history **historia de cuerpos** poetic history **historia poética modernismos pasados y futuros** past and future modernisms **vanguardias imposibles** impossible vanguards **visiones hemisféricas** hemispheric visions from Julia de Burgos to punk and hip-hop **de Julia de Burgos al punk y el hip-hop el swing salsoul de estas coordenadas** the salsoul swing of these coordinates an insubordinate language **un lenguaje insub... insubordinado** now micromanaged **ahora...**

4

quedará algo más? does something else remain in these post-postindustrial shores **en estas riberas post-post-industriales y qué más post** and what's more post than newspaper ideologies **que las ideologías de los diarios a la cual sirve como alternativa la poesía?** to which poetry is an alternative? and I say a litoral one   **y digo que es litoral**   **como manera de resaltar**   as a way to underscore   **que no hay nada de monolito en esta literatura**   that there's no monolith in this literature   **la ciudad letrada hace mucho que murió**   the lettered city died long ago   **lo dijo Jean Franco**   quoth Jean Franco   **y yo por eso me desbarranco**   and that's why I tumble   into these screens   **hacia esas pantallas**   donde **se reproduce el sentido**   where meaning is reproduced

5

y se hace memes   and it's memed   **y se jashtaguea**   and it's hashtagged   **y vende comunidades**   and it sells communities   even as it promises to liberate them   **así como promete liberarlas qué liberación en estas deliberaciones digitales?**   what liberation in these digital deliberations?   all is delivery   all is global flow   **todo es flujo global**   **todo es encargo**   and I know that *delivery* is not *encargo*   **y sé que encargo no traduce delivery**   **pero ése es mi letargo dulce-amargo**   but that's my sweet and bitter lethargy   of smartphone improvisations   **de improvisaciones de teléfonos móviles**   so what are mine   but smartphone nations?   **pues qué son las mías sino naciones del teléfono inteligente   ininteligible?**   unintelligible   **nombremos los litorales**   let us name the litorals   **éste es el Bronx Kill**   this is the Bronx Kill   **nombre apropiadamente mortal**   an appropriate...

6

an appropriately mortal name   fatal name   **nombre fatal   para marcar mis cruces**   to mark my crosses   it separates the southernmost tip of the Bronx   the South Bronx   **separa al punto más al sur del sur del Bronx   Port Morris   de Randalls Island**   from   Randalls   Island   **y   por   lo   tanto**   and therefore   **emblematiza**   epitomizes   **mi condición de isla**   my condition of islandness   **como boricua**   as a Puerto Rican   **términos que no se traducen**   terms that don't translate one another   but also as a translator   **pero también como traductor**   whose business is traducing   **cuyo negocio es la traición**   **cuyo negocio es la traslación**   whose business is translation   trains overhead   **trenes pasando**   voice   overheard   **voz   en   el   trasfondo**   that tension   **esa   tensión**   traducing   **trasladando**   to   betray **desplazarse**   somehow marks my endeavor   **de alguna manera** caracteriza a mi empresa   y es más que *traditore, traduttore*   and it's more than *traditore, traduttore*

7

I keep returning   **sigo volviendo**   a la voz   to the voice   **a la página**   to the page   **vienen a ser no lo mismo**   they end up being not the same   but a reflected smudge   **sino un reflejo borroso inexacto**   inexact refraction of self   **refracción del yo**   I keep returning   **y sigo volviendo**   to Palés Matos and Williams   **a Palés Matos y a Williams**   Williams es claro tradujo a Palés Matos   Wiliams, of course, translated Palés Matos   but one might say   **pero podría decirse**   that he did so litorally   **que lo hizo litoralmente**   for Williams's American grain   **pues el grano americano de Williams**   **siempre tuvo una granulosidad caribeña**   always had a Caribbean graininess   even if unacknowledged by WCW himself   **si bien no reconocida por el mismo William Carlos**   **el litoral jodido de Palés**   Palés Matos's fucked up littoral   appropriated voices   **voces apropiadas**   stereotyped bodies   **cuerpos estereotipados**   gendered violence   **violencia de género**   genre violence   **violencia de género**   **oralidad violenta y hermosa**   beautiful violent orality   **recalibrada hacia un barroco**   recalibrated as baroque   as Lezama told us   **como nos dijo Lezama Lima**   **nuestras voces poéticas**   our poetic voices

8

no son sino accidentes   are little more than accidents of the landscape   **del paisaje**   and that's beautiful   **y eso es hermoso**   **extensiones del roquedal americano**   extensions of our hemispheric American cragginess   the rock formations and voice formations   **las formaciones de roca y de voces**   that define our cities   **que definen nuestras ciudades**   thus the ship of translation   **por lo tanto el barco de la traducción**   is

9

vale solo lo que valen sus rocas   the obstacle to translation   **el obstáculo a la traducción**   is translation   **es la traducción**   and embodying that obstacle   **y darle cuerpo a ese obstáculo**   is always litoral translation **traducción litoral**

a litoral wager **es siempre una apuesta litoral** veamos dónde acabamos let's see where we've ended up

10

let's think back on the history of modern poetry **recordemos la historia de la poesía moderna** acaso el flâneur no depende doesn't the flâneur depend on a discreet legibility **de una legi legibilidad discreta** even a national visibility? **incluso una visibilidad nacional?** Baudelaire's modern poet **el poeta moderno de Baudelaire** is then a French poet **es por lo tanto un poeta francés y al traducir a Poe** and upon translating Poe **lo afrancesa** makes him French too **pues qué hacemos los flâneurs** what is there to do for those of us flâneurs who claim no nation **que no reclaman nación alguna** except pronomination **salvo la pronominación** improvisation **improvisación** the desecration **la desacralización** of our colonial histories **de nuestras historias coloniales** and the search for alternative ones **y la búsqueda de alternativas** breathing leaving living ones **con aliento prófugas vivas** in our aimless meander **en nuestro caminar sin rumbo meando** pissing on meaning **en el sentido** in modern poetry **en la poesía moderna** and the poetry of the modern city **y la poesía de la ciudad moderna** are always discrete national affairs **son siempre asuntos discretamente nacionales** **apostemos a lo nocional** let's wager on the notional **la náusea de nacer en este no ser** the nausea of being reborn in this unbeing meaning fleeing **el sentido huyendo** **palabras en el viento** words in the wind **animal sediento que hace rimas** **para aproximarse al sentido** a thirsty animal that makes up rhymes to approximate meaning meaning's undermining **el socavamiento del sentido** **yo soy yo y mis aspavientos** I am myself and my flailings that is perhaps the dictum **es tal vez el dictum** of a litoral poetics **de una poética litoral** let us collapse **colapsemos las fronteras** the borders **no traduce frontiers** *lo liminal* ain't the same borders that separate **las fronteras que separan** the Latin American baroque **al barroco latinoamericano** **del gringo American grain** from the gringo American grano urban poets have always been walking **los poetas urbanos siempre han estado caminando** **por lo menos los que tienen ese privilegio** at least those that f   but what of the Black and the Brown   the gendered   and queered   and un-able   **y qué de los oscuros y los negros   de los que sufren por género   los queer   los que no pueden caminar   los que no pueden pagar la renta en la ciudad**   the ones that can't make rent in the city   the ones who die every day   **los que mueren todos los días   sin nombre**   without a name   even when documented   **si bien documentados**   on smartphones like these   **en teléfonos como éste**   their bodies in the wind must become our voices   **sus cuerpos en el viento tendrán que volverse nuestras voces   para imaginar otros litorales**   to imagine other littorals   our responsibility   **nuestra responsabilidad**   it turns out that walking the city   **sucede que caminar la ciudad**   is also a translation   **es también una traducción**   like all of them   **como todas**   marked by nonequivalence   **marcada por la no-equivalencia**   **algunos la logran caminar**   some manage to walk it   **otros son caminados por ella**   others are walked by it   we walk by them   **les caminanos por el lado**   as if our walking made its own meaning   **como si nuestro caminar creara su propio significado   somos monumentos al lado de la nada**   we are monuments next to the void   somehow enamored with our own presence   **por alguna razón enamorados de nuestra propia presencia   la quintaesencia de habitar ciudades**   the quintessence of living in cities   jogging?   **jogueando?**   the mind   I mean   **el cerebro   quiero decir**   my rumination is my ruination is my nation   **mi rumiación es mi ruina es mi nación   a eso apuesto   por lo que tenga de apuesta mi voz**   that's what I wager on   however fly my flighty voice might be   I apologize if I've sounded humanistic   **me disculpo si he sonado humanista**   I don't believe in such things   **no creo en tales cosas**   at least not in any essential sense   **por lo menos en ningún sentido esencialista**   I'm all down with apps   **le someto a las aplicaciones telefónicas   las uso para improvisar**   I use them to improvise   **y hacer traducciones falsas**   and to produce mistranslations   I see the potential for irreverence   **veo el potencial de traducciones irreverentes   en estas coordenadas digitales**   in these digital coordinates   and I take solace in that   **y me refugio en eso   en lo tonto y lindo**   in the silly and pretty   **en el derecho de jugar**   in the right to play   not by the rules   **no por las reglas**   but to survive   **sino para sobrevivir   para supercar el sentido**   to surpass meaning   and to know my body in its failings   **y conocer mi cuerpo en sus fracasos**   **ésa es la verdad que busco**   that's the truth I search for   **si bien la ofusco**   even if I obfus obfuscate it   with all my trickery   **con todos mis truquitos**   I see a joy in litoral translation   **traducción litoral**   139

Netlish   quoth Emily Apter   **le veo su deleite al Netlish   como le llama Emily Apter   al app-lish**   to App-lish   **mi ingles y mi español   los dos caseros   pero   no domesticados   no aplicados**   my English and my Spanish both home languages   homebodies but not domesticated   unwilling to apply themselves   I express myself against the backdrop of expressways and bridges   **me expreso bordeado de expresos   autopistas y puentes   pero también en mi pulsión gigabyteada**   but also in these pulsating gigabytes   in neural flash   **en el destello neural   en mi ciudad convulsa**   in my city and its seizure   one thing I don't get about translation   **algo que no entiendo de la traducción**   the transprefix   **el prefijo trans-**   especially when the way it's practiced seems so butch   so cis   **sobre todo cuando la manera en que se practica parece tan butch   tan cis**   and I'm addressing myself here   **y me dirijo a mí mismo**   nothing cool about this mea culpa   **este mea culpa no culipandea**   translation   as least as practiced quasi-institutionally in the U.S.   **la traducción   por lo menos como se practica cuasi-institucionalmente en los Estados Unidos**   and again I mean myself   **y de nuevo me refiero a mí mismo   también**   also   seems insufferably boutique-y   **me parece insufriblemente parroquial   y no es pa' rockear**   and it's not for those about to rock   it's not about the rocks of meaning and unmeaning   **las rocas del sentido y sinsentido**   in these litoral shores   **en estas riberas litorales   matorrales neuronales**   neuronal shrubs   and this is not a manifesto   **y esto no es un manifesto manifiesto**   so I don't have a program   **o sea que no tengo programa**   I don't have an answer   **no tengo respuesta**   I'll take the Socratic way out   **me conformo con la ruta socrática   sonrisa hierática**   hieratic smile   **en mi walking talking teching**   in my walking talking teching   **este wokitokiteki errático**   this erratic wokitokiteki   from the lit**oral** zones   **desde las zonas lit**orales   maybe   **tal vez**   one alternative   **una alternativa**   is to think of translation as remediation   **es pensar la traducción como remediación   por ejemplo**   for example   **este poema**   this poem   **lo voy a transcribir**   I'm going to transcribe it   as soon as I get home   **tan pronto llegue a casa**   and it will become a print text   **y se volverá un texto impreso**   and unless I put this up somewhere online   **y a menos que ponga esto en línea en algún lado**   nobody will know   **nadie sabrá**   unless they're reading carefully   **a menos que lean cuidadosamente**   and what does that even mean   **y qué quiere decir eso**   these days   **en estos días**   that this began as a smartphone improvisation   **que esto comenzó como una** improvisación en el teléfono móvil y que por ende and that therefore **es una traición** it's a traducing it's a displacement **es una traslación** **un traslado de sentido?** a displacement of meaning? from the beginning **desde el comienzo** its transcription **su transcripción** its irruption on the page **su irrupción en la página** a mere afterthought **casi dado por sentado** so translation cannot be easily disentangled from remediation **y pues la traducción no se puede desenmarañar de la remediación** and what if we added that translation is embodiment? **y que si añadiéramos que la traducción es un volverse cuerpo?** you could say Haroldo's transcreation pointed us there perhaps **pudiera alegar que la transcreación de Haroldo de Campos nos señaló ese camino hace un tiempo** pero me interesa más but I'm more interested in poetics that unsettle discrete languages **poéticas que desestabilizan los lenguajes discretos devolviéndonos al cuerpo** returning us to the body think of Anzaldúa **pensemos en Anzaldúa** fighting off the guards **sacándose de encima a los centinelas** her only weapon **su única arma** **la agudeza** the wit that lets her undo **que le permite deshacer** juridical borders **fronteras jurídicas** logical borders **fronteras lógicas** the borders that legitimize **las fronteras que legitiman** **la violencia contra esos otros cuerpos** the violence against those other bodies which are most bodies **que son la mayoría de los cuerpos** all bodies really **todos los cuerpos de hecho**

1 1

I say all of this to mean **digo todo esto para constatar** **para preguntar** to ask what are translation's bodies that matter? **cuáles son los cuerpos que importan de la traducción?** what are its antibodies? **cuáles son sus anticuerpos?** what is its antimatter? **cuál es su antimateria?** what is its center? **cuál es su centro?** **cuál es su periferia?** what is its periphery? **cuál es su barrio?** what is its neighborhood? and what is its hemisphere? **y cuál es su hemisferio?** no answer **no respuesta** **pero sí la colocación** but yes the colocation **la eco-locación** the eco-location the language ecology **la ecología del lenguaje** **no siempreverde** not evergreen but inseparable from these gritty litorals **pero inseparable de estos sucios litorales** a litoral translation **una traducción** litoral wouldn't just be site-specific **no sería solo localizada** **ni translocal** nor glocal but instead   **por el contrario**   turn its verbal glocks upon itself   **se apuntaría pistolas verbales a sí mismo**   **provocando un paroxismo**   leading to a paroxysm   **del sentido**   of meaning   that would return us to the beautiful problem   **que nos devolvería al hermoso problema   de la ciudad que somos**   of the city we are   and we do not know   **y no conocemos   improvisazón**   improviseizure   improvisoupçon   **improsospecha   improvisura**   improvisuture   meaning no longer lateral   lit**oral**   always lit   about to be on fire   always latent across these latitudes   always too late or too early   **el significado siempre abismado   siempre en fuego   y siempre latiendo latente   las laderas   los linderos   de estas latitudes   litoral no litúrgico**   litoral not liturgical   lit**oral**   little but looming lit**oral   leve   lúgubre   pero   circunlocutorio**   lit**oral improvisación   diaria   precaria   y   necesaria**   lit**oral**   daily improvisation   our first and final station   our only nation

10 · CODA
The City of a Translator's Mind

PETER BUSH

I lived in many imaginary cities before ever living in a real one. I grew up in a small rural town, and when I started reading Balzac at the age of seventeen, I felt his Tours or Saumur or even Paris, those finite fictional urban spaces, were not totally alien to the city already in my head, a palimpsest of shards of historical experience, its social dislocations seen and articulated first through the prism of dialects of English and then through French, Spanish, and Latin, with their respective histories and imaginaries. The town was Spalding, in the county of Lincolnshire. My father had come to live there in 1921 from nearby Pinchbeck as a young boy when my grandfather, a shepherd, was evicted from a tied cottage by the landowner when he fell ill. The youngest of a family of sixteen, he was determined not to work on the land and entered an apprenticeship as a typographer. He spoke a nonstandard Lincolnshire dialect and the standard English, which was at the center of his craft as a printer. My mother was born in the center of the steel city of Sheffield, in a tenement on Pond Street, also the youngest of sixteen. Her father had migrated from the Rhondda mining valley in Wales to find work as a carpenter; her mother had left Liverpool, where her Irish father was a captain of a tugboat on Merseyside. My mother was happy at school; enjoyed the urban working-class culture of dance halls, socialist cycling clubs, and American movies; and from her street watched men making steel. An uncle was the manager of the Hippodrome Theatre, so they got complimentary tickets to classical concerts and plays. That all came to an end when she was put into service with another uncle, and when she could stand that servitude no longer, she went down to the labor exchange and signed up to travel to Lincolnshire, where strawberry pickers were needed for the harvest. It was 1929, the year of the Great Depression. She stayed on and rented a room with another Sheffield lass, who was a single mother. And in what could hardly be a more English circumstance, she met my father in a queue outside a fish and chip shop. Strong-minded, she changed her name from Emma (too old-fashioned and Victorian) to Muriel (more Hollywood). Naturally, she spoke the Yorkshire dialect of English but not very strongly, as her parents were from Wales and the Liverpool Irish community.

However, a relationship that was forged by migration and eviction and soon had two young daughters was to be tested by war. My father volunteered in 1939—when he read about the fall of the Spanish Republic—and only returned home after two years in northern France and four in a desert hospital in the Middle East. So my mother had to endure those six years living with a cantankerous mother-in-law, surrounded by my uncles and aunts who regarded her as an "uppity" urban creature, with two young kids. Some of that time was alleviated by the presence of a family evacuated from London. My sisters didn't recognize their father when he returned in 1945, and emotional recovery for them was hampered when I was born in 1946—a boy who had been longed for in that lengthy separation. Dad went back to his old job, where he refused to accept the pay rate from 1939 and started to unionize the printshop. Like many workers returning from the war, he wasn't prepared to go back to the 1930s; they wanted a piece of that freedom they had been fighting for.

All or none of this predisposed me to be a literary translator. It meant that in the small rural town, I coexisted with a series of worlds that were the subject of the tales told within my family and that were nurtured by visits to relatives in small local villages or the city of knives—train drivers, tractor drivers, postmen, potato/bulb pickers, sugar-beet workers, road menders, bartenders, park attendants, school cooks, dykers, a commercial rep for Craven A . . . all with a halo of stories around them from Ypres to Ilkley Moor. One was a community where I felt I knew everyone or, certainly, that my parents knew everyone and what they had done and stood for over the previous forty years. The other seemed exotic and exciting and, in the many daily conversations with my mum, a city that was a constant source of nostalgia and absence. Spalding was face-to-face and later for me became increasingly claustrophobic. It was a home without a television, telephone, or car but with lots of newspapers and radio and, before I was eleven, sporadic visits to see relatives in Sheffield (another, less dour world where people smiled and spoke to you on the trams) and to London (work trips to see a football match—the Spurs before the Man U. crash—and go to a West End show in the evening: The Crazy Gang at the Victoria Palace). The first real shock to my psyche occurred when I went to primary school at the age of five, by which time I was a fluent speaker but clearly not a skilled enough code-switcher between nonstandard, which was my mother tongue, and standard, which you spoke to doctors, parsons, insurance men, rent collectors, and essentially anyone middle class you ever encountered. My teacher pronounced that my accent and language—and by extension, those of my parents and their social milieu—were not "proper."

From then on, what happened was an often tense, juddering, painful journey on a road that continuously expanded the city of my mind by locating me in a series of situations I could never have anticipated: microuniverses I experienced intensely and then departed having picked up knowledge and realms of language way beyond my stuttering steps into literacy with "The cat sat on the mat." Another way of describing it would be to use the Renaissance image of the Palace of Memories, though rather than being stored in separate rooms in a palatial construction, those knowledges and realms of language rest semihidden, often resurfacing in consciousness in response to the latest microuniverse I find myself inhabiting for real, in the imagination, or via an interplay between both, now specifically in a series of acts of literary translation. However, I didn't start translating until I was forty-one, so perhaps I will mention just the first of those previous encounters that I believe helped form me as such a beast.

A scholarship to the local grammar school at the age of ten symbolized how successfully "proper" I had become—I now clearly was into the "grammar" that my parents had been denied access to. From being a bubbly, very jokey lad, I suddenly became taciturn in that world full of people who had been "proper" from their day one, and I excelled in French, Latin, and Spanish, where we all started from scratch. At sixteen, those were the languages I studied for the advanced-level exams, and I embraced the urban and rural worlds of Balzac, Flaubert, Molière, Fernando de Rojas, Virgil, Cicero, Horace, and Tacitus. In parallel, there was a subject called "General English" where arts and science students came together to read and write about realist novels and plays, such as *Saturday Night and Sunday Morning* or *Roots* or *The Grapes of Wrath*, and books of cultural criticism like *The Uses of Literacy* (essay title set for homework—"What Does It Teach Us about the Working-Classes?") and *The Hidden Persuaders*. It was the heyday of the "Two Cultures" debate in the United Kingdom, and the science students, true to stereotype, were continual disrupters. One day, I walked home with a bank manager's son who lived on a road of detached houses before you reached my council estate. He remarked how deadening it must be to live surrounded by houses that were all the same. From the age of eleven, I had always gone to the movies on a Friday or Saturday night—the latest at the Odeon and Savoy—with my parents. Now at sixteen, I joined the town film society, where films were shown on a small screen in the school library, and I became hooked on Bergman, Buñuel, and Antonioni; Mexico City, Rome, and Sweden; and the strange beauty of a Japanese film, *Ugetsu Monogatari*.

I had never lived in a city, but already, quite unawares, surrounded by Lincolnshire's fertile flatlands and open horizons, I was creating a translator's city of the mind.

ACKNOWLEDGMENTS

The idea for this book stemmed from the American Comparative Literature Association (ACLA) 2013 annual meeting held at the University of Toronto. Our call for papers for a seminar titled "Translating the City" yielded an overwhelming response from scholars and translators. We thank the ACLA for giving us the opportunity to offer the seminar. This volume would not have been possible without the quality and intellectual creativity of the conversations that took place during and after the seminar. Some of the contributors to this volume participated in the ACLA seminar, while others joined as the project developed. At some point, each of the contributors offered direction and ideas that shaped the overall design of this project. We are honored to have worked with such an outstanding list of contributors, and we thank them immensely for their dedication to this project, their patience during its many stages, and their intellectual and creative vigor and depth. We thank Heather Dubnick for her meticulousness and patience with us throughout the process of preparing the numerous pieces of the manuscript for submission. At Bucknell University Press, we especially thank Greg Clingham and Pam Dailey, who guided this project through its multiple editorial layers; the anonymous reader of the manuscript, who offered valuable feedback; and the rest of the hardworking editorial team.

We are grateful for the support we received from our respective institutions. At the University of Massachusetts Amherst, Regina Galasso would like to thank her colleagues and students in the Spanish and Portuguese Program and the Comparative Literature Program of the Department of Languages, Literatures, and Cultures, as well as William Moebius, chair of the department, and Julie Candler Hayes, dean of the College of Humanities and Fine Arts. She also thanks the Institute for Teaching Excellence and Faculty Development for the generous support in the form of a Flex Grant to assist with the manuscript preparation. At Manhattan College, Evelyn Scaramella would like to thank her colleagues in the Department of Modern Languages and Literatures, Marlene Gottlieb, Joan Cammarata, Antonio Córdoba, Laura Redruello, Samira Hassa, and Nonie Wanger, as well as the dean of the School of Liberal Arts, Keith Brower. She would also like to thank the Faculty Resource Network at New York University for its generous support while she worked on this project.

Our walk down this avenue would have had zero zest were it not for the support, love, and inspiring energy of our family members: Albert, Julia, Natalia, Carson, Bess, and Tommy. The words "Moltes gràcies!" and "Thank you!" will never be enough.

BIBLIOGRAPHY

Alonso Gamo, José María. Introductory note to Roy Campbell, "Tendencias de la poesía inglesa." *Escorial* 20, no. 60 (August 1949): 1021–1037.

Anderson, Andrew A. "The Evolution of García Lorca's Poetic Projects 1929–1936 and the Textual Status of *Poeta en Nueva York*." *Bulletin of Hispanic Studies* 60 (1983): 221–246.

———. "La trayectoria de *Poeta en Nueva York* a través de sus traductores estadounidenses: Humphries, Belitt, Simon/White y después." In *El impacto de la metrópolis: La experiencia americana en Lorca, Dalí y Buñuel*, edited by José M. del Pino, 93–115. Frankfurt: Vervuert, 2018.

Aquin, Hubert. "La fatigue culturelle du Canada français." In *Blocs erratiques*, 69–103. Montreal: Les Quinzes, 1982.

Armony, Víctor. "La 'latinité' des Québécois à l'épreuve." In *Canadian Cultural Exchange / Échanges culturels au Canada: Translation and Transculturation / Traduction et transculturation*, edited by Norman Cheadle and Lucien Pelletier, 247–267. Waterloo, Ontario: Wilfrid Laurier University Press, 2007.

———. *Le Québec expliqué aux immigrants*. Montreal: VLB, 2007.

Barthes, Roland. "Semiology and the Urban." In *The City and the Sign: An Introduction to Urban Semiotics*, edited by M. Gottdiener and Alexandros Ph. Lagopoulos, 87–98. New York: Columbia University Press, 1986.

Bartles, Jason. "Calvert Casey's Wasted Narratives." *Revista Hispánica Moderna* 70, no. 1 (2017): 19–35.

Bassnett, Susan. "Travelling and Translating." *World Literature Written in English* 40, no. 2 (2008): 66–76.

———, and Peter Bush, eds. *The Translator as Writer*. New York: Continuum, 2007.

———, and André Lefevere, eds. *Constructing Cultures: Essays on Literary Translation*. Clevedon, UK: Multilingual Matters, 1998.

Bastin, Georges L., Álvaro Echeverri, and Ángela Campos. "La traducción en América Latina: Propia y apropiada." *Estudios* 24 (2004): 69–94. http://www.revistaestudios.ll.usb.ve/es/node/61.

Bellos, David. *Is That a Fish in Your Ear? Translation and the Meaning of Everything*. New York: Farrar, Straus and Giroux, 2012.

Benet i Jornet, Josep Maria. *La Plaça del Diamant*. Barcelona: Proa, 2007.

Benjamin, Thomas. *La Revolución: Mexico's Great Revolution as Memory, Myth, and History*. Austin: University of Texas Press, 2000.

Benjamin, Walter. "The Task of the Translator," translated by Harry Zohn. In *Selected Writings, 1913–1926*. Vol. 1, edited by Marcus Bullock and Michael W. Jennings, 253–263. Cambridge, Mass.: Belknap Press of Harvard University Press, 1996.

Bernadete, M. J., and Rolfe Humphries, eds. *". . . And Spain Sings": Fifty Loyalist Ballads Adapted by American Poets*. New York: Vanguard Press, 1937.

Blanco, José Joaquín. "¿Por qué nadie lee las *Memorias de Pancho Villa*?" In *Veinte aventuras de la literatura mexicana*, 91–112. Mexico City: CONACULTA, 2006.

Blasier, Cole. *The Hovering Giant: U.S. Responses to Revolutionary Change in Latin America*. Pittsburgh, Pa.: University of Pittsburgh Press, 1985.

Borduas, Paul. *Refus global et autres écrits*. Montreal: Typo, 1991.
Borges, Jorge Luis. "The Intruder," translated by Alastair Reid. *Encounter*, April 1969, 15–17.
———. "La intrusa." In *El Aleph*. Buenos Aires: Emecé Editores, 1995.
———. *Para las seis cuerdas*. Buenos Aires: Emecé Editores, 1965.
Bosteels, Bruno. *Marx and Freud in Latin America: Politics, Psychoanalysis, and Religion in Times of Terror*. London: Verso, 2012.
Bou, Enric. *Invention of Space: City, Travel and Literature*. Madrid: Iberoamericana Vervuert, 2013.
Brooks, David. "José Martí, the National Poet." *New York Times*, April 22, 2016.
Cabrera Infante, Guillermo. "Who Killed Calvert Casey?" In *Mea Cuba*, translated by Kenneth Hall with the author, 114–137. New York: Farrar, Straus and Giroux, 1994.
Callahan, David. "Stephen Spender, the 1930s, and Spanish Writing." *Miscelánea. A Journal of English and American Studies* 32 (2005): 39–55.
Camba, Julio. *Maneras de ser periodista*, edited by Francisco Fuster. Madrid: Libros del K. O., 2013.
Campbell, Roy. *The Collected Poems*. Vol. 2. London: Bodley Head, 1957.
———. *Collected Works*. Vols. 2 and 4, edited by Peter Alexander, Michael Chapman, and Marcia Leveson. Craighall, South Africa: Ad Donker, 1985.
———. *Flowering Rifle: A Poem from the Battlefield of Spain*. London: Longmans, Green and Co, 1939.
———. *Lorca: An Appreciation of His Poetry*. New Haven, Conn.: Yale University Press, 1952.
Carballo, Emmanuel. "Glorieta y no gloria: Pancho Villa convertido en estatua." *Excélsior*, November 22, 1969, 7.
———. "Martín Luis Guzmán." 1965. In *Protagonistas de la literatura mexicana*, 91–112. Mexico City: Porrúa, 1994.
Carranza, Luis E. *Architecture as Revolution: Episodes in the History of Modern Mexico*. Austin: University of Texas Press, 2010.
Casey, Calvert. *Calvert Casey: Tres relatos rituales*, edited by Alberto Ruy Sánchez. Mexico City: Coordinación de Difusión Cultural, Dirección de Literatura, Universidad Nacional Autónoma de México, 2008.
———. *The Collected Stories*, edited by Ilan Stavans, translated by John H. R. Holt. Durham, N.C.: Duke University Press, 1998.
———. "Cuba: Nación y nacionalidad." *Lunes de Revolución* no. 28 (September 28, 1959): 2.
Centeno, Miguel Ángel. "War and Memories: Symbols of State Nationalism in Latin America." *Revista Europea de Estudios Latinoamericanos y del Caribe / European Review of Latin American and Caribbean Studies* 66 (June 1999): 75–105. http://www.jstor.org/stable/25675821.
Chambers, Iain. "The Translated City." *Translation* 1, no. 1 (2011): 101–106.
Cheadle, Norman. "Canadian Counterpoint: Don Latino and Doña Canadiense in José Leandro Urbina's *Collect Call* (1992) and Ann Ireland's *Exile* (2002)." In *Canadian Cultural Exchange / Échanges culturels au Canada: Translation and Transculturation / Traduction et transculturation*, edited by Norman Cheadle and Lucien Pelletier, 269–304. Waterloo, Ontario: Wilfrid Laurier University Press, 2007.
———. "Emerging from a Cloud: The Inter-American Discursive Position of Hispano-Canadian Literature." *Interfaces Brasil/Canada* 13, no. 17 (2013): 17–55.
Ching Vega, Oscar W. *La última cabalgata de Pancho Villa*. Chihuahua, Mexico: Centro Librero La Prensa, 1977.

Cho, Jinwoo. "All in the Tone: A Korean Translation in Queens Strikes Wrong Note," translated by Hyemi Lee. *Voices of New York*, June 7, 2012. https://voicesofny.org/2012/06/all-in-the-tone-a-korean-translation-in-queens-strikes-wrong-note/. Originally published in *Korea Times*.

Cifuentes-Goodbody, Nicholas. *The Man Who Wrote Pancho Villa: Martín Luis Guzmán and the Politics of Life Writing*. Nashville, Tenn.: Vanderbilt University Press, 2016.

———. "Translation, Space, and Power in Martín Luis Guzmán's *Memorias de Pancho Villa*." *Translator* 23, no. 3 (2017): 279–291.

Clifford, James. *Routes: Travel and Translation in the Late Twentieth Century*. Cambridge, Mass.: Harvard University Press, 1997.

Corona, Dolores, and Ofelia García. "English in Cuba: From the Imperial Design to the Imperative Need." In *Post-Imperial English: Status Change in Former British and American Colonies, 1940–1990*, edited by Joshua A. Fishman, Andrew W. Conrad, and Alma Rubal-López, 85–112. New York: Mouton de Gruyter, 1996.

Crampton, Jeremy W., and Stuart Elden, eds. *Space, Knowledge and Power: Foucault and Geography*. Surrey, UK: Ashgate, 2007.

Cronin, Michael. *Across the Lines: Travel, Language, Translation*. Cork, Ireland: Cork University Press, 2000.

———. "Digital Dublin: Translating the Cybercity." In *Speaking Memory: How Translation Shapes City Life*, edited by Sherry Simon, 103–116. Montreal: McGill-Queen's University Press, 2016.

———. *Translation and Identity*. New York: Routledge, 2006.

———, and Sherry Simon. "Introduction: The City as Translation Zone." *Translation Studies* 7, no. 2 (2014): 119–132, doi:10.1080/14781700.2014.897641.

Darroch, Michael. "Language in the City, Language of the City." In *Circulation and the City: Essays on Urban Culture*, edited by Alexandra Boutros and William Straw, 23–47. Montreal: McGill-Queen's University Press, 2010.

Desnoes, Edmundo. *Memorias del subdesarrollo*. Mexico City: Joaquín Mortiz, 1980.

Díaz, Roberto Ignacio. *Unhomely Rooms: Foreign Tongues and Spanish American Literature*. Lewisburg, Pa.: Bucknell University Press, 2002.

Dongchan Shin. "Korean 'Comfort Women' Demand Apology," translated by Heesook Choi. *Voices of New York*, December 21, 2011. http://voicesofny.org/2011/12/korean-comfort-women-meet-with-holocaust-survivors/. Originally published in *Korea Daily*.

Donovan, Aaron. "Connecting Large Advertisers and Ethnic Newspapers." *New York Times*, May 22, 2002.

Eisenberg, Daniel. *"Poeta en Nueva York": Historia y problemas de un texto de Lorca*. Barcelona: Editorial Ariel, 1976.

Ellis, Keith. *Cuba's Nicolás Guillén: Poetry and Ideology*. Toronto: University of Toronto Press, 1983.

Fernández Retamar, Roberto. "Caliban: Notes toward a Discussion of Culture in Our America." In *Caliban and Other Essays*, translated by Edward Baker, 3–45. Minneapolis: University of Minnesota Press, 1989.

Fost, Dan. "S.F. Nonprofit Helps Small Magazines Stay Alive." *SFGate*, December 12, 2002. https://www.sfgate.com/business/article/S-F-nonprofit-helps-small-magazines-stay-alive-2711854.php.

Foucault, Michel. "Of Other Spaces," translated by Jay Miskowiec. *Diacritics* 16 (1986): 22–27.

———. *Power/Knowledge: Selected Interviews and Other Writings, 1972–1977*, edited by Colin Gordon, translated by Colin Gordon et al. New York: Pantheon, 1980.

Fountain, Anne. *José Martí and U.S. Writers*. Gainesville: University Press of Florida, 2003.

García Canclini, Néstor. "From National Capital to Global Capital: Urban Change in Mexico City," translated by Paul Liffman. *Public Culture* 12, no. 1 (2000): 207–213. https://muse.jhu.edu/article/26182.

———. *L'Amérique latine au XXIe siècle*, translated by Emmanuelle Tremblay. Quebec City: Les Presses de l'Université Laval, 2007.

García Carpio, Antonio. "Poeta en Nueva York de Federico García Lorca y las artes plásticas." PhD diss., Universidad Politécnica de Valencia, 2004.

García Lorca, Federico. *Gypsy Ballads*, translated by Jane Duran and Gloria García Lorca. London: Enitharmon Press, 2011.

———. "Lorca's New York Poems: *Poet in New York / Earth and Moon*," translated by Ben Belitt, introduction by Piero Menarini. Unpublished manuscript. Edwin Honig Papers, Ms. 97–96, box 4, folders 22–23.

———. *Lorca, Songs*, edited by Daniel Eisenberg, translated by Philip Cummings. Pittsburgh, Pa.: Duquesne University Press, 1976.

———. *Poems*, translated by Stephen Spender and J. L. Gili. London: Dolphin, 1939.

———. *Poeta en Nueva York*, edited by Andrew A. Anderson. Barcelona: Galaxia Gutenberg / Círculo de Lectores, 2013.

———. *Poeta en Nueva York: Tierra y luna*, edited by Eutimio Martín. Barcelona: Ariel, 1981.

———. *Poet in New York*, translated by Ben Belitt, introduction by Ángel del Río. New York: Grove Press, 1955.

———. *Poet in New York*, translated and with a new preface and critical chronology by Ben Belitt, introduction by Ángel del Río. New York: Grove Press (An Evergreen Book, E-815), 1983.

———. *Songs*, translated by Philip H. Cummings, edited by Daniel Eisenberg. Pittsburgh, Pa.: Duquesne University Press, 1976.

———. *Poet in New York*, translated by Pablo Medina and Mark Statman. New York: Grove Press, 2008.

———. *Poet in New York. 1988*, edited by Christopher Maurer, translated by Greg Simon and Steven F. White. New York: Farrar, Straus and Giroux, 2013.

———. *The Poet in New York and Other Poems*, translated by Rolfe Humphries. New York: W. W. Norton, 1940.

———. *Poet in New York: Bilingual Edition*, translated by Greg Simon and Steven F. White, edited by Christopher Maurer. New York: Farrar, Straus and Giroux, 2013.

García Lorca, Francisco. *Federico y su mundo*, edited by Mario Hernández. Madrid: Alianza, 1980.

García Márquez, Gabriel. *One Hundred Years of Solitude*, translated by Gregory Rabassa. New York: Avon, 1970.

Gentzler, Edwin. *Translation and Identity in the Americas: New Directions in Translation Theory*. New York: Routledge, 2007.

Gillman, Richard, and Michael Paul Novak, eds. *Poets, Poetics, and Politics: America's Literary Community Viewed from the Letters of Rolfe Humphries, 1910–1969*. Lawrence: University Press of Kansas, 1992.

Giménez Micó, José Antonio. "Latin-Americanizing Canada." In *Canadian Cultural Exchange / Échanges culturels au Canada: Translation and Transculturation / Traduction et transculturation*, translated by Kate Alvo, edited by Norman Cheadle and Lucien Pelletier, 59–74. Waterloo, Ontario: Wilfrid Laurier University Press, 2007.

Ginsberg, Allen. *Howl and Other Poems*, introduction by William Carlos Williams. San Francisco: City Lights, 1956.

Glass, Loren. *Counterculture Colophon: Grove Press, the Evergreen Review, and the Incorporation of the Avant-Garde.* Stanford, Calif.: Stanford University Press, 2013.

Gómez, Mayte. "Soldier of Franco, Soldier of Christ: Roy Campbell and Spain in the 1930s." *English in Africa* 34, no. 1 (May 2007): 21–41.

González, Carina Fernanda. "La odisea del retorno: Calvert Casey y el regreso que se repite." *Hispamérica* 45, no. 134 (2016): 3–12.

González Echevarría, Roberto. "*Biografía de un cimarrón* and the Novel of the Cuban Revolution." *NOVEL* 13, no. 3 (1980): 249–263.

Guillén, Nicolás. *Nicolás Guillén: A Bilingual Anthology*, edited and translated by Keith Ellis. Havana: Editorial José Martí, 2003.

Guzmán, Martín Luis. *Discurso en el 50 aniversario de la muerte de Villa.* Mexico City: Archivo Histórico de la UNAM, Archivo Martín Luis Guzmán Franco, June 20, 1973.

———. *Discurso pronunciado por el señor Martín Luis Guzmán en el mitin que el Partido Revolucionario Institucional llevo a cabo, para apoyar a sus candidatos a senadores por el Distrito federal.* Mexico City: Archivo Histórico de la UNAM, Archivo Martín Luis Guzmán Franco, June 5, 1970.

———. *Memoirs of Pancho Villa*, translated by Virginia H. Taylor. Austin: University of Texas Press, 1975.

———. *Memorias de Pancho Villa.* 1951. In *Obras completas*, 3:25–908. Mexico City: INEHRM, 2010.

Harel, Simon. *Le voleur de parcours: Identité et cosmopolitisme dans la littérature québécoise contemporaine.* Montreal: Éditions XYZ, 1999.

Harvey, David. Afterword to *The Production of Space*. By Henry Lefebvre, 426–432. Malden, Mass.: Blackwell, 1991.

Haslip-Viera, Gabriel. "The Evolution of the Latino Community." In *Hispanic New York: A Sourcebook*, edited by Claudio Remeseira, 35–56. New York: Columbia University Press, 2010.

Hazelton, Hugh. *Latinocanadá: A Critical Study of Ten Latin American Writers of Canada.* Montreal: McGill-Queen's University Press, 2007.

———. "Polylingual Identities: Writing in Multiple Languages." In *Canadian Cultural Exchange / Échanges culturels au Canada: Translation and Transculturation / Traduction et transculturation*, edited by Norman Cheadle and Lucien Pelletier, 225–245. Waterloo, Ontario: Wilfrid Laurier University Press, 2007.

———. "Québec Hispánico: Themes of Exile and Integration in the Writing of Latin Americans Living in Quebec." *Canadian Literature / Littérature canadienne* 142, no. 43 (1994): 120–135.

———. "Transculturation and National Identity in the Novel *Rojo, amarillo y verde* by Alejandro Saravia." In *Canada and Its Americas: Transnational Navigations*, edited by Winfried Siemerling and Sarah Phillips Casteel, 219–230. Montreal: McGill-Queen's University Press, 2010.

Henighan, Stephen. "From Exile to the Pandilla: The Construction of the Hispanic-Canadian Masculine Subject." In *Cobro revertido* and *Côte-des-Nègres*, edited by Gordana Yovanovich and Amy Huras, 285–298. Waterloo, Ontario: Sir Wilfrid Laurier University Press, 2010.

Hernández, Mario. "Los manuscritos de *Poeta en Nueva York.*" In *Manuscritos neoyorquinos: "Poeta en Nueva York" y otras hojas y poemas*, by Federico García Lorca, edited by Mario Hernández, 13–29. Madrid: Tabapress / Fundación García Lorca, 1990.

Honig, Edwin. *The Poet's Other Voice: Conversations on Literary Translation.* Amherst: University of Massachusetts Press, 1985.

Hughes, Langston. *I Wonder as I Wander.* New York: Hill and Wang, 1993.

Illas, Edgar. *Thinking Barcelona: Ideologies of a Global City.* Liverpool, UK: Liverpool University Press, 2012.

Jakobson, Roman. "On Linguistic Aspects of Translation." In *On Translation*, edited by Arthur Reuben Brower, 232–239. Cambridge, Mass.: Harvard University Press, 1959.

Jörgensen, Beth E. *Documents in Crisis: Nonfiction Literatures in Twentieth-Century Mexico.* Albany: SUNY Press, 2011. http://muse.jhu.edu/book/12688.

Katz, Friedrich. *The Life and Times of Pancho Villa.* Stanford, Calif.: Stanford University Press, 1998.

Kazin, Alfred. *A Walker in the City.* Orlando, Fla.: Harcourt, 1951.

Kristal, Efraín. "Philosophical/Theoretical Approaches to Translation." In *The Blackwell Companion to Translation Studies*, edited by Sandra Berman and Catherine Porter, 28–40. Chichester: Wiley-Blackwell, 2014.

Kutzinski, Vera M. *The Worlds of Langston Hughes: Modernism and Translation in the Americas.* Ithaca, N.Y.: Cornell University Press, 2012.

Lalo, Eduardo. *Uselessness: A Novel*, translated by Suzanne Jill Levine. Chicago: University of Chicago Press, 2017.

"La muerte de Axkaná." *Tiempo*, January 1977, 5–23.

Larson, Susan. *Constructing and Resisting Modernity: Madrid 1900–1936.* Madrid: Iberoamericana Vervuert, 2011.

Lea, Richard. "Fiction v. Nonfiction: English Literatures' Made-Up Divide." *Guardian*, March 24, 2016.

Lefebvre, Henri. *The Production of Space*, translated by Donald Nicholson-Smith. Cambridge, Mass.: Blackwell, 1991.

Lefevere, André. *Translation/History/Culture: A Sourcebook.* New York: Routledge, 1992.

———. *Translation, Rewriting, and the Manipulation of Literary Fame.* New York: Routledge, 1992.

Legrás, Horacio. "El Ateneo y los orígenes del estado ético en México." *Latin American Research Review* 38, no. 2 (January 2003): 34–60. http://www.jstor.org/stable/1555419.

———. "Martín Luis Guzmán: El viaje de la revolución." *MLN* 118, no. 2 (March 2003): 427–454. http://www.jstor.org/stable/3252014.

Londero, Renata. "Roy Campbell, traduttore di Lorca: La metafora nel *Romancero gitano.*" In *La luna e la morte: Atti dell'incontro internazionale su Federico García Lorca*, edited by Giancarlo Ricci, Luis Luque Toro, and Sagrario del Río, 55–65. Udine, Italy: Forum Edizioni, 2001.

Mabrey, María Cristina C. "Mapping Homoerotic Feelings and Contested Modernity: Whitman, Lorca, Ginsberg, and Hispanic Modernist Poets." *South Atlantic Review* 75, no. 1 (2010): 83–98.

MacDiarmid, Hugh. *Complete Poems.* Vol. 2, edited by Michael Grieve and W. R. Aitken. Manchester, UK: Carcanet, 1994.

Manzoni, Celina. "Poéticas del retorno: Tres pesadillas cubanas." *Hispamérica* 45, no. 134 (2016): 3–12.

Marti, José. *The America of José Martí*, translated by Juan de Onís, edited and with a preface by Federico de Onís. New York: Noonday Press, 1953.

———. *La comunidad cubana de New York: Siglo XIX*. Havana: Centro de estudios martianos, 2002.

———. *José Martí: Selected Writings*, translated by Esther Allen. New York: Penguin Classics, 2002.

———. *Obras completas*. Havana: Editorial de Ciencias Sociales, 1975.

Maurer, Christopher, and Andrew A. Anderson. *Federico García Lorca en Nueva York y La Habana: Cartas y recuerdos*. Barcelona: Galaxia Gutenberg / Círculo de Lectores, 2013.

Mayhew, Jonathan. *Apocryphal Lorca: Translation, Parody, Kitsch*. Chicago: University of Chicago Press, 2009.

McGee, Anne Marie. "Body Politics and the Figure of Pancho Villa: From National Exclusion to Regional Resurrection." *Anuario de Estudios Americanos* 67, no. 2 (2010): 425–444. http://biblioteca.ues.edu.sv/revistas/10800305-2.pdf.

Menton, Seymour. *Prose Fiction of the Cuban Revolution*. Austin: University of Texas Press, 1975.

Molloy, Sylvia. *At Face Value: Autobiographical Writing in Spanish America*. Cambridge: Cambridge University Press, 1991.

———. "Postcolonial Latin America and the Magic Realist Imperative: A Report to an Academy." In *Nation, Language, and the Ethics of Translation*, edited by Sandra Bermann and Michael Wood, 370–379. Princeton, N.J.: Princeton University Press, 2005.

Monsiváis, Carlos. "El hastío es pavo real que se aburre de luz en la tarde: Notas del camp en México." 1965. In *Días de guardar*, 171–197. Mexico City: Ediciones Era, 1991.

Neruda, Pablo. *Obras escogidas*, edited by Francisco Coloane. Santiago, Chile: Editorial Andrés Bello, 1972.

O'Brien, Justin. "Poet on Horseback." *Kenyon Review* 4, no. 1 (1942): 75–86.

Palmero González, Elena. "Desplazamiento cultural y procesos literarios en las letras hispanoamericanas contemporáneas: La literatura hispano-canadiense." *Contexto* 15, no. 17 (2011): 57–81.

Parra, Max. *Writing Pancho Villa's Revolution: Rebels in the Literary Imagination of Mexico*. Austin: University of Texas Press, 2006.

Pérez, Louis A. *On Becoming Cuban: Identity, Nationality and Culture*. Chapel Hill: University of North Carolina Press, 1999.

Pérez Firmat, Gustavo. *Tongue Ties: Logo-Eroticism in Anglo-Hispanic Literature*. New York: Palgrave Macmillan, 2003.

Perulero Pardo-Balmonte, Elena. "Recepción y repercusión de la poesía de Federico García Lorca en la poesía norteamericana del siglo XX: El caso de *Poeta en Nueva York*." In *Actas, XV Congreso de la Asociación Internacional de Hispanistas, Tomo III*. http://cvc.cervantes.es/literatura/aih/pdf/15/aih_15_3_027.pdf.

Polezzi, Loredana. *Translating Travel: Contemporary Italian Travel Writing in English Translation*. Aldershot, UK: Ashgate, 2001.

Portal, Marta. "Conversación con Martín Luis Guzmán." *ABC*, October 29, 1971, 122–123.

Quintero-Herencia, Juan Carlos. "'El regreso' de Calvert Casey: Una exposición en la playa." *Cuadernos de literatura* 27, no. 33 (2013): 337–403.

Ramos, Julio. *Desencuentros de la modernidad en América Latina*. Santiago, Chile: Ediciones Callejón, 2003.

Ricci, Giancarlo, Luis Luque Toro, and Sagrario del Río, eds. *La luna e la morte: Atti dell'incontro internazionale su Federico García Lorca*. Udine, Italy: Forum Edizioni, 2001.

Robinson, Sal. "The Nonfiction Gap." *Three Percent*, September 19, 2001. http://www.rochester.edu/College/translation/threepercent/?id=3613.
Rodoreda, Mercé. *In Diamond Square*, translated by Peter Bush. London: Virago, 2013.
Rodríguez-Hernández, Raúl. *Mexico's Ruins: Juan García Ponce and the Writing of Modernity*. Albany: SUNY Press, 2007.
Rogers, Gayle. *Incomparable Empires: Modernism and the Translation of American and Spanish Literatures*. New York: Columbia University Press, 2016.
———. *Modernism and the New Spain: Britain, Cosmopolitan Europe and Literary History*. Oxford: Oxford University Press, 2012.
Rojas, Rafael. *La vanguardia peregrina: El escritor cubano, la tradición y el exilio*. Mexico City: Fondo de Cultura Económica, 2013.
Rowlandson, William. *Sartre in Cuba—Cuba in Sartre*. New York: Palgrave Macmillan, 2018.
Sanguinetti, Pablo. "La doble invisibilidad del periodista-traductor." In *Hijos de Babel: Reflexiones sobre el oficio de traductor en el siglo XXI*, edited by Mercedes Cebrián Coello et al., 141–142. Madrid: Fórcola Ediciones, 2013.
Scher, Abby. "Reading, PA." *Dissent*, Winter 2015. http://www.dissentmagazine.org/article/reading-pa-solidarity-economy.
Scorer, James. *City in Common: Culture and Community in Buenos Aires*. Albany: SUNY Press, 2016.
Sheridan, Guillermo. "Monuments." In *The Mexico City Reader*, edited by Rubén Gallo and Lorna Scott Fox, 149–151. Madison: University of Wisconsin Press, 2004.
Simon, Sherry. "Across Troubled Divides: Translation, Gender, and Memory." Lecture presented at Nida School of Translation Studies, Session 22, San Pellegrino University Foundation, Misano Adriatico, Italy, May 27, 2013.
———. *Cities in Translation: Intersections of Language and Memory*. New York: Routledge, 2012.
———. "Translating in the Multilingual City: Montreal as a City of the Americas." In *Canada and Its Americas: Transnational Navigations*, edited by Winfried Siemerling and Sarah Phillips Casteel, 171–185. Montreal: McGill-Queen's University Press, 2010.
———. *Translating Montreal: Episodes in the Life of a Divided City*. Montreal: McGill-Queen's University Press, 2006.
Soja, Edward W. *Postmodern Geographies: The Reassertion of Space in Critical Social Theory*. New York: Verso, 1989.
Sommer, Doris, ed. *Bilingual Games: Some Literary Investigations*. New York: Palgrave Macmillan, 2003.
Sommerville, Henry S. "Commerce and Culture in the Career of the Permanent Innovative Press: New Directions, Grove Press, and George Braziller, Inc." PhD diss., University of Rochester, 2009.
Stein, Bernard L. "A New 'Voices' for a New Decade." *Voices of New York*, September 7, 2011. https://voicesofny.org/2011/09/411/.
Torres, Luis. "Writings of the Latin American Exile." *Revista Canadiense de Estudios Hispánicos* 26, no. 1–2 (October 2001 / Winter 2002): 179–198.
Tymoczko, Maria, and Edwin Gentzler, eds. *Translation and Power*. Amherst: University of Massachusetts Press, 2002.
"Una Estatua." *Tiempo*, November 1969, 43–44.
Valis, Noël. "Lorca's *Agonía republicana* and Its Aftermath." *Bulletin of Spanish Studies* 91, no. 1–2 (2014): 267–294.

Venuti, Lawrence. *The Translator's Invisibility: A History of Translation*. New York: Routledge, 1995.

Villa, Guadalupe, and Rosa Helia Villa de Mebius, eds. *Pancho Villa: Retrato autobiográfico, 1894–1914*. Mexico City: Santillana Ediciones Generales, 2004.

Walsh, Andrew Samuel. "Lorca's *Poet in New York* as a Paradigm of Poetic Retranslation." In *Literary Retranslation in Context*, edited by Susanne Cadera and Andrew Samuel Walsh, 21–51. New York: Peter Lang, 2017.

Winks, Christopher. *Symbolic Cities in Caribbean Literature*. New York: Palgrave Macmillan, 2009.

Wittgenstein, Ludwig. *Philosophical Investigations*, translated by G. E. Anscombe. Malden, Mass.: Wiley-Blackwell, 2009.

Yaffe, Helen. *Che Guevara: The Economics of Revolution*. New York: Palgrave Macmillan, 2009.

Young, Howard. "La primera recepción de Federico García Lorca en los Estados Unidos (1931–1941)." In *América en un poeta: Los viajes de Federico García Lorca al nuevo mundo y la repercusión de su obra en la literatura americana*, edited by Andrew A. Anderson, 105–108. Seville, Spain: Universidad Internacional de Andalucía / Fundación Focus-Abengoa, 1999.

Zambrano, María. *Islas*, edited by Jorge Luis Arcos. Madrid: Editorial Verbum, 2007.

NOTES ON CONTRIBUTORS

ESTHER ALLEN is a writer and translator who teaches in both the Hispanic and Luso-Brazilian and the French programs at the Graduate Center and Baruch College of the City University of New York (CUNY). A two-time recipient of the National Endowment for the Arts Translation Fellowship (1995 and 2010), she was a 2009–2010 fellow at the Cullman Center for Scholars and Writers at the New York Public Library. In 2014–2015, she was a biography fellow at the Leon Levy Center for Biography, working on a biography of José Martí now under contract with Henry Holt and Co. She cofounded the PEN World Voices Festival in 2005 and guided the work of the PEN/Heim Translation Fund from its inception in 2003 to 2010. In 2006, the French government named her a Chevalier de l'ordre des arts et des lettres; in 2012, she received the Feliks Gross Award from the CUNY Academy for the Arts and Sciences.

ALICIA BORINSKY is a fiction writer, poet, and literary critic who published extensively in English and Spanish in the United States, Latin America, and Europe. Her most recent books are *La mujer de mi marido / My Husband's Woman*, translated with Natasha Hakimi (poetry; Literal, 2016); *Las ciudades perdidas van al paraíso / Lost Cities Go to Paradise* (poetry; Swan Isle Press, 2015), translated with Regina Galasso; *Low Blows / Golpes Bajos* (short fictions; University of Wisconsin Press, 2007); *Frivolous Women and Other Sinners* (poetry; Swan Isle Press, 2009), all published bilingually; and *One Way Tickets: Writers and the Culture of Exile* (literary criticism; Trinity Press, 2001). She is the recipient of several awards, including the Latino Literature Prize for Fiction and a John Simon Guggenheim Foundation Fellowship. Her research interests include the theory and practice of literary translation, transnational cultural studies, contemporary gender and literary theory, Latino literature and the legacy of the Latin American avant-garde from Huidobro to Borges, and the writers of the "Boom" to the present. She is a professor of Spanish and the director of the Summer Cultural Studies Program in Buenos Aires at Boston University.

PETER BUSH is a freelance literary translator and scholar who lives in Oxford. He has translated eighteen works from Catalan by authors such as Najat El Hachmi, Quim Monzó, Josep Pla, Mercè Rodoreda, Joan Sales, and Teresa Solana. His translation of Pla's *The Gray Notebook* won the 2014 Ramon Llull Literary Translation Prize, and he was awarded the Creu de Sant Jordi in 2015 for his translation and promotion of Catalan literature. He has translated Juan Goytisolo, Juan Carlos Onetti, Leonardo Padura, and Senel Paz and classics by Federico García Lorca, Fernando de Rojas, and Ramón del Valle-Inclán. His most recent translation from Catalan is Emili Teixidor's *Black Bread*; from French, Alain Badiou's *In Praise of Love*; from Mexican Spanish, Carmen Boullosa's *Before*; and from peninsular Spanish, Fernando Royuela's *A Bad End*. A former director of the British Centre for Literary Translation (BCLT), he founded the journal *In Other Words* and the BCLT Literary Translation Summer School and was a professor of literary translation at both Middlesex University and the University of East Anglia.

NICHOLAS CIFUENTES-GOODBODY is the associate director of the Dornsife Language Center at the University of Southern California. He has published articles on Mexican and Latin American literature as well as translation studies. His recently published book, *The Man Who Wrote Pancho Villa: Martín Luis Guzmán and the Politics of Life Writing* (Vanderbilt University Press, 2016), places Guzmán's work in a biographical context, shedding light on the immediate motivations behind his writing in a given moment and the subsequent ways in which he rewrote or repackaged that work over the course of his life.

JENNIFER DUPREY is an associate professor of Spanish and Catalan studies at Rutgers University Newark. She is the author of *The Aesthetics of the Ephemeral: Memory Theaters in Contemporary Barcelona* (SUNY Press, 2014).

REGINA GALASSO is an associate professor of Spanish and the director of the Translation Center at the University of Massachusetts Amherst. She is the translator of *A True Story: A Cuban in New York* (by Miguel Barnet; Jorge Pinto, 2010) and *Lost Cities Go to Paradise* (by Alicia Borinsky; Swan Isle Press, 2015) and the editor with Carmen Boullosa of a special "Nueva York" issue of *Translation Review*. Her book, *Translating New York: The City's Languages in Iberian Literatures* (Liverpool University Press, 2018), won the 2017 Northeast Modern Language Association Book Award.

CHARLES HATFIELD is an associate professor of Latin American studies at the University of Texas at Dallas, where he is also the associate director of the Center for Translation Studies and an editor of the journal *Translation Review*. Hatfield is the author of *The Limits of Identity: Politics and Poetics in Latin America* (University of Texas Press, 2015).

HUGH HAZELTON is a writer and translator who specializes in the comparison of Canadian and Quebec literatures with those of Latin America, as well as in the work of Latin American writers of Canada and in Quebec poetry. He has written four books of poetry and translates from Spanish, French, and Portuguese into English; his translation of *Vétiver* (Signature, 2005), a book of poems by Joël

Des Rosiers, won the governor general's award for French-English translation in 2006. He is a professor emeritus of Spanish at Concordia University in Montreal and former codirector of the Banff International Literary Translation Centre (BILTC). In 2016, he received the Linda Gaboriau Award from BILTC and the Literary Translators' Association of Canada (LTAC) for his work on behalf of literary translation in Canada.

SUZANNE JILL LEVINE is a writer and renowned translator of canonical Latin American writers, including Guillermo Cabrera Infante, Julio Cortázar, Manuel Puig, Severo Sarduy, and Adolfo Bioy Casares. She has received many honors, including a PEN Career Achievement Award in Hispanic studies, several grants from the National Endowments for the Arts and for the Humanities, a Guggenheim Foundation Fellowship, and, most recently, the PEN USA award for José Donoso's *The Lizard's Tale* (2012). A professor of Latin American literature and the director of literary translation studies at the University of California Santa Barbara, her books include *The Subversive Scribe: Translating Latin American Fiction* and the biography *Manuel Puig and the Spiderwoman: His Life and Fictions* (FSG; Seix Barral). As the general editor of Penguin's paperback classics of Jorge Luis Borges's poetry and essays, she has recently translated Eduardo Lalo's *Uselessness* for the University of Chicago Press and coedited, for the Routledge "Advances in Translation and Interpreting Studies" series, *Untranslatability Goes Global* (2018).

CHRISTOPHER MAURER is a professor of Spanish at Boston University. He writes about Spanish poetry from Garcilaso to the Generación del 27. His most recent book, coauthored with Andrew A. Anderson, is *Federico García Lorca en Nueva York y La Habana: Cartas y recuerdos* (Galaxia Gutenberg, 2013). His biography of American painter and writer Walter Inglis Anderson won the 2003 Eudora Welty Award and the Nonfiction Prize of the Mississippi Academy of Arts and Letters.

URAYOÁN NOEL is an associate professor of English and Spanish at New York University and the author of seven books of poetry, the most recent of which is *Buzzing Hemisphere / Rumor Hemisférico* (University of Arizona Press, 2015), as well as the critical study *In Visible Movement: Nuyorican Poetry from the Sixties to Slam* (University of Iowa Press, 2014), winner of the LASA (Latin American Studies Association) Latina/o Studies Section Book Award and an honorable mention in the MLA Prize in Latina/o and Chicana/o Literary and Cultural Studies. He has received fellowships from the Ford Foundation, the Howard Foundation, and CantoMundo and is currently completing a bilingual edition of the poetry of Pablo de Rokha for Shearsman Books. Learn more at urayoannoel.com and wokitokiteki.com, a bilingual, improvisational poetry vlog.

EVELYN SCARAMELLA is an associate professor of Spanish at Manhattan College in Riverdale, New York. She has published articles about translation studies, Federico García Lorca, Langston Hughes, and race relations during the Spanish avant-garde period. Her work on Langston Hughes and Dorothy Peterson as translators of Hispanic poets appeared in the special "Nueva York" issue of *Translation Review*. She recovered and published Langston Hughes translations of Spanish Civil War poetry accompanied by a critical essay in the *Massachusetts Review*. She is currently working on a book manuscript, *Translating the Spanish Civil War: The Avant-Garde, Anti-fascism, and Literary History*, which explores the literary and political history of translation practices between Hispanophone and Anglophone avant-garde writers during the Spanish Civil War.

ILAN STAVANS is the Lewis-Sebring Professor in Latin American and Latino Culture at Amherst College. He is also the publisher of Restless Books, host of the NPR podcast *In Contrast*, and the cofounder and academic director of Great Books Summer Program. His best-selling books include *On Borrowed Words* (2001), *Spanglish* (2003), *Dictionary Days* (2005), *Love and Language* (2008), *Gabriel García Márquez: The Early Years* (2010), *A Critic's Journey* (2011), *Quixote: The Novel and the World* (2015), and *Borges, the Jew* (2016). His graphic novels are *Latino USA: A Cartoon History* (2000, with Lalo Alcaraz), *Mister Spic Goes to Washington* (2007, with Roberto Weil), *El Iluminado* (2012, with Steve Sheinkin), *A Most Imperfect Union* (2014, with Lalo Alcaraz), and *Angelitos* (2018, with Santiago Cohen). His work, adapted into radio, film, and theater, has been translated into twenty languages. He edited *Tropical Synagogues* (1994), *The Oxford Book of Jewish Stories* (1998), *The Shocken Book of Modern Sephardic Literature* (2005), *Becoming Americans* (2008), *The Norton Anthology of Latino Literature* (2011), *The FSG Book of Twentieth-Century Latin American Poetry* (2013), and *Oy, Caramba! An Anthology of Jewish Stories from Latin America* (2016). He has translated Borges, Neruda, Mariano Azuela, Juan Rulfo, Ricardo Piglia, and *El Lazarillo de Tormes* into English; Isaac Bashevis Singer from Yiddish; Yehuda Halevi from Hebrew; Emily Dickinson, Elizabeth Bishop, and Richard Wilbur into Spanish; and Shakespeare and Cervantes into Spanglish. His many honors include the Rubén Darío Distinction, the Pablo Neruda Presidential Medal, the National Jewish Book Award, three International Latino Book Awards, an Emmy nomination, and a Guggenheim Fellowship.

INDEX

Page numbers in italics refer to figures.

accents, 17, 19, 20
Adams, Mildred, 34, 35, 46n11, 47–48n26
adaptation, 82–96, 95n10, 95n17
Aguilar, 42
Alberti, Rafael, 3
Alexievich, Svetlana, 114
Alianza de Intelectuales Antifascistas (Alliance of Antifascist Intellectuals), 3, 4
All Communities Advertising Service, 123, 124
Allen, Donald M., 36, 39, 40, 44–45, 51n70
Alonso Gamo, José María, 47n24
Altolaguirre, Manuel, 3
Alvarado, Tito, 103
Amerikai Népszava, 112
Anderson, Andrew A., 34, 45n2, 50n58
Anglophone media, Martí and, 117–119
Apollinaire, Guillaume, 102
Apostles Review, The, 103
appropriation, translation as, 58
"Aquel Tapado de armiño," 26–27
Aquin, Hubert, 99, 108
Arabic, 125
Arbeiter-Zeitung, 117
Aridjis, Homero, 104
Armony, Victor, 108
Auden, W. H., 32, 45
automatistes, 99
avenue, 1–2

Banff International Literary Translation Centre, 107
Bangla, 125
Barcelona, Spain, 11, 81–96; history of, 82–83, 85, 95n8; as linguistically dual city, 127, 128; multilingualism and, 127, 128; 1992 Olympic Games in, 82; in 1930s, 83; as palimpsest, 82; social formation of, 81–82; theater in, 81; Universal Expositions in, 82

Barthes, Roland, 6–7
Bassnett, Susan, 7
Bastin, George, 58
Batista, Fulgencio, 76
Batista regime, 72–73
Bauche Alcalde, Manuel, 55–56
Beauvoir, Simone de, 73
Beckett, Samuel, *Waiting for Godot*, 39
Bel, Pepe, 95n13
Belamich, André, 34
Belitt, Ben, 39, 47–48n26, 48–49n35, 49n37, 49n44, 49n45, 50n49, 51n70; correspondence with Del Río, 40; "Lorca's New York Poems: Poet in New York / Earth and Moon," 42–44; plans a bifurcated translation, 42–44; translation of García Lorca's *Poet in New York*, 10, 33, 34, 36, 39, 40–41, 42–44
Bellemare, Gaston, 104
Bellos, David, 113, 114, 121
Benet i Jornet, Josep M., stage adaptation of Rodoreda's *La Plaça del Diamant*, 11, 81–96, 89, 93, 94
Benjamin, Walter, 6–7, 93–94
Bergamín, José, 10, 43, 50n58
Bernd, Zilá, 105, 107
Betanzos Santos, Manuel, 100, 102
Betriu, Francesc, *The Time of the Doves*, 82
bilingualism, 4, 5, 10–11, 71. See also multilingualism
Blake, William, 20
Blanchot, Maurice, viii
Blue Metropolis / Métropolis bleu, Premio Azul award given at, 106
Bodega y Quadra, Juan Francisco, 98
Bogan, Louise, 35
Bolaño, Roberto, 105
book-publishing industry, 11–12, 101–108, 114. See also specific publishers

books, monuments and, 61
Borduas, Paul-Émile, 99
Boreal, 100
Borges, Jorge Luis, 30–31n4, 30n2; on concept of "definitive" text, 33; "La instrusa," 26; *Para las seis cuerdas*, 25
Bou, Enric, 1
Bouchard, Brigitte, 105
Bouchard, Michel Marc, 106
Brazilian Association of Canadian Studies (ABECAN), 106
Brickell, Herschel, 34, 46n11
Brooklyn, 20
Brossard, Nicole, 103, 105
Brown, Francis, 47–48n26
Brownsville, Brooklyn, New York, 16, 19
Bryant, Arthur, 48n34
Bryce, James, 129
Bryson, Eugene, 118
Buenos Aires, Argentina, ix, 9, 25, 27–30, 30–31n4
Burns, Robert, 37, 48n27
Burnshaw, Stanley, 49n47

Cabrera Infante, Guillermo, vii, viii–ix, 71–72
californios, 120–121
Calles, Plutarco Elías, 53, 54, 59, 65
Camba, Julio, 2–3, 6
Campbell, Roy, 32, 36–37, 47, 47n18, 47n21, 47n24, 48–49n35, 48n26, 48n28, 48n33, 48n34; *The Flowering Rifle*, 38; "On the Martyrdom of F. García Lorca," 38–39; *Talking Bronco*, 38–39
Campillo, María, 95n14
Campo, Ángela, 58
Campobello, Nellie, 3
Canada Council, 103–104
Canadian Cultural Exchange / Échanges culturels au Canada: Translation and Transculturation / Traduction et transculturation, 108
Cancino, Jorge, *Juglario / Jongleries*, 102
capitalism, 81–82
Cárdenas, Lázaro, 53, 54, 56, 59, 61, 65
Caribbean press, 122
Carlos Vélez Journalism Prize, 126
Carlson, Marvin, 91
Carranza, Luis, *Architecture as Revolution*, 59, 64

Casa de las Américas, 69
Casares, Toni, 82
Casey, Calvert; bilingualism of, 71; biography of, 71–72; "Cuba: Nación y nacionalidad," 73; "El regreso," 69–80; "linguistic self-consciousness" of, 71; writings for *Lunes de Revolución*, 73
Castellanos Moya, Horacio, 105
Catalan history, 91
Catalan language and culture, 83, 92
Catalan literature, 81–96, 91
Catalan theater, 82–83
censorship, 40, 83
Centeno, Miguel Angel, 66
Center for Community and Ethnic Media (CCEM) at the City University of New York's (CUNY) Graduate School of Journalism, 124, 127
Central and Eastern European languages, viii. *See also specific languages*
Centre des auteurs dramatiques (CEAD), 105
Centro de Estudios Martianos, 120
Césaire, Aimé, 100
Chamberland, Paul, 100
Chambers, Iain, 7–8, 64
Charter of the French Language, 99
Chávez, Denise, 121
Chenelière, Évelyne de la, 105
Chicago, Illinois, 117–118
Chihuahua, Mexico, 52, 53, 58
Chinatown, 18–19
Chinese, 18, 125–126, 127
Chinese Exclusion Act, 117
Chinese press, 122, 123, 125–126
Choi, Heesook, 124–125
Cifuentes-Goodbody, Nicholas, 10
cities/the city: in Casey's work, 75–76; diversity and, 54–55; history and, 5; identity and, 5; landscape of, 55; languages and, 5, 54–55, 69–80; modernity and, 4; monuments and, 64; multilingualism and, 5, 54–55; political conflict and, 60; power and, 64; soundscape of, 5, 55–58; space and, 64; space of, 1, 5–6; theater and, 81; translation and, 7–8, 9, 64–65; translators and, vii–ix (*see also specific translators*). *See also specific cities*

citizenship, translation and, 5
City University of New York (CUNY) Craig Newmark Graduate School of Journalism, 124, 125; subject concentration in Spanish-language journalism, 127–128
class, language and, 77
Clifford, James, 1
Cobb, Carl, 32
code-switching, 25, 77, 143
Cohen, Leonard, 99
comfort women, 124–125
Confluences littéraires Brésil-Québec: Les bases d'une comparaison, 107
connectedness, 114–115, 128
Conseil des arts et des lettres du Québec (CALQ), 105
Consejo Nacional para la Cultura y las Artes (CONACULTA), 105
Contursi, Pascual; "Flor de fango," 30; "Mi noche triste," 27–28
Cormorán y Delfín, 100
Cortes, Zaira, 126
cosmopolitanism, ix, 70, 112–132
Cronin, Michael, 7, 13n4, 55, 113
Cross, Elsa, 104
Crow, John, 37
Cuba, 3, 72–73, 74, 75–76, 115–116, 118–119, 129
Cubanidad, 10–11
Cuban independence movement, 115, 116
Cuban literature, 72, 78
Cuban Revolution, 76–77, 78
Cuban Revolutionary Party, 119
Cubans, in New York City, 116
cultural heterogeneity, 70
Cummings, Philip, 37, 40–41, 48n27, 49n44, 49n45

Dalí, Salvador, 37
Dana, Charles Anderson, 117–118
Daoust, Jean-Paul, 108
D. Appleton & Company, 120
Darroch, Michael, 13n10
Del Río, Ángel, 40–41, 46n12, 49n44, 49n47
democracy, 82
Dennis, Nigel, 50n58
Dérives, 107
desencuentro, 129

Desnoes, Edmundo, *Memorias del subdesarrollo*, 74–75
Díaz, Junot, 106
Díaz, Porfirio, 115
Díaz, Roberto Ignacio, 77, 79n14
Díaz Ordaz, Gustavo, 53, 59–60
Díaz-Plaja, Guillermo, 41
digital communication, 113
Dinkins, David, 117
Dinverno, Melissa, 33
distancing, 128
diversity: cities and, 54–55; linguistic, 122 (*see also* multilingualism)
División del Norte, 52, 53, 65
domestication, translation and, 55–58
Dorion, Hélène, 105
dualities, linguistic, 127–129
Ducharme, Réjean, 105
Dutch fur traders, 112
Duvalier, François "Papa Doc," 100, 105

Echeverri, Álvaro, 58
Echeverría, Luis, 53, 58, 63
economic localism, 123
Éditions d'Orphée, 103
Éditions du Boréal, 103
Éditions Fides, 103
Éditions Les Allusifs, 105
Eisenberg, Daniel, 34
El Avisador Hispano-Americano, 119
El Diario / La Prensa, 123, 126
Elía, Ramón de, 103
Eliot, T. S., 36, 47n18
Ellipse: Canadian Writing in Translation / Textes littéraires canadiens en traduction, 107
El Partido Liberal, 119
English, 16–19, 21, 22, 76–77, 125, 127, 128, 142
Escomel, Gloria, 108
"Espanglish," 9, 20
Etcheverry, Jorge, 109n6
ethnic media, 113, 122, 131–132n36
Étienne, Gérard, 105
Exit, 107

Faber and Faber, 36, 47n18
Faleiros, Álvaro, 102
Fanon, Frantz, 100

Farheit, 117
Farrar, Straus and Giroux, 50n58
Faura, Albert, 95n13
Fernández-Montesinos, José, 41, 42
Fernández-Montesinos, Manuel, 42–43
Ferron, Jacques, 103
Festival de la poésie, 106
Festival de Théâtre des Amériques (Festival TransAmériques), 105
Festival International de la Poésie, 106
fiction, Anglophone publishers' preference for translating, 114
Flores Patiño, Gilberto, 103
Fom Ling-Cho, 117
Fondo de Cultura Económica, 105
Foucault, Michel, 65
France, 4
Franco, Francisco, 47n21, 83, 91, 100
Fraser, G. S., 48n28
Fréchette, Louis, *La légende d'un peuple*, 98
freedom of speech, 115–117
French, 24, 125, 142, 144
Fuentes, Manuel, 118
furthering, 128

Galician authors. *See* Betanzos Santos, Manuel; Camba, Julio
García Lorca, Federico, 3, 32–51; American perceptions of, 44; assasination of, 3; becomes better known in United States, 39; *Bodas de sangre*, 4; "Canción de jinete," 32; *El público*, 34; estate of, 42–43; *Gypsy Ballads*, 32; homosexuality of, 35, 38, 40, 48n33; lecture on *Poeta en Nueva York*, 50n58; New York poetry and, 9; *Obras completas*, 42; "Poemas de la soledad en Vermont," 40–41; *Poeta en Nueva York*, 9–10, 32–51; possible influence of Belitt's translation on Ginsberg, 44–45; *Primer romancero gitano*, 32; problem of "definitive" version, 33; *Romancero gitano*, 3, 4, 35; as rural poet, 37–38, 42, 44–45; *Suites*, 33; *Three Tragedies*, 39; *Tierra y luna*, 42; translations of, 32–51; as universal poet, 37; in Vermont, 40–41; "Vuelta de paseo" ("After a Walk"), 9
García Lorca, Francisco, 33–34, 36, 41, 47n19, 51n70; death of, 42; edits Federico García Lorca's *Selected Poems*, 36, 39

García Márquez, Gabriel, 82
Gardel, Carlos, 29–30; "Victoria," 27
Gauvreau, Claude, 99, 103
gaze, 86, 95n16
Gelman, Juan, 104
Generation of 1927, 4
Genette, Gerard, 84
Gentzler, Edwin, 8, 63
geography, 1, 58, 65. *See also* space
Gili, J. L., 47n18, 48–49n35
Ginsberg, Allen; *Howl*, 44–45; "A Supermarket in California," 44
Giovanni da Verrazzano, 112
global translation industry, 123
Glorieta del Riviera, Navarte neighborhood, Mexico City, Mexico, 60–61, 65
Godbout, Jacques, 105
Goldman, Francisco, 106
González, Rodrigo, *Cuentos de la cabeza y la cola / Contes de la tête et de la queue*, 102
González Echevarría, Roberto, 78
Google translator, 121
Goulet, André, 103
Gousse, Edgard, 102
Graham, W. S., 39
Great Depression, 142
Greek tragedy, 81
Green, John, 36, 47n21
Grossman, Edith, 5, 6
Grove Press, 36, 39–40, 43, 44, 45, 47n19, 49n37, 51n70
Guachiac Ambrocio, Francisco, 126
Guadalajara Book Fair, 105
Guatemala, 115, 116
Guerra Da Cal, Ernesto, 34, 35, 46n11, 47–48n26
Guillén, Nicolás, 3, 76–77, 79n14; "Tengo," 76–77
Guzmán, Martín Luis, 10, 52–68; *Memorias de Pancho Villa*, 54–58, 60–63
Guzmán, Martín Luis, 67n26; at ceremony interring Villa at Monument of the Revolution, 65; claim of authenticity as translator, 55–57; conception of the intellectual, 57–58; conception of translation, 55–58; *El águila y la serpiente* (*The Eagle and the Serpent*), 57; exile of, 59; nominated to represent Mexico City in the Senate, 61;

represents himself as Villa's biographer, 62–63; represents himself as Villa's translator, 55–58
Guzmán Blanco, Antonio, 115

Hardy, Ginette, 103
Harlem, New York, 15–16
Hasenclever Montesinos, Nora, 41
"haunted stage," 91
Havana, Cuba, ix, 3, 10–11, 69, 71, 74, 116; in Casey's work, 75–76; Centro de Estudios Martianos, 120; monument to Martí in, 122
Hayes, Francis C., 47–48n26
Hazelton, Hugh, 107
Heritage Canada, 104
Hernández, Mario, 34, 50n58
heterosexuality, 25
Hindi, 125
Hispanic journalists, 122
history: cities and, 5; "law of historical memory," 92; materialization of, 82, 83–84; memory and, 83, 92
homosexuality, 35, 38, 40
Honig, Edwin, 33, 43
Hour magazine, 117–118
Housman, A. E., 32
Hughes, Langston, 3, 6; *I Wonder as I Wander*, 4; translation of Lorca, 3–4
Hugo, Victor, 120
Humanitas, 103
Humphries, Rolfe, 38, 49–50n49; *". . . And Spain Sings": Fifty Loyalist Ballads Adapted by American Poets*, 34–35; translation of García Lorca's *The Gypsy Ballads*, 35; translation of García Lorca's *The Poet in New York and Other Poems*, 10, 34, 35, 37, 41, 46n11
Hutcheon, Linda, 11, 82, 83–84, 86, 91, 92, 95n10
hyperlocal media hubs, 114–115, 122–127, 131–132n36

identity: cities and, 5; translation and, 58, 128
ideology, literature and, 77–78
Idling, Peter Fröberg, 130n9
Illas, Edgar, 1
immigrants/immigration, 100–101, 113. See also *specific communities*

Independent Press Association (IPA), 122–123, 124
individualism, bourgeois, 75
industrialization, 81–82
Institutional Revolutionary Party (PRI), 52, 53, 54, 60, 62, 64–65
Interfaces Brasil/Canadá, 106
interior monologues, adaptation of, 86
interlingualism, 79n14
interpreters, 127
"intersemiotic transposition," 82
Irish press, 122
Italian, 17, 18, 22, 24

Jack, Peter Monro, 45n2
Jackson, Helen Hunt, 120–121
Jakobson, Roman, 7, 13n4
Jarrell, Randall, 38
Jewish Daily Forward, 114
Jiménez, Juan Ramón, 3
Jörgenson, Beth, 55
journalism, 12; linguistic alterity and, 120; Martí and, 116–122, 131n23; multilingualism and, 124–127; translation and, 113–114, 121–122, 125–127
journalists, Hispanic, 122
Joyce, James, viii
Junco, Maite, 125
justice, 91–92

Kapuscinski, Ryszard, 113
Katz, Friedrich, 67n26
Kazin, Alfred, *A Walker in the City*, 9, 16–17, 19, 21
K'iché, 126
Kokis, Sergio, 108
Korea Daily, 125
Korean press, 125
Korea Times, 125
Kuhlman, Roy, 43
Kurapel, Alberto, 104
Kutzinski, Vera, 1

La Compagnie des Arts Exilio, 104
La Edad de Oro, 119
Lalanda, Marcial, 48n33
Lalo, Eduardo, vii
La Nación, 119
Langlois, Henri, vii

language(s), 113; cities and, 69–80; class and, 77; foreignness of, viii; public sphere and, 5; travel and, 7. *See also specific languages*
La Opinion Nacional, 119
Larsen, Susan, 1
late modernity, 70–71
Latin, 142, 144
Latin American literature: and authors' flight from tyranny/repression, 100–101; in francophone Canada, 11–12, 97–109; Montreal and, 11–12, 97–110; publication/translation of, 101–108; second generation of, 108–109; translation and, 58
La Vérendrye, Louis-Joseph Gaultier de, 98
La Vérendrye, Pierre Gaultier de, 98
Lavergne, Alfredo, 103
Lavigerie, Guy, 106
"law of historical memory," 92
Lawrence, D. H., 39, 40
Lefebvre, Henri, 60
Legrás, Horacio, 57
Leguizamo, John, 128
Leméac Éditeur, 105
Lenape natives, 112
Lepage, Robert, 105
Les Écrits des Forges, 104, 106
Librería las Américas, 106
Li-In-Du, 117
Lincolnshire, England, 144
Lindo, Elvira, 48n32
linguistic alterity, journalism and, 120
linguistic communities, 113
linguistic diversity, 122
listening, translation and, 5
literary circulation, networks of, 1
literary production, translation and, 6
Literary Translators' Association of Canada (LTAC / ATTLC): John Glassco prize awarded by, 103
Literatura francófona II: América, 105
literature, ideology and, 77–78
Little Italy, 18
Liverpool, England, 142, 143
Lloyd, A. L., 48–49n35
the local, translating, 112–132
localism, 123
localization, 123
location, 1, 65. *See also* cities/the city; space

London, England, ix
López Morales, Laura, 105
Lorca, Federico García. *See* García Lorca, Federico
loss, viii. *See also* memory
Lower East Side, 17–18
Lunes de Revolución, 73
lunfardo, 24, 27, 30, 30n2

MacDiarmid, Hugh, 48n34
MacGregor, Robert, 36
Mackenzie, Alexander, 98
MacLennan, Hugh, *Two Solitudes*, 100
Madrid, Spain, 3, 4
Magarshack David, 39
Malamud, Bernard, 16
Malaspina, Alejandro, 98
"Malevaje," 25, 27, 31n5
Manahatta, 112
Manhattan, New York, 17–18, 122. *See also* New York, New York
Many Voices, One City, 123, 124
"María," 29
Marquette, Jacques, 98
Martel, Émile, 104
Martel, Nicole, 104
Martí, José, 12, 73, 112, 127, 131n23; Anglophone audience and, 118, 128, 129; Anglophone media and, 117–119; *crónicas* by, 116–117, 120, 123, 129; in Cuba, 115–116; death of, 115–116, 119–120; as foreign correspondent, 119; freedom of speech and, 115, 116–117; in Guatemala, 115; *Impressions of America (By a Very Fresh Spaniard)*, 118; journalism and, 116–122, 131n23; letter to *New York Evening Post*, 122; *Lucía Jérez*, 120; in Mexico City, Mexico, 115, 116; multilingualism and, 115–122; in New York, 115–122; "Nuestra América," 120; *Obras completas*, 120, 121; translation of Helen Hunt Jackson's *Ramona*, 120–121; translation of Victor Hugo's *Mes fils*, 120; in Venezuela, 115, 116; "Vindicación de Cuba," 119; writings on the United States, 118, 120, 129
Martín, Eutimio, critical edition of García Lorca's *Poeta en Nueva York*, 41–42, 43

Martínez Nadal, Rafael, 34, 47n18
Mayhew, Jonathan, 1, 33
Mayoral, Elsa María, 30n3
Mayoral, Héctor, 24, 30n3
McGee, Anne Marie, 59
McGill University, 100
media localism, 123
Medina, Pablo, translation of García Lorca's *Poet in New York*, 34
Melançon, Joseph, 105
memory, 91; collective, 91, 92; as a form of justice, 92; history and, 83, 92; "law of historical memory," 92
Menarini, Piero, 42, 43
Menton, Seymour, 72
Mexican Revolution, 52, 53, 57, 58–59, 60, 62–63, 66
Mexico, 3. *See also* Mexico City, Mexico
Mexico City, Mexico, ix, 3, 9, 10, 52–68; Jews in, 16, 21; Martí in, 115, 116; monuments of, 53, 54, 58–61, 64; politics in, 59–60; student movement of 1968 in, 59, 61
microcosmopolitan, 113–114
microcosmopolitan media, 112–132
milongas, 23–25, 27–29, 30n1, 30–31n4
minority communities, 129. *See also* linguistic communities
minority languages, 126. *See also* linguistic alterity; linguistic diversity
Mistral, Gabriela, 3
Mochkofsky, Graciela, 128
modernity, 4, 70–71
Molloy, Sylvia, 58
monolingualism, 79n14
Montreal, Quebec, Canada, 6, 11–12, 97–110; Haitian authors in, 100, 102; as hub of Hispano-Québécois literature/culture, 11–12, 97–110; Iberian authors in, 100; Latin American authors in, 100–101; Latin American literature/scholarship in, 101–103, 106–107; as linguistically dual city, 127, 128; literary festivals in, 106; literary reviews/journals founded in, 100, 102–103, 106–107; multilingualism and, 127, 128; publication/translation in, 101–108; publishing industry in, 11–12, 101–108; small presses in, 102–103; theater in, 104, 105–106; trilingual/multilingual approaches in, 100, 101–104, 106, 107–108; university courses/programs in, 106–108
Monument of the Revolution, 53, 54, 59, 60, 63, 64, 65–66
monuments, 53–54, 59–60, 63–66; books and, 61; cities and, 64
Moreno Villa, José, 3
multiculturalism, 11
multilingualism, 11, 73–74, 76–77; in Barcelona, Spain, 76–77, 127, 128; cities and, 54–55; journalism and, 124–127; Martí and, 115–122; in Montreal, Quebec, Canada, 127, 128; in New York, New York, 112–113, 115–123, 127, 128, 130n2; nineteenth-century, 115–122

National Association for Hispanic Publications, José Martí Prize given by, 122
nationalism, 70, 73
Nationalists, 38
Nelligan, Émile, 98
Nemerov, Howard, 44
Nepalese community, 126
Nepali, 125
Nerudo, Pablo, *Canto General*, 78
New America Media, 131–132n36
New Directions, 36–37, 43
news agencies, 113–114
New York, New York, ix, 3, 6, 8–11, 15–22, 69, 74; African American communities in, 117; in Casey's work, 75–76; Chinese newspapers in, 117; Cubans in, 116; Irish communities in, 117; Jewish communities in, 16–17, 19, 21, 117; Martí, José in, 115–122; microcosmopolitan media of, 112–132; multilingualism and, 112–113, 115–123, 127, 128, 130n2; Muslim community publications in, 122; Russian communities in, 117; September 11, 2001, terrorist attacks and, 122; Spanish language speakers in, 116
New York daily Sun, 117–118
New York Evening Post, 118–119, 122
New York Herald, 118, 124
New York Ilbo, 125
New York Times, 125, 126; Spanish and Chinese editions of, 124, 126

New York University, MFA in creative writing in Spanish, 128
New York World, 118
Nicholson and Watson, 47n18
Noel, Urayoán, 12–13
nonfiction, 12, 130n8, 130n9; translation and, 12, 114–115
Nordstjernan, 112
Norton, William Warder, 46n11
nostalgia, viii, ix. *See also* memory

Obama, Barack, 122
Ollé, Joan, 82
O'Rell, Max, 129

Pacific News Service, 131–132n36
Palin, Laure, 103
Palisades Park, New Jersey, 125
Paris, France, ix, 4
Park, Chloe B., 125
Parra, Max, 57
Parti Québécois, 99, 101
Patria, 119–120, 121
Paz, Octavio, 39–40
Pelletier, Lucien, 108
Pennar, Karen, 125, 126, 127
PEN World Voices festival, 113
Percovich, Mariana, *Jocasta*, 106
Pérez Firmat, Gustavo, 71, 72–73
performance, 86
periodical media, 113–114
Perron, Sylvie, 103
Peterson, Michel, 107
Philadelphia Manufacturer, 118–119
Piazzolla, Astor, 25, 30–31n4
poetry: at festivals, 106; Hispano-Québécois, 100, 101, 102–105; publication of, 100, 102–103, 104–105, 107–108; readings of, 102–103. *See also specific poets*
Poetry London, 47n18
Polezzi, Loredana, 7, 13n4
polis, 81
Polish, 125
Polish press, 122
political conflict, cities and, 60
politics, rewriting and, 63–64
polyglossia. *See* multilingualism
Portuguese, 125

post–Spanish Civil War period (1936–1939), 83, 85, 86
Pound, Ezra, 36
power: cities and, 64; space and, 63–66; translation and, 64
Pozier, Bernard, 104
Primo de Rivera, Miguel, dictatorship of, 83
propaganda, translation and, 4
public sphere, language and, 5
publishing industry, 11–12, 101–108, 114. *See also specific publishers*
Puig, Manuel, vii, viii–ix, 3

Quebec, Canada, 97–110; under British rule, 98–99, 109n3; early Iberian/French presence in, 98; francophone nationalism in, 98–99, 101; French Caribbean community in, 100, 102; Latin America and, 11–12; Latin American and, 97–110; Latin American immigration to, 100–101; Latin American literature/scholarship in, 101–103, 106–107; literary/artistic contacts and exchanges in, 105–106; literary festivals in, 106; literary reviews/journals founded in, 100, 102–103, 106–107; literature of, as read in Spain/Latin America, 105; publication/translation in, 101–108; trilingual/multilingual approaches in, 98, 100, 101–104, 106, 107–108; university courses/programs in, 106–108. *See also* Montreal, Quebec, Canada
Queens, New York, 19–20, 125
Queens Chronicle, 125
Queens Tribune, 125
Quintero-Herencia, Juan Carlos, 77–78

Rabassa, Gregory, viii
Radiguet, Raymond, 39
Ramos, Julio, 120, 129
Record, The, 125
Refus global (Automatiste manifesto), 99
Reid, Alistair, translation of Borges's "The Intruder," 26
Republican propaganda, 4
Republican Spain, 4, 34–35
Republican writers, translation and, 4
Revista de Estudios Canadienses, 107
Revista de la Universidad Complutense, 100

Revista Mexicana de Estudios Canadienses, 106–107
Revolutionary Family, 59, 60, 65
Revolution of 1910, 52
rewriting: politics and, 63–64; translation as, 57–58
Richler, Mordecai, 99
Riopelle, Jean-Paul, 99
Rivero, Edmundo, 30–31n4
Robinson, Sal, 114, 130n9
Rodoreda, Mercé, *La Plaça del Diamant*, 11, 82, 89, 93, 94
Roethke, Theodore, 44
Rogers, Gayle, 1
Roig, Jordi, 84–85
Roig, Oscar, 85
Rosset, Barney, 39, 40, 44
Rothenberg, Jonathan, 33
Rotker, Susana, 120
Ruiz, Hector, 108
Ruptures: La revue des Trois Amériques, 102–103, 107
Russian, 125

Sabines, Jaime, 104
Sackett, William L., 49n45
Saint-Denys Garneau, Hector de, 104
Sala Gran, Teatre Nacional de Catalunya, 82
S. A. La Nación, 123
Salazar, António de Oliveira, 100
Samson, Pierre, 108
Sanguinetti, Pablo, 121
Saravia, Alejandro: *Lettres de Nootka*, 98; *L'homme polyphonique*, 108
Sarmiento, Domingo Faustino, 120
Sartre, Jean-Paul, 73, 78
Saura, Carlos, *Bodas de sangre*, 33
Scher, Abby, 122, 123
Schleiermacher, Friedrich, 113
Schoemann, Boris, 106
Scorer, James, 1
Second Spanish Republic, 83, 87
Segura, Mauricio, 108
self-translation, 12
Sellars, Peter, 48n32
Sender, Ramón, 37, 47–48n26
September 11, 2001, terrorist attacks of, 122
September 11 Digital Archive, 122

Severo, Severo, ix
Sheffield, England, 142, 143
Shin, Dongshan, 124–125
Simon, Greg, translation of García Lorca's *Poeta en Nueva York*, 34, 50n58
Simon, Sherry, 4–5, 6, 7, 54–55, 113, 127, 128
Singer, Isaac Bashevis, 114
Sing Tao Daily, 123
Singulier Pluriel, 106
Socialist Workers Party (PSOE), 91
social production, space and, 60
Soja, Edward, 60, 64, 65
Sommer, Doris, 5, 70–71, 127
soundscapes, 5, 55–58
source texts, versions of, 32–33
space, 58, 64, 65; cities and, 64; power and, 63–66; social production and, 60
Spain, 3–4
Spalding, Lincolnshire, England, 142–143
Spanish, 16–18, 19, 21–22, 76–77, 116, 125–128, 142, 144
Spanish-American War, 116
Spanish Civil War, 3, 4, 34–35, 38, 47n21, 82, 83, 85–87
Spanish Civil War ballads, 4
Spanish-language journalism, 127–128. *See also* Spanish-language press
Spanish-language press, 122, 123, 125–126
Spanish Republic, 143
Spender, Stephen, 36, 47n18, 48–49n35
Statman, Mark, translation of García Lorca's *Poeta en Nueva York*, 34
Stavans, Ilan, 8–9, 15, 72
Stowe, Harriet Beecher, *Uncle Tom's Cabin*, 120–121
stream of consciousness, 86
Sullivan, Françoise, 99
surrealism, 35, 36, 37

tango, 9, 23–31
Teatro de la Capilla, 105–106
testimonio, 57
textual instability, 33
Thames and Hudson, 44
theater, 11; in Barcelona, Spain, 81; cities and, 81; Hispano-Québécois, 104–106
theatron, 84
time, spatialization of, 82, 83–84

Times Literary Supplement, 47n18
Tlatelolco Massacre, 59, 61
Tocqueville, Alexis de, 129
Torres, Luis, 107
Torres, Salvador, 108; *Dieuseries et odieuseries / Dioserías y odioserías*, 103
Tower of Babel, 6
transformation, poetics of, 84
translation(s), 58, 126–127, 143–144; as appropriation, 58; domestication and, 55–58; early days of, 101–102; funding of, 103–104; identity construction and, 58, 128; as inevitably partial, 63; Jakobson's three definitions of, 13n4; journalism and, 113–114, 121–122, 125–127; listening and, 5; as a local, urban phenomenon, 114–115; loss and, viii, ix; as a native langauge, 23–31; as part of everyday life, 113; of plays, 104, 105–106; power and, 63–66, 64; propaganda and, 4; refusal of, 76; as rewriting, 57–58; "translation acts," 2–3; travel and, 2–3, 5, 6, 7; urban-centric literature and, 7; as a violent political act, 58. See also specific translators; translation studies; translation theory
translation studies, 2, 8, 12, 113–114
translation theory, 7
translators, vii–ix, 4, 114. See also specific translators
transnationalism, 113
travel, 113; language and, 7; translation and, 2–3, 5, 6, 7
Tremblay, Michel, 105
trilingualism, 11–12
Truque, Yvonne América, 102
Tymoczko, Maria, 63

Ucelay, Margarita, 34, 46n11
Ukrainian, 125
Union des écrivaines et écrivains Québécois (UNEQ), 105
United States, 3, 120, 129. See also specific cities
Universidade de São Paulo, 102
Universidade Federal de Rio Grande do Sul, 105
Université de Sherbrooke, 100

Université du Québec à Montréal (UQAM), 102
urban-centric literature, translation and, 7
urban space, 1, 5–6
urban theory, 6
Urbanyi, Pablo, 103
Urbina, José Leandro, *Cobro revertido*, 103
Urdu, 125
U.S. Census Bureau, 112

Valencia, Spain, 4
Valis, Noël, 47–48n26, 48n33
Varela, Félix, 119
Varin, Claire, 108
Venezuela, 115, 116
Venuti, Lawrence, 58, 64, 115
versioning, textual theory of, 33
Vice Versa, 107
Villa, Francisco "Pancho," 52–68
Villa, Pancho, 10; assasination of, 59, 62; legacy of, 59; name on Wall of Honor, Mexican Congress, 59, 64; statue of, 52, 53, 54, 59–61, 62, 64, 65–66
Villemaire, Yolande, 104
Vincent, Julie, 106
Voices of New York, 124–129; "Translating NYC," 127
Voices That Must Be Heard website, 122, 124, 127
Vozes do Quebec: Antologia, 105

Wales, 142, 143
walking, 8–9, 15
White, Steven F., translation of García Lorca's *Poeta en Nueva York*, 34, 50n58
Whitman, Walt, 38, 39, 44, 45
Wilson, Edmund, 34
Winks, Christopher, 75
Wittgenstein, Ludwig, 6–7
Wordsworth, William, 32
World War II, 143
W. W. Norton, 34–35, 41, 46n11

Xiaoqing, Rong, 126

Year of Historical Memory (Spain), 91
Yiddish, viii, 16, 17, 21, 114